THE ECONOMICS OF SMALL BUSINESSES

THE ECONOMICS OF SMALL BUSINESSES

Their Role and Regulation in the U.S. Economy

A CERA RESEARCH STUDY

William A. Brock
and
David S. Evans

with contributions by Bruce D. Phillips

HOLMES & MEIER
New York • London

First published in the United States of America 1986 by

Holmes & Meier Publishers, Inc.
30 Irving Place
New York, N.Y. 10003

Great Britain:
Holmes & Meier Publishers, Ltd.
Pindar Road, Hoddesdon
Hertfordshire, EN11 0HF, England

Book design by Ellen Foos

Library of Congress Cataloging in Publication Data

Brock, William A.
The economics of small businesses. Their role
and regulation in the U.S. Economy.
Bibliography: p.
Includes index.
1. Small business—Government policy—United
States.
2. Small business—United States—
Management. 3. Small
business—taxation—Law and legislation—United States.
I. Evans, David S. (David Sparks), 1954–
II. Phillips, Bruce D. (Bruce Dana) III. Title.
HD2346.U5B76 1986 338.6′42′0973 84-25138
ISBN 0-8419-0848-6

Manufactured in the United States of America.

CONTENTS

LIST OF TABLES

LIST OF FIGURES

PREFACE

Few businesses own Manhattan skyscrapers, issue publicly traded stock, have thousands of workers at plants spread across the country, or capture headlines when they bounce their president or they become targeted for a takeover. Yet readers of the economics literature are likely to encounter little discussion of any businesses but these. The reasons are clear. Economic theory has trouble explaining the continual coexistence of monoliths and midgets and even more trouble explaining where upstarts like Apple, MCI, and that new gourmet food store around the corner from you came from. Scant economic data are available on businesses that do not get sued under the antitrust laws or that do not have to file extensive financial reports with the government as a result of issuing stock.

Is there anything wrong with this skewed emphasis? After all, the ten thousand largest businesses in this country produce almost two-thirds of the Gross National Product (GNP) and employ more than half the work force. We believe there is something wrong. First, although many of the 17 million businesses are inactive or part-time enterprises, about 9 million individuals rely on their own business for their livelihood. Studied by neither industrial organization scholars nor labor economists, these businessmen have fallen through the cracks of economic research. Second, the industrial giants of today were the small businesses of yesterday; some of the small businesses of today will become the industrial giants of tomorrow. The environment that nurtures these future industrial giants deserves study. Third, small businesses have a hallowed place in this country's political traditions, extending from Jeffersonian notions of a democratic society, through the philosophy that underlies the antitrust laws, and through many federal policies that favor small businesses. Yet there is little economic research that can guide federal policies toward small businesses. Fourth, the businesses that are not among the largest ten thousand employ almost half the work force and produce almost a third of the GNP. Small business may not have the biggest slice of the economic pie, but it has a healthy slice nonetheless.

This book examines the role of small businesses in the economy. It has four major objectives: first, to summarize what is known about the role small businesses play in this country's economy and to develop a theoretical framework for examining the formation, dissolution, and growth of these businesses; second, to illustrate how this theoretical framework together with available data can be used to investigate a variety of empirical issues concerning small businesses; third, to examine the impact of government policies—in particular the increasingly burdensome federal health and safety regulations—on the success and survival of small businesses; fourth, to examine the optimal design of regulations across firm size and to determine the circumstances under which lighter regulations on smaller businesses are desirable.

Researchers who are interested in concise summaries of theories and facts concerning small businesses will find these in Chapters 1, 2, and 3. Policy makers who are concerned with the impact of government actions on small businesses or who are entrusted with implementing the provisions of the Regulatory Flexibility Act should find this book especially useful. They will find prescriptive and practical advice in Chapters 3 and 4. Economists who are interested in the normative theory of regulation—that is, in how regulation *should* be designed in order to maximize some measure of social welfare—will find much that is new in our analysis of tiering in Chapter 4. A summary of the evidence concerning the differential impact of regulations across business sizes appears as Chapter 5. Three empirical studies that we hope will stimulate research on small businesses are discussed in Chapter 6.

In choosing the level of presentation for this book, we were guided on the one hand by our belief that we must provide sufficient detail for our fellow economists to evaluate the validity of our results and on the other hand by the hope that many noneconomists will find our work useful. Our attempt to serve two masters may give portions of this book a schizophrenic tone. Where new results are developed we have not avoided using advanced mathematics. Some of the material is unavoidably difficult. But readers with a less mathematical bent need not despair. We always precede technical material with nontechnical explanations and examples, and we note sections that readers may skip without loss of continuity.

Portions of this book are based on research performed by CERA Economic Consultants, Inc., under contract to the Small Business Administration (contract nos. SBA-1A-01-0, SBA-212-VA-83, SBA-7186-OA-83) and the Environmental Protection Agency (purchase order no. 1W-1939-NASX). We wish to thank these agencies for their interest in sponsoring our work. Of course, these agencies do not necessarily share our views. Earlier versions of portions of Chapters 3, 4, and 5 appeared in a report prepared for the Small Business Administration, and in Evans's doctoral dissertation at the University of Chicago.

This book has benefited throughout from the careful and insightful comments of Bruce D. Phillips, senior economist with the Office of Advocacy of the Small Business Administration. The presence of his name on the title page is a small measure of our appreciation for the assistance he provided us. William Dechert, Robert Lucas, Sherwin Rosen, José Scheinkman, and Michael Shapiro also made helpful comments at various stages of our research. These individuals naturally do not share our responsibility for the opinions expressed in the following pages. Kathryn Evans typed portions of the manuscript and prepared the index. Nan Roche transformed our scratchings into fine-looking graphs. Thanks to all.

William A. Brock
Madison, Wisconsin

David S. Evans
Greenwich, Connecticut

To Joan and Kathy

THE ECONOMICS OF SMALL BUSINESSES

1

INTRODUCTION

Federal regulation of business has increased dramatically over the last fifteen years. During the 1970s, the federal regulatory budget grew sixfold, federal regulatory employment nearly tripled, and the number of pages in the *Federal Register* reporting new regulations increased threefold.[1] By the late 1970s businesses were spending substantial sums of money in order to comply with federal regulations. Robert DeFina estimated that in 1977 businesses spent roughly $75 billion, 2.3 percent of business sales, as a result of federal regulation.[2] Arthur Andersen found that forty-eight large businesses spent $2.6 billion, 1.2 percent of their total sales, in order to comply with federal regulations in 1977.[3] The Council on Environmental Quality estimated that businesses spent $12.8 billion, 0.5 percent of business sales, as a result of pollution control requirements alone in 1977.[4] By comparison, businesses spent 2.5 percent of business sales for corporate income taxes in 1977.[5]

Policy makers have expressed increasing concern that these regulations have a disparate impact on small businesses. These concerns have led to the passage of legislation that either explicitly exempts smaller businesses from certain regulations or encourages regulatory agencies to impose lighter regulatory burdens on these businesses. A 1981 survey found forty-three examples of regulations that give smaller businesses a break, by way of reduced reporting requirements, fewer inspections, lighter requirements, or outright exemptions.[6] The Regulatory Flexibility Act of 1980 encourages agencies to impose lighter regulatory burdens on smaller businesses.

Despite this obvious interest in small businesses, readers will find little serious economic research on these businesses, much less on whether regulations have a disparate impact on small businesses or on whether there are economic grounds for regulating smaller businesses differently from larger businesses. The Regulatory Flexibility Act encourages policy makers to "tier" regulations—to create different requirements for different business sizes—but the policy maker who looks for economic guidance on when and how to tier will search in vain. The reader who seeks to document the impact of regulation on small businesses will find much talk and few facts, with the "facts" scattered across numerous, often unpublished, studies. Students learn little about small businesses from economics textbooks.

This book helps fill these gaps. It is about small businesses, their role in the economy, the impact of government regulations on them, and the optimal design of government policies toward them. It pulls together a considerable body of theory and fact from both published and unpublished sources on the role small businesses play in the economy and the impact of government regulations on them. It contains an original analysis of tiering that examines when regulators should impose lighter regulatory requirements on smaller businesses and discusses the merits of alternative tiering schemes. It reviews existing studies, some published and some unpublished, of the differential impact of federal regulations across business sizes. It also presents three original empirical studies concerning business formation, dissolution, and growth.

Whether a small business is one with fewer than one hundred employees or fewer than five hundred employees or with sales of less than $500,000 or sales of under $1 million—criteria sometimes used by the government—need not concern us. Such definitions are arbitrary and not particularly helpful. Whether a business is small depends upon the particular industry in which it operates. MCI is a small telecommunications company and American Motors is a small automobile company, although both have sales in the millions. Sidley and Austin is a large law firm and Wharton Econometrics is a large economic consulting firm, although both have fewer than five hundred employees. Whether a business is small also depends upon our reasons for talking about small versus large. Jurists who speak of small businessmen as the backbone of our society apparently refer to the guys who run the corner gas station and not Marathon Oil, the "small" oil company that was devoured by U.S. Steel.[7] For our purposes, we simply view small businesses as those businesses that are much smaller than the largest businesses in the same industry.[8]

Since George Stigler observed that often regulated firms gain and society as a whole loses from regulations, a cottage industry has developed around the positive theory of regulation.[9] The positive theory of regulation seeks to explain the imposition of regulation on businesses by examining the demand for regulation by businesses (who may gain from certain kinds of regulation) and the supply of regulation by politicians and bureaucrats (who get votes or power or whatever by imposing certain desired regulations). The positive theory of regulation stands in sharp contrast to the normative theory of regulation that seeks (1) to identify situations where the competitive process breaks down (pollution is an example), and (2) to devise government policies that make the economy more efficient (a pollution tax is an example).

Most of this book is in the normative tradition. We take as given that there are circumstances where regulation is desirable, either because of a legitimate market failure or because society wishes to achieve some non-market objective, and then examine the optimal design of such regulation. We do not deny that some regulations merely redistribute income toward powerful special interest groups. But for many regulations redistribution of income is ancillary to the main objective of policy makers.

A common criticism of the normative approach is that policy makers ignore economists' prescriptions. We do not believe we are vain in rejecting this criticism. Maybe economic advice on how to make regulations as efficient as possible is not heeded as quickly or as completely as some economists would like, but it is heeded nonetheless. Regulatory agencies are increasingly using cost-benefit analysis in designing and enforcing regulations. The Environmental Protection Agency has recently adopted on an experimental basis some of the market-based regulatory schemes long advocated by economists.[10] The recent partial deregulation of the airline, cable, trucking, banking, securities, and telecommunications industries resulted at least partly from the response of policy makers to economic evidence that regulation was not socially beneficial in those industries.[11]

The following six chapters develop a framework for analyzing small business problems, use this framework to develop regulatory schemes that are sensitive to the special role played by small businesses in the economy, and examine the empirical evidence concerning the differential impact of regulations across business sizes. Chapter 2 surveys the role of small businesses in the economy. After showing that most businesses are small by almost any reasonable measure, it examines how the importance of small business has changed over the last quarter-century in each of our major industries and in the economy as a whole. It then discusses some of the reasons policy makers and economists are concerned about small businesses. It concludes by examining how these smaller businesses differ from larger ones.

Our framework for analyzing the impact of government policies on small businesses is developed in Chapter 3. After reviewing some of the traits possessed by people who start businesses, we discuss several recently developed economic theories concerning the determinants of business formation, dissolution, and growth. We then use this framework to examine the impact of government regulations and taxes on smaller versus larger businesses.

The model of the size distribution of businesses that we develop in Chapter 3 provides a powerful vehicle for analyzing the differential impact of government policies across business sizes. But its power comes from its simplicity, and its simplicity comes at the expense of ignoring several important aspects of the real business world. First, it ignores the fact that the goods or services produced by most businesses are differentiated from the goods or services produced by most other businesses in the same industry. Product differentiation is the norm in most industries. Smaller businesses produce different products than do larger businesses. But taking product differentiation into account would add few insights into the impact of government policies on small businesses and make our model much less tractable and informative. Second, by assuming that perfect competition prevails, it ignores the fact that entry into many industries is limited, including many that are commonly associated with smaller businesses. For example, federal, state, and local regulations hinder competitive entry into the banking, cable, and telephone industries, and anticompetitive industry practices sometimes hinder competitive entry into the real estate, medical, and construction industries.

We can see from casual observation that the fact that an industry has a lot of small businesses does not necessarily make it competitive. An example that we mention frequently in the sequel is the real estate industry. Most real estate agencies are tiny. Yet there is evidence that residential real estate commissions are not competitively determined and that entry into local markets is difficult. The development of large nationwide realtors may actually improve competition in this industry. The results we obtain from our model are not applicable to industries characterized by extensive entry barriers. Policy makers will not improve economic efficiency by giving small firms a break if these same small firms hinder rather than promote competition.

Many regulatory requirements are tiered according to the specific circumstances of the regulated firm. Chapter 4 examines the circumstances under which tiering is socially desirable and develops socially optimal tiering schemes under alternative assumptions concerning the information available to regulators. In order to capture the salient aspects of tiering, it assumes that regulators use taxes to mitigate a negative externality (such as pollution), the collection of taxes imposes administrative costs on the taxed firm and the regulatory agency, and firms differ in size because they have differential access to a scarce factor. The scarce factor is taken as managerial ability, although this identity is not essential for any of the results obtained. Chapter 4 develops some rules of thumb that policy makers can use in order to determine whether an industry is a good candidate for tiering. It also compares and contrasts existing tiering schemes with those we propose. Major portions of Chapter 4 are highly technical. Readers who are more interested in the relevance of our results to policy making than in mathematical details can skip the technical portions of this chapter without loss of continuity. Nontechnical introductions and conclusions summarize the major results.

The most frequent justification for tiering is that imposing uniform regulatory requirements across all types of businesses has a disparate impact on smaller businesses because there are scale economies in regulatory compliance. Scale economies arise because regulations impose fixed costs. Larger businesses can average fixed costs over a larger quantity of output and thereby achieve a competitive advantage over their smaller rivals. Chapter 5 examines the empirical evidence that there are scale economies in complying with federal regulation. Chapter 5 provides little support for the assertion that regulations have had a disparate impact on smaller businesses. Of course, the fact that regulations do not appear to have a disparate impact on smaller businesses does not imply that tiering and the provisions of the Regulatory Flexibility Act are unjustified. Rather, it attests to the success of tiering in attenuating the impact of regulations on smaller businesses.

Chapter 6 reports some preliminary results from three empirical studies we are conducting concerning the determinants of business formation, dissolution, and growth. The first study examines the relationship between firm growth, size, and age for a sample of about 20,000 manufacturing firms observed between 1976 and 1982. The second study examines the determinants of the decision to become self-employed and self-employment earnings using data drawn from the 1980 census. The third study examines the impact of environmental and safety regulations on changes in the size distribution of establishments between 1967 and 1977.

We present our conclusions in Chapter 7.

2

SMALL BUSINESS IN THE U.S. ECONOMY

What are small businesses? Are they a vanishing breed? Why should we care about them? How are they different from large businesses? The following four sections address these questions. The first section reviews data on small businesses in the overall economy and in the various industries that make up the economy. It shows that most businesses are small compared with the handful of firms that garner the majority of sales. The second section analyzes the changing role of small business in the economy over the last twenty-five years. It examines changes in the small business share of employment, sales, and value-added for the economy and the major industries that comprise it. The third section examines the importance of small businesses from the standpoint of three theories: the populist theory that underlies a considerable body of antitrust precedent in this country; classical economic theory, which extols the merits of competition between atomistic competitors in a static world; and Austrian economic theory, which emphasizes the importance of the entrepreneur in the dynamic competitive process. The fourth section summarizes some of the empirical regularities that characterize small businesses and distinguish them from large businesses.

Overview

Most of the 16.8 million businesses that filed tax returns in 1980 are small by any standard.[1] Eighty percent of 12.7 million are sole proprietorships, 60 percent of 1.4 million are partnerships, and 40 percent of the 2.7 million corporations filing in that year had annual business receipts of under $50,000.[2] Many of these small businesses are operated on a part-time basis, are in their infancy, or are operated by individuals who alternate between wage and salary employment and self-employment.[3]

Detailed data are entirely lacking on most of these tiny businesses.[4]

More than 10 million businesses that file tax returns are not picked up by the Census Bureau's quinquennial survey of businesses or by Dun and Bradstreet's continual survey of businesses; most of these businesses are sole proprietorships with no employees. The Census Bureau's 1977 *Enterprise Statistics* obtained data from roughly 25 percent of the businesses that filed tax returns in that year.[5] The 1980 Dun and Bradstreet Market Identifier File (DMI), from which the Small Business Data Base (SBDB) of the U.S. Small Business Administration is derived, contained data on 24 percent of the businesses that filed tax returns in that year.[6]

Of the 4.0 million businesses on the 1980 SBDB, 3.4 million (85 percent) had business receipts of $50,000 or more.[7] Of the 16.8 million businesses that filed tax returns in 1980, 5.1 million (30.4 percent) had business receipts of $50,000 or more. The SBDB therefore contains data on 67 percent of businesses that have receipts of $50,000 or more, but on only 5 percent of businesses that have receipts of less than $50,000.[8]

Even excluding tiny businesses with annual business receipts below $50,000, most businesses are small compared with the monoliths that produce the major share of this country's goods and services. Of every thousand businesses on the DMI, 981 have fewer than one hundred employees and 997 have fewer than five hundred employees.[9] Yet businesses with more than five hundred employees accounted for 57 percent of all business receipts, and businesses with more than one hundred employees accounted for 65.9 percent of all business receipts.[10] The ten thousand largest businesses produced more than 62 percent of GNP and employed 53 percent of the nongovernment work force in 1978.[11] Most of these large businesses are corporations that operate on a national basis, have many subordinate establishments and places of business and issue publicly traded stock.[12]

The vast majority of the 16.8 million businesses in this country are small concerns with fewer than five employees. These companies are retail stores (such as small groceries and clothing boutiques), wholesale trade and construction firms, and service firms (such as data processing firms, medical laboratories, and automobile garages, and, increasingly, transportation and finance firms). Almost 9 million businesses have no employees except for the owner and perhaps members of his family.

With the exception of professional services, the easy entry into and exit out of the markets served by "mom and pop" concerns keep profits low and lead to a high rate of business formation and dissolution. The minimal entry requirements encourage entrepreneurs to test their abilities at these ventures. The low sunk investment cost facilitates the exit of entrepreneurs who do not pass muster at the hands of consumers.[13] Notably, the relatively high rates of business formation that the economy has had in the last several years have been accompanied by high rates of business dissolution. This observation is particularly true for retail trade.[14]

Although it is generally true that profits per dollar of sale are higher in larger firms than in smaller firms, there are many industries in which the opposite is true.[15] As shown in Table 2.1, some of the industries in which profits are higher in smaller firms include those dominated by smaller businesses, e.g., general construction, instrument manufacturing, truck, real estate, credit agencies, and education service firms.[16] In those industries entrepreneurs, whether through experience or detailed knowledge of a local market, appear to have competed successfully with large firms.[17]

Diseconomies of scale coupled with deregulation have recently created many profitable opportunities for smaller businesses. Take the case of airlines. Prior to deregulation in 1978, United Airlines was flying short-haul passengers from Fort Wayne, Indiana, to Chicago to switch them to longer flights. However, United was losing $2 million a month on this and other short-haul services. It dropped the Fort Wayne–Chicago run in 1981. As the chairman of United put it at the time, "Allowing a commuter carrier or a regional airline to ferry traffic from Fort Wayne to Chicago makes better economic sense than for United to do the job itself."[18]

Most mom and pop businesses are sole proprietorships. The distribution of sole proprietorships across industries therefore provides a good

TABLE 2.1

Industries in Which Firms with 20–99 Employees Had the Highest Profits per Dollar of Sales in 1978

SIC Code	*Industry*
12	Bituminous coal
15	General contractors*
17	Special trade construction*
27	Printing and publishing*
30	Rubber products
31	Leather products
38	Instruments
42	Trucking and warehousing*
50	Wholesale-Durables
61	Credit agencies*
65	Real estate*
70	Hotels, motels*
82	Educational services
89	Miscellaneous services

SOURCE: Executive Office of the President, *The State of Small Business: A Report of the President* (Washington, D.C.: Government Printing Office, March 1982), table A1.31.

*This industry contains a greater than average concentration of small firms.

picture of the distribution of mom and pop businesses across the economy. Table 2.2 shows the percent of all businesses that were sole proprietorships in 1980 for nine broad industries. The three industries with the largest percentage of sole proprietorships were agriculture, services, and construction. The three industries with the smallest percentage of sole proprietorships were finance, wholesale trade, and manufacturing.

Although most sole proprietorships provide their owners with paltry incomes—in 1980, 27 (55) percent of proprietorships reported before-tax income of less than $10,000 ($20,000)[19]—many small businesses are, as Table 2.1 suggests, profitable and dynamic enterprises. It is useful to divide these businesses into two types. Stable, profitable small businesses have found market niches that provide little room for expansion but yield high incomes for their proprietors. Some of these businesses are run by entrepreneurs who are exceptionally able at running a small concern but who could not leverage their expertise enough for them to run profitable, larger concerns. Others have obtained a monopoly in a small geographic area either because of locational advantage or because they have succeeded in erecting entry barriers. Some researchers have argued, for example, that local building codes help protect local building companies from competition.[20] Real estate agencies allegedly impede competition in order to preserve local market power. The Federal Trade Commission mounted an investigation of the real estate industry several years ago but has yet to bring charges.[21] California, Connecticut, and Massachusetts have also mounted antitrust investigations into the residential real estate industry. There is some evidence that local real estate boards use their control over multiple listings to discourage competitive entry.[22]

Rapid growth companies start out small and grow quickly. Often these businesses have developed a new product or service or have developed methods for producing existing product or services more cheaply. These businesses sometimes evolve into gigantic enterprises. Indeed, many "household names" began as rapidly growing small businesses. Examples abound. McDonalds started out as a small chain of family-run hamburger restaurants. DuPont began as a small gunpowder manufacturer. ITT was originally a small manufacturer of telephone equipment. MCI, now the second largest long-distance telephone company, began as a small company providing microwave service between Chicago and St. Louis.

Entrepreneurs who expect their businesses to grow over time usually form corporations. The corporation's ability to issue stock and its stockholders' freedom to resell their stock either on organized markets or in individual transactions provide several advantages that are unavailable to proprietorships or partnerships. The corporation's ability to issue stock facilitates the process of raising capital for expansion since it can sell a slice of future profits to investors in return for needed capital. Neither the proprietorship nor the partnership provides an easy mechanism for selling

TABLE 2.2
Sole Proprietorships, Partnerships, and Corporations That Filed Tax Returns in 1980

Industry	*Total (thousands)*	*Proprietorships (percentage)*	*Partnerships (percentage)*	*Corporations (percentage)*
Agriculture	3,486	94.6	3.1	2.3
Mining	180	66.4	19.4	14.2
Construction	1,412	76.0	4.7	19.3
Manufacturing	569	52.0	5.3	42.7
Transportation	571	76.9	3.6	19.5
Wholesale	643	51.3	5.0	43.7
Retail	2,749	75.2	6.1	18.7
Finance	2,180	48.1	29.2	22.6
Services	4,778	80.4	5.5	14.1
All industries*	16,568	75.5	8.2	16.3

SOURCE: Executive Office of the President, *The State of Small Businesses: A Report of the President* (Washington, D.C.: Government Printing Office, March 1983), table 2.2, p. 33. Data from Internal Revenue Service, *1980 Partnership Returns, 1980 Sole Proprietorship Returns, 1980 Corporation Income Tax Returns* (preliminary data).

NOTE: Columns and rows may not sum because of rounding.
*Excludes 224,000 businesses that could not be allocated to an industry.

equity in the business. The stockholders' freedom to sell their stock on the open market makes it easy for them to capitalize on their investment with minimal interference with the daily operation of the business. A proprietorship or partnership technically loses its identity when it is sold. By divorcing ownership from control, the corporation enables individuals to pursue their comparative advantages as capitalists, entrepreneurs, or managers. Table 2.2 shows the percent of all businesses that are corporations. The three industries with the largest percent of corporations are wholesale trade, manufacturing, and finance. The three industries with the smallest percent of corporations are agriculture, services, and mining.

Small businesses are a much more important economic factor in some industries than in others. Table 2.3 reports the percentage of industry sales made by businesses in each of several size categories for 1980.[23] A third of all sales on average are made by firms with fewer than one hundred employees, and 45 percent of all sales are made by firms with fewer than five hundred employees. But a majority of sales are made by firms with fewer than one hundred employees in agriculture, construction, wholesale trade, retail trade, and services. A majority of all sales are made by firms with more than five hundred employees in mining and manufacturing.

Another measure of the relative economic importance of small busi-

TABLE 2.3

Share of Sales by Firm-Size Category

Industry	*Number of Employees in Firm*										
	1–4	*1–9*	*1–19*	*1–49*	*1–99*	*1–249*	*1–499*	*1–999*	*1–4,999*	*1–9,999*	*All Firms*
All industries	6.0	12.0	18.5	27.2	33.4	40.3	45.3	49.6	60.7	66.3	100.0
Agriculture	23.8	40.6	53.5	68.4	75.3	82.0	86.7	90.4	95.5	96.9	100.0
Mining	1.1	2.1	3.4	5.0	6.3	8.3	9.5	10.5	15.0	20.1	100.0
Construction	19.4	30.6	42.2	56.9	66.1	74.8	79.8	83.4	89.4	91.9	100.0
Manufacturing	0.8	2.2	4.4	8.7	12.5	17.9	22.1	26.1	36.7	43.5	100.0
Transportation	2.3	5.4	9.0	13.6	16.9	21.2	24.1	27.7	43.9	55.9	100.0
Wholesale	8.7	20.5	33.5	48.8	58.2	66.8	73.9	79.0	90.6	92.4	100.0
Retail	10.5	21.3	31.7	46.2	55.5	62.0	65.1	67.5	73.2	77.3	100.0
Finance	5.8	11.0	17.1	25.2	32.3	41.5	49.5	55.2	70.6	77.3	100.0
Services	8.5	15.8	23.2	31.8	38.1	48.1	55.1	62.8	80.1	86.9	100.0

SOURCE: Executive Office of the President, *State of Small Business: A Report of the President* (Washington, D.C.: Government Printing Office, March 1983). Based on data from the Small Business Administration's Small Business Data Base.

nesses across industries is the share of value added contributed by small businesses. Table 2.4 reports the share of gross product—a modified measure of value added—created by businesses with fewer than five hundred employees by industry for 1977.[24] Businesses with fewer than five hundred employees contributed slightly less than half—46.5 percent—of gross product in 1977. They contributed more than half in contract construction, wholesale trade, retail trade, and services. They contributed less than half in transportation, manufacturing, mining, and finance. It is notable that small businesses contribute only a fifth of gross product in manufacturing, which is by far the largest industrial sector (almost 30 percent of gross product originates in manufacturing).

Why are small businesses more prevalent in some industries than in others? Lawrence White has examined this question by regressing the small business share of industry sales against possible determinants of the size distribution of firms.[25] He conjectured that the minimum efficient firm size would be smaller and therefore the small business share would be larger the less capital-intensive the industry (the lower the ratio of capital to labor), the less vertically integrated the industry (the lower the ratio of value added to sales), the more localized the industry's markets (the higher

TABLE 2.4

Gross Product Originating in Firms with Fewer than 500 Employees for 1977

Industry	*Gross Product Originating* (billions of dollars)*	*Small Business Share (percentage)*
Mining	14	29.8
Construction	87	80.5
Manufacturing	465	19.8
Transportation, communications, and public utilities	171	18.7
Wholesale trade	139	79.9
Retail trade	184	60.3
Finance, insurance, and real estate	276	47.8
Services	228	78.9
All industries	1,596	46.5

SOURCE: Executive Office of the President, *The State of Small Business: A Report of the President* (Washington, D.C.: Government Printing Office, March 1983), appendix table 2.15, p. 214. Based on Joel Popkin and Company, *Estimates of Gross Product Originating in Small Business: 1977 Benchmark and Revisions of Intervening Years Since 1972* (Washington, D.C.: Office of Advocacy, Small Business Administration, September 1982).

*Gross Product Originating includes employee compensation, net interest, indirect business taxes, and capital consumption allowances. It does not include rents paid to others, which is usually included in value added.

the average shipping distance of the industry's products), the more rapidly the industry is growing (the higher the average annual growth rate between 1958 and 1971), and the smaller the ratio of advertising to sales.

Using data on 111 manufacturing industries from the 1972 *Enterprise Statistics,* he found that all of these variables with the exception of advertising had the conjectured impact on the small business share of sales.[26] Table 2.5 shows the estimated percent changes in the small business share due to a 1 percent change in the value of each determinant of the importance of small businesses. A 1 percent increase in the capital-labor ratio leads to a 1.24 percent decrease in the small business share, whereas a 1 percent increase in the historical growth rate leads to a .59 percent increase in the small business share. These findings confirm casual observation that small businesses are least prevalent in stable, capital-intensive, and vertically integrated industries that serve national markets.[27]

With this snapshot view of the small business sector in mind, let us now examine how this sector has changed over the last quarter of a century.

Changes in Businesses over Time

There are many more small businesses today than there were even twenty-five years ago. The total number of businesses increased from 10.7 million in 1958 to 16.8 million in 1980.[28] Yet the relative economic importance of small business in the overall economy declined over this period. The fraction of the work force employed by businesses with fewer than five hundred employees, the share of business receipts garnered by small businesses, and the share of value added created by small businesses have all declined. Between 1958 and 1977, the share of employment held by firms with fewer than five hundred employees decreased from 41.3 percent to 40.1 percent. Between 1958 and 1979 the share of business receipts obtained by companies with less than $5 million in receipts declined from 51.5 percent to 28.7 percent.[29] Between 1958 and 1977 the share of value added contributed by firms with five hundred or fewer employees decreased from 52 percent to 47 percent.[30]

Changes in the relative importance of small businesses in the economy as a whole are determined by changes in the relative importance of small businesses in each industry and by changes in the relative importance of these industries in the economy. For example, the share of gross product originating in firms with fewer than five hundred employees declined from 28 percent in 1958 to 20 percent in 1977 in the manufacturing industries and from 85 percent in 1958 to 79 percent in the service industries. Over this same period, the share of gross product originating in manufacturing decreased from 33 percent to 30 percent, while the share contributed by

TABLE 2.5

Estimated Impact of a One Percent Change in Small Business Determinants on the Small Business Share of Sales

Variable	*Estimated Elasticities*	*T-statistics*
Capital-labor ratio	−1.24	(7.40)
Value added-sales ratio	−0.31	(0.82)
Average growth rate	0.59	(2.42)
Average transportation distance	−0.43	(3.44)
Consumer goods dummy*	−0.16	(3.13)
Advertising-sales ratio	0.23	(1.74)

SOURCE: Lawrence J. White, "The Determinants of the Relative Importance of Small Business," *Review of Economics and Statistics* (February 1982): 42–49.

NOTE: The dependant variable was the log of the small business share of industry sales. Other specifications including a logit transform of the small business share yielded similar results.

*Equal to 1 if observation for a consumer goods industry and 0 otherwise.

services increased from 10 percent to 14 percent.[31] The increased importance of the small business–dominated service industries and the decreased importance of the large business–dominated manufacturing industries helped maintain the relative importance of small business in the overall economy despite the decreased relative importance of small business in each of these industrial sectors.

Lawrence White has examined the changing importance of small business in the economy in great detail.[32] He used employment, sales, and value added to measure the importance of small business. He also decomposed the changes in the small business share into that due to changes in the relative importance of small business within industries and that due to changes in the relative importance of industries with different small business shares. The remainder of this section reviews and updates his findings.[33]

The change in the fraction of employment at small companies between 1958 and 1977 is shown in the third column of Table 2.6 for the economy as a whole and for eight major industrial sectors. The small business share of employment declined for every industry between 1958 and 1977. The ratio of the 1977 share to the 1958 share reported in the fourth column of the table measures the severity of the decline across industries. The relative importance of small businesses has declined most severely in mining and least severely in services.

Despite the sharp decline in the small business share within most industries, the small business share of total employment declined by a modest 2.6 percentage points (a 5 percent decrease according to column 4) from 55.1 percent to 52.5 percent. The shift in employment over time from big business–dominated industries such as manufacturing to small business–dominated industries such as wholesale trade, documented in Table 2.7, has clearly cushioned the impact of intraindustry decreases in the small business share on the small business share for the economy as a whole.

In order to gauge the relative importance of intraindustry changes and interindustry changes on the small business share of employment, it is useful to decompose the change in the small business share between 1958 and 1977 into the change due to intraindustry changes in the relative importance of small business and into the change due to changes in the relative importance of different industrial sectors.[34] Excluding the construction and public warehousing industry, for which we do not have consistent data for 1958 and 1977, the small business share declined by six percentage points, from 55 percent in 1958 to 49 percent in 1977. Had the employment share of each industry remained constant between 1958 and 1977, the small business share of employment would have fallen by nine percentage points, from 55 percent in 1958 to 46 percent in 1977, as a result of the decreasing importance of small business in each industry. Had the relative importance of small businesses in each industry remained constant between 1958 and 1977, the small business share of employment would have risen four percentage points, from 55 percent in 1958 to 59

TABLE 2.6

Small Business Share of Employment, 1958–1977

Industry	*1958*	*1977*	*Change*[a]	*Ratio*[b]
All industries	55.1	52.5	−2.6	95
Minerals	62.2	44.3	−17.9	71
Construction[c]	85.7	82.1	−3.6	96
Manufacturing	37.1	29.0	−8.1	78
Transportation[d]	—	—	—	—
Public warehousing[e]	86.1	—	—	—
Wholesale trade	94.1	83.1	−11.0	88
Retail trade	72.5	62.3	−10.2	86
Services	84.0	75.6	−8.4	90

SOURCE: U.S. Department of Commerce, Bureau of the Census, *Enterprise Statistics,* 1958 and 1977.

NOTE: Small businesses are those enterprises with fewer than one hundred employees. Note that enterprises with no employees but the owner are excluded from these calculations.

[a] Change is calculated as 1977 share minus 1958 share.

[b] Ratio is calculated as 1977 share divided by 1958 share times 100.

[c] 1972 data substituted for 1958 data, since 1958 data were not available.

[d] No data available.

[e] Post-1958 data not available.

TABLE 2.7
Industry Share of Employment, 1958 and 1977

Industry	*1958*	*1977*
Mineral	1.8	1.3
Construction*	—	7.8
Manufacturing	55.8	44.1
Wholesale trade	6.8	7.2
Retail trade	25.9	27.2
Selected services	9.3	12.4

SOURCE: U.S. Department of Commerce, Bureau of the Census, *Enterprise Statistics,* 1958 and 1977.

*Data on the construction industry are not available for 1958.

percent in 1977, as a result of the increasing importance of small business–dominated industries such as services. The changing composition of the economy clearly cushioned the fall in the small business share.

The change in the fraction of business receipts made by small companies between 1958 and 1979 is shown in Table 2.8 for the economy and for eight major industrial sectors. The figures show a dramatic decrease in the small business share of business receipts for all industries. The small business share has declined most severely in mining and manufacturing and least severely in agriculture and services.[35]

In contrast to employment, changes in the share of business receipts obtained by each industry slightly accentuated the decline in the small business share of business receipts for the overall economy. Large business–dominated industries such as manufacturing maintained their shares of business receipts between 1958 and 1979, while some small business–dominated industries such as agriculture had smaller shares of business receipts in 1979 than in 1958, as documented in Table 2.9. The small business share of business receipts declined by twenty-three percentage points from 52 to 29 percent, between 1958 and 1979. Had the share of business receipts obtained by each industry remained constant between 1958 and 1979, the small business share of business receipts would have declined by twenty-one percentage points, from 52 to 31 percent. Had the small business share of business receipts remained constant for each industry between 1958 and 1979, the small business share of business receipts would have declined by only two percentage points, from 52 to 50 percent.

The share of gross product originating from businesses with fewer than five hundred employees is reported in Table 2.10 for the economy and for eight industry sectors for 1958 and 1977. All industries experienced decreases in the small business share of gross product originating. Mining suffered the most severe decline, and finance, insurance, and real estate suffered the least severe decline.

As with employment and in contrast to business receipts, the changing composition of the economy attenuated the decrease in the small business share of gross product originating for the economy. As documented in Table 2.11, the share of gross product originating in large business–dominated industries such as mining and manufacturing has decreased over time, while the share of gross product originating in small business–dominated industries such as services has increased over time. The small business share of gross product originating decreased by four percentage points, from 51 percent to 47 percent, between 1958 and 1977. Had the relative importance of small business in each industry remained constant between 1958 and 1977, the share of gross product originating from small businesses would have increased three percentage points, from 51 percent in 1958 to 54 percent in 1977, as a result of the increasing importance of small business–dominated industries. Had the share of value added contributed by each industry between 1958 and 1977 remained constant, the share of value added contributed by small businesses would have declined by seven percentage points, from 51 percent in 1958 to 44 percent in 1977.

Table 2.12 summarizes the changes in the small business share of employment (1958–1977), of business receipts (1958–1979), and of gross product originating (1958–1977) due to intraindustry shifts in the relative importance of small businesses and shifts in the industrial composition of the economy. All three measures show that the relative importance of

TABLE 2.8

Small Business Share of Business Receipts, 1958–1979

Industry	*1958*	*1979*	*Change*	*Ratio*[a]
All industries	51.5	28.7	−22.8	56
Agriculture	97.0	82.7	−14.3	85
Mining	44.3	14.4	−29.9	33
Construction	80.7	60.0	−20.7	74
Manufacturing	26.1	8.5	−17.6	33
Transportation	22.5	14.2	−8.3	62
Wholesale and retail trade	67.9	36.4	−31.5	54
Finance, insurance, real estate	43.4	30.6	−12.8	71
Services	88.4	72.6	−15.8	82

SOURCE: U.S. Department of the Treasury, *Statistics of Income* (Washington, D.C.: Government Printing Office, 1958 and 1980).

[a] Ratio is calculated as 1979 share divided by 1958 shares times 100.

NOTE: Small firms are those with business receipts of $5 million or less. Because the price level increased by 250 percent between 1958 and 1979, these comparisons vastly overstate the real decline in the small business share.

TABLE 2.9

Share of Business Receipts by Industry, 1958 and 1979

Industry	*1958*	*1979*
Agriculture	3.6	2.9
Mining	1.2	2.4
Construction	5.2	5.4
Manufacturing	35.7	35.7
Transportation	6.3	7.7
Wholesale and retail trade	35.4	33.5
Finance	7.4	6.0
Services	5.0	6.3

SOURCE: U.S. Department of the Treasury, Internal Revenue Service, *Statistics of Income* (Washington, D.C.: Government Printing Office, 1958 and 1979), for corporations, sole proprietorships, and partnerships.

NOTE: Shares exclude unclassified categories.

TABLE 2.10

Small Business Share of Gross Product Originating, 1958–1977

Industry	*1958*	*1977*	*Change*	*Ratio**
All industries	51	47	−4	.92
Mining	52	30	−12	.58
Construction	88	80	−8	.92
Manufacturing	28	20	−8	.71
Transportation, communications, and utilities	19	18	−1	.95
Wholesale trade	89	80	−9	.90
Retail trade	75	60	−15	.80
Finance, insurance, and real estate	49	48	−1	.98
Services	86	79	−7	.92

SOURCE: Joel Popkin and Company, "Measuring Gross Product Originating in Business: Methodology and Annual Estimates, 1955–1977," prepared under contract for the Small Business Administration, 1981.

*Ratio is calculated as 1977 share divided by 1958 share times 100.

small businesses has declined dramatically holding the industrial composition of the economy constant. The employment and gross product originating measures show that the decline in the relative importance of small businesses in the overall economy was cushioned by the increased share of employment and gross product taken by small business–dominated industries such as services and trade. The sales measure shows that the decline in the small business share of sales was magnified slightly by the decreased share of sales made by small business–dominated industries.

Why the difference between the sales measure on the one hand and the gross product originating and employment measures on the other hand?

TABLE 2.11
Industry Shares of Gross Product Originating, 1958 and 1977

Industry	*1958*	*1977*
Mining	3.3	2.9
Construction	5.6	5.4
Manufacturing	33.3	29.1
Transportation, communications, and utilities	10.9	10.7
Wholesale trade	8.2	8.7
Retail trade	12.0	11.5
Finance, insurance, and real estate	16.3	17.3
Services	10.4	14.3

SOURCE: Executive Office of the President, *The State of Small Business* (Washington, D.C.: Government Printing Office, March 1983), appendix table 2.15, pp. 213–214.

TABLE 2.12
Changes in the Small Business Share of Employment, Sales, and Gross Product Originating

	Employment[a] *(1958–1977)*	*Business Receipts (1958–1979)*	*Gross Product Originating (1958–1977)*
Total Change	−6	−23	−4
Change due to shifts in industry composition[b]	+4	−2	+3
Change due to shifts in small business share within industries[c]	−9	−21	−7

SOURCE: Calculations by the authors.

NOTE: Small businesses are those with fewer than 500 employees for the employment and value added measures and those with sales of under $5 million in 1958 dollars for the sales measure.

[a] Excludes the construction industry.

[b] Calculated under the assumption that each industry's share of total employment, sales, or value added, respectively, remained constant over the time period under consideration.

[c] Calculated under the assumption that small businesses' share of employment, sales, or value added, respectively, remained constant for each industry over the time period under consideration.

One possibility, suggested by White, is that the decline in vertical integration of manufacturing relative to other sectors and the rise in capital-labor ratios of manufacturing relative to other sectors has enabled manufacturing to support a greater value of sales with a smaller amount of employment and value added.

The small business share of value added is the best single measure of the relative importance of small business in the economy. Value added measures the amount of capital and labor the firm applies to materials purchased from other sectors of the economy in order to produce a final product. Sales tend to understate the importance of small businesses for the reasons discussed above. Employment tends to overstate the importance of small businesses because small businesses are more labor-intensive than large businesses. The small business share of value added has declined modestly overall—by about 8 percent, according to the fourth column of Table 2.10—despite dramatic declines in particular sectors—42 percent in mining, 29 percent in manufacturing, and 20 percent in retail trade according to the fourth column of Table 2.10.

The Role of Small Business

Although small businesses constitute an important albeit declining sector of our economy, they have received more attention from politicians than from economists. Their sheer number makes them an attractive constituency for politicians. Their meager market shares in many industries and the lack of detailed data on them have placed them at the bottom of most economists' research agendas.

Politicians have had a special concern for small businesses.[36] Congress codified this concern with the passage of the Small Business Act in 1953, which established the Small Business Administration. It directed the SBA to help small businesses obtain government loans, government contracts, and technical and managerial know-how.[37] Congress strengthened this act in 1958 by requiring government agencies to conduct a representative share of their business with small firms. It also passed the Small Business Investment Act in 1958, which encouraged the creation of investment companies that could provide small businesses with venture capital. The thrust of these pieces of legislation was to improve the competitive position of small businesses.

Dissatisfaction with the performance of the SBA among small businesses led Congress to strengthen the SBA's role as ombudsman for small businesses within the government. In 1976, Congress established the Office of Advocacy at the SBA.[38] This office was directed to "measure the direct costs and other effects of government regulation on small businesses and make legislative and nonlegislative proposals for eliminating excessive or unnecessary regulations of small businesses."[39] Other government agencies were directed to cooperate with the Office of Advocacy in this endeavor.

The creation of the Office of Advocacy "marked a dramatic shift of emphasis for the SBA," as Paul Verkuil has noted, "from protecting small business against a harsh economy to protecting it against a harsh bureaucracy."[40] This shift was due to the increasing role played by government regulations in the marketplace and also reflected the discontent of many businesses with the burdens imposed on them by the health and safety regulations erected during the early 1970s.

Congress reemphasized its concern over the impact of government policies on small businesses by passing, in 1980, four pieces of legislation that deal directly with small business problems.[41] The Small Business Economic Policy Act of 1980 "mandates the coordination of all federal departments and agencies in fostering the economic interests of small business and requires the President to submit an annual report to Congress assessing the impact of federal law and policies on small business."[42] It also provides for the creation of the SBDB mentioned earlier. The Paperwork Reduction Act of 1980 empowers the Office of Management and Budget to limit the paperwork generated by governmental agencies. Small businesses were seen as a major beneficiary of this legislation. The Regulatory Flexibility Act of 1980 encourages federal agencies to impose lighter regulatory burdens on small businesses by requiring these agencies to prepare regulatory analyses of proposed rules that would exert a "significant economic impact on a substantial number of small entities" and to review the existing rules that affect small businesses in a significant way.[43] The Equal Access to Justice Act (1980) enables small businesses to recover legal costs when they prevail in litigation with the federal government.

These four pieces of legislation reflect congressional concern that small businesses bear a disproportionate share of the regulatory burden and are therefore placed at a competitive disadvantage relative to larger businesses. For example, the main impetus behind the Regulatory Flexibility Act was the belief that larger businesses can average regulatory costs over a larger quantity of output and thereby obtain a cost advantage over their smaller rivals. The thrust of the four bills enacted in 1980 was to make federal policy makers more aware of the impact of their policies on small businesses and to establish broad guidelines for incorporating small business interests in the social calculus. It is important to note, however, that these bills do not automatically condemn policies that have a disparate impact on smaller businesses. They merely ask policy makers to weigh small business interests along with other competing social interests.

Congress seldom provides a clear rationale for the legislation it enacts. Bill promoters appeal to many often conflicting rationales in order to maximize their bill's chance of passage. The three theories reviewed in the remainder of this section articulate the potential merits and demerits of small businesses and encompass most of the major arguments made during congressional debate on small businesses issues.

POPULIST THEORY

The courts have expressed special concern for small businesses in antitrust case law. Justice Rufus Wheeler Peckham, speaking for a majority of the Supreme Court in its first substantive interpretation of the Sherman Act, noted that business combinations

> may even temporarily, or perhaps permanently, reduce the price of the article traded in or manufactured, by reducing the expense inseparable from the running of many different companies for the same purpose. Trade or commerce under those circumstances may nevertheless be badly and unfortunately restrained by driving out of business the small dealers and worthy men whose lives have been spent therein and who might be unable to readjust themselves to their altered surroundings. Mere reduction in the price of the commodity dealt in might be dearly paid for by the ruin of such a class.[44]

This apparent willingness to sacrifice the efficiencies gained from business competition in order to protect small businesses was echoed repeatedly in subsequent decisions. Judge Hand noted for the majority in *Alcoa,* "It is possible, because of its indirect social and moral effect, to prefer a system of small producers, each depending for his success on his own skill and character, to one in which the great mass of those engaged must accept the direction of the few."[45] Judge Douglas, in his *Columbia Steel* dissent, argued, "Industrial power should be decentralized, it should be scattered into many hands so that the fortunes of the people will not be dependent on the whims and caprice, the political prejudices, the emotional stability of a few self-appointed men."[46] Finally, Judge Warren, in the majority opinion for *Brown Shoe,* argued that one of the purposes of the Clayton Act was to protect "viable, small, locally owned businesses," even if that resulted in "occasional higher costs and prices."[47]

The solicitude the courts have shown toward small businesses is apparently based on two value judgments. The first is a preference for a maximally decentralized society where production is at the hands of the "worthy" men who operate small businesses and provide the "moral backbone" to society. As Kaysen and Turner remark, this preference is based on "Jeffersonian symbols of wide political appeal and great persistence in American life."[48] Small businesses are the backbone of local communities and thus of democracy itself. Large businesses threaten the power of small businesses and of local communities. The loss of local power may lead to the increase of federal power. Therefore, society must curtail the power of big businesses and other agglomerations of economic and social power.

The second value judgment is based on a belief that the superior bargaining ability and efficiency sometimes achieved by big businesses are inherently unfair to small businesses that are thereby placed at a competitive disadvantage. This concern for the underdog is seen most clearly in the enforcement of the Clayton Act. Neale's comment is on point:

> An element of "underdoggery" has been noted in the enforcement of the Clayton Act prohibitions. The way in which the courts pay less heed to economic effects once there is proof of coercion, the way in which they focus on the competitive viability of small firms rather than on the competition between large ones—all this points to a tendency in antitrust administration to extend the sway of the policy to the correction of apparent hardship and "unfairness" in the private commercial relations, rather than to confine it to the control of the monopoly power in the public interest.[49]

Whether Congress intended the antitrust statutes to protect small businesses is open to question. Bork argues persuasively that the sole purpose of the Sherman Act was to protect consumers by condemning combinations that create inefficiencies. Turner disputes Judge Warren's interpretation of the Clayton Act. He says that there is "no credible support for the statement in *Brown Shoe* that Congress appreciated the possible efficiency cost of attempting to preserve fragmented industries and consciously resolved the competing considerations in favor of centralization."[50]

The goals of the Robinson-Patman Act are less clear. This act was passed in the midst of the Great Depression, at a time when small businesses faced contracting markets and the expansion of large retail chains. Neale notes that this legislation, which strengthened the Clayton Act prohibition against price discrimination, was designed to aid small merchants. These merchants were convinced that the large chains were using their buying power to extract discounts from their suppliers and were thereby securing an unfair competitive edge over small business.[51] But whatever the congressional intent behind the statutes, the case law clearly holds the protection of small businesses as a major charter.

CLASSICAL ECONOMIC THEORY

Textbook economic theory gives small businesses mixed reviews. It extols their virtue in facilitating the invisible hand of perfect competition. But it sometimes condemns their failure to achieve efficiencies supposedly available from operating at a large scale.

In the traditional theory of competitive markets, the equilibrium price equals two different measures of cost. First, price equals the cost of supplying an additional unit, the so-called marginal or incremental cost of production. Second, price equals the average cost of providing the quantity demanded at this price. This twofold equality guarantees that society uses its scarce resources as efficiently as possible and that businesses earn no more than a competitive rate of return. Part of the reason for this desirable property is that average cost is smallest when it equals marginal cost. When there are a large number of identical firms, the industry and each firm in it operate at the so-called efficient scale of operation, where the average cost of production is smallest (the point of least average cost).

The equality of price, average cost, and marginal cost follows from three basic assumptions. First, there are no entry restrictions that prevent firms from entering the market, competing price down to least average cost, and thereby eliminating excess profits. Second, the average cost of production eventually increases with increases in production so that scale economies are exhausted at an output level that is small relative to market demand. Third, the output supplied by all firms, each producing at a common efficient scale of operation, equals the output demanded when price equals the least average cost.

With these and many other technical assumptions, modern economists have proved Adam Smith's famous invisible hand theorem:

> As every individual, therefore, endeavors as much as he can both to employ his capital in the support of domestic industry, and so to direct that industry that its produce may be of the greatest value; every individual necessarily labours to render the annual revenue of the society as great as he can. He generally, indeed, neither intends to promote the public interest, nor knows how much he is promoting it. . . . By directing that industry in such a manner as its produce may be of the greatest value, he intends only his own gain, and he is in this, as in many other cases, led by an invisible hand to promote an end which was no part of his intention.[52]

Perfect competition, in modern terms, promotes an allocation of resources from which it is impossible to make anyone better off without making someone else worse off.

An essential characteristic of competitive markets is that no firm can by itself affect the market price. Each firm must take price as given. Firms are individually powerless because they are so small relative to the market that any reduction in their output level will have no discernible effect on market price and any increase in their price will drive their customers to other sellers. Another essential characteristic of competitive markets is that firms cannot readily conspire to fix market price. Firms are collectively powerless because the costs of organizing and policing a cartel are prohibitive and opportunities for tacit collusion are limited.

Small business therefore provides a bulwark against market power. For this reason some economists have supported policies that prevent industries from becoming too concentrated. For example, a vigorous antimerger policy receives support from at least some segments of the economics profession. F. M. Scherer argues, "There is much to be said for a policy that errs on the side of a hard line against mergers, accepting the risk that occasionally mergers offering substantial efficiency benefits will be barred because the judicial system is such an imperfect screen."[53]

Small businesses are not always as innocent as traditional industrial organization theory characterizes them. Although most theories of tacit and explicit collusion suggest that anticompetitive behavior is difficult in markets with a large number of small firms, casual observation suggests otherwise. Doctors, lawyers, dentists, real estate brokers, and opticians—all basically small businessmen—have been remarkably successful at inhibiting competition, as have other professional groups. Local building codes, local zoning restrictions, and certain real estate practices have inhibited competition in the construction and sale of residential real estate.[54] Several important antitrust cases in the last decade have involved businesses that most observers would call small. Corrugated container manufacturers have lost or settled under unfavorable terms several major private antitrust cases that accused them of price fixing. Paper product companies have also lost price-fixing cases. Finally, several grand juries have returned sweeping indictments against construction companies for rigging bids on government contracts.

The traditional theory of competitive markets breaks down when firms have an efficient scale of operation that is large relative to market demand. In the extreme case where a single firm can meet all market demand at a lower cost than two or more firms could—the case of natural monopoly—the market process generally imposes few constraints on the power of this firm to set prices and production levels. The firm will charge a price and set a production level that maximizes its profit. Although economists have not reached a consensus on how prices and production levels are determined in less extreme cases where a few large firms dominate the market, most theories suggest that such firms will continue to set prices above and production levels below the competitive levels.

Large businesses may achieve various economies that are unavailable to smaller businesses. There are three possible sources of economies.

First, the most efficient technology for serving a market may entail fixed costs—for capital equipment, for developing a distribution system, or to meet regulatory requirements, for example—that are largely independent of output or may involve network economies that can only be achieved by large-scale operation. Telephone service and trucking, for example, arguably benefit from networking. The efficient scale of operation is undoubtedly larger in some industries than in others. Few economists would argue that thousands of small firms could produce automobiles or provide telephone service more efficiently than a few industrial giants. But, often, the case for size is overstated. Peters and Waterman, drawing upon their own study of top-performing companies and academic studies of business organizations, argue that the best companies are often run as a collection of small businesses.[55] These companies have lean corporate staffs, decentralize responsibility and control into small divisions usually hiring fewer than five hundred employees, and avoid diversifying into unrelated areas in which they have no special expertise. These companies recognize that scale economies that exist in theory often evaporate in practice, particularly in the efficient training of workers. Peters and Waterman claim that "smallness . . . induces manageability and, above all, commitment. A manager can really understand something that is small and in which one central discipline prevails."[56] The better firms also stick to their knitting—they either specialize in a narrowly defined service or product line or they diversify in closely related lines of business. Peters and Waterman argue, "It is a simple fact that most acquisitions go awry. Not only are the synergies to which so many executives pay lip service seldom realized; more often than not the result is catastrophic."[57] The companies surveyed by Peters and Waterman must realize some advantage from bigness, since most are quite large. Peters and Waterman do not address this paradox directly. But the answer may be that these companies have highly developed corporate cultures, imparted by the company founders and refined over the years, that bind the corporate divisions and give them a competitive advantage.

Second, centralized control of economic activity through a corporate bureaucracy may achieve efficiencies unavailable from decentralized market coordination. The transaction cost theory of the firm, for example, identifies circumstances in which market transactions are cumbersome and for which integration across firms is therefore desirable. Evans and Grossman argue, however, that the problems that afflict market transactions also afflict internal transactions within integrated firms. The transactions cost theory fails to show how integration makes cumbersome market transactions less cumbersome.[58]

Third, large businesses may engage in more innovation and thereby achieve more dynamic efficiencies than can small businesses. Schumpeter, for example, argues that businesses will underinvest in research and development unless they are protected from parasitic competitors. Larger and more monopolistic firms can capture a greater share of the gains from their innovations than can smaller and less monopolistic firms. They therefore have a greater incentive to invest in innovation in the first place. There is little empirical support for the proposition that larger businesses are more innovative than smaller businesses, however, and recent theoretical work on innovation suggests that there is no strong link between market structure and innovative activity.[59]

The invisible hand may operate poorly in markets where the efficient scale of operation is large relative to market demand and where atomistic competition is therefore not feasible. In these markets economists have traditionally recommended substituting the visible hand of government regulation for the ineffectual invisible hand of competition. Government regulation has taken several forms. The first form of regulation inhibits the development of large firms by limiting mergers. The policy advocated by economists involves trading off the gains from efficiency potentially available from mergers into large productive units against the loss in efficiency from possible anticompetitive behavior. The policy adopted by the courts places a great deal of weight on the inequities of monopoly power and the loss of small businesses as well as on the efficiency losses of anticompetitive behavior. The Reagan administration, however, has placed a greater weight on the efficiency gains from merger than have previous administrations or the courts. The Justice Department and the Federal Trade Commission, which have jurisdiction over mergers, have opposed few mergers since 1981.

The second form of regulation promotes the development of large firms by allowing mergers, granting exclusive franchises, and prohibiting entry. The policy advocated by many economists and generally adopted in the regulation of public utilities recognizes that some industries are natural monopolies and that competition is wasteful. It therefore designates a single firm to serve these markets. But in order to prevent this firm from exercising monopoly power, it regulates the prices charged and the rate of return earned by these firms. This policy has come into increasing disrepute among economists for two reasons: (1) there is some evidence that many public utility monopolies are less natural than economists once thought;[60] (2) there is some evidence that regulation is less effective than competition in controlling prices and profits in these industries.[61]

The third form of regulation is a hybrid called "regulated competition." The dissatisfaction with the second form of regulation has led policy makers to allow restricted competition in banking, trucking, and telecommunications in the last several years. Regulators have made it easier for businesses to enter these fields and challenge dominant incumbent firms. At the same time, regulators have retained a measure of control over the prices charged, services offered, and rates of return earned by the firms in these industries. Typically, regulators give small competitors much more leeway than the large dominant firms. The FCC, for example, is considering exempting all long-distance companies except AT&T from having to seek FCC approval for rate changes and new service offerings. The major pitfall of regulated competition is that firms sometimes find trying to convince regulators to place constraints on their rivals more profitable than trying to provide customers with the best products at the best price.[62] The Civil Aeronautics Board, recognizing that competition and regulation are anathema, promoted its own destruction.[63]

Since the Carter administration came into office in 1977, the government has placed increasing reliance on the competitive process and decreasing reliance on the visible hand of government regulation. Small business may benefit from this policy drift. It is true that the Reagan administration's liberal attitude toward mergers may increase concentration and possibly place small businesses at a disadvantage in some industries, but increased merger freedom may also encourage the formation of more small businesses. Mergers enable businesses to capitalize on their investments. The freedom to sell out for a profit may encourage more entrepreneurs to test the waters. Moreover, the freedom of particularly able entrepreneurs to capitalize on their abilities by becoming large through mergers may also encourage small business formation. Deregulation on the other hand has clearly stimulated the formation of small businesses in airlines, financial services, trucking, and telecommunications.[64]

THE AUSTRIAN SCHOOL

Textbook economic theory and the more academic discussion of antitrust and regulatory policy are often at odds with an alternative tradition in economics, the Austrian school, which is currently experiencing a renaissance among economists.[65] Austrian economics views competition as a process of dynamic change, in contrast to neoclassical economics, which views competition as a state of equilibrium. Hayek argued that "competition is by its nature a dynamic process whose essential characteristics are assumed away by the assumptions underlying static analysis" and that equilibrium theory "deals almost exclusively with a state . . . in which it is assumed that the data for the different individuals are fully adjusted to each other, while the problem which requires explanation is the value of the process by which the data are thus adjusted."[66]

The entrepreneur is the mover and shaker in the dynamic process. His alertness to hitherto unnoticed profit opportunities enables him to improve the allocation of scarce resources and to make a profit in the process. He is the innovator who introduces new products or services or who introduces more efficient methods for providing existing products or services. As Schumpeter put it, his role in the capitalist system

> is to reform or revolutionize the pattern of production by exploiting an invention or, more generally, an untried technological possibility for producing a new commodity or producing an old one in a new way, by opening up a new source of supply of materials or a new outlet for products, by reorganizing an industry.[67]

Ownership over the means of production is not a prerequisite to entrepreneurship in the Austrian school, in contrast to the neoclassical theory. The successful entrepreneur, like the successful commodity broker, is a better judge of the future than his fellow man. He helps arbitrage between different states of the world and earns a profit on his superior ability to do so.

He may need investment capital in order to accomplish this arbitrage. If he has a successful track record as an entrepreneur, he will have little difficulty raising the necessary capital. If he is unable to convince potential creditors of his superior foresight, he may have to act as his own capitalist or pay a substantial premium for risk capital. But in either case, he earns a profit on his entrepreneurial ability that is distinct, at least in theory, from the profit on capital.

Small businesses, at least the kind that test new ideas in the marketplace, have a more hallowed place in Austrian than in neoclassical economics. These businesses are often the source of Schumpeter's perennial gale that shakes up the capitalist system. From them today emerge the great industries of tomorrow. This point is brought home by the industrial revolution in electronics, computers, and telecommunications. In the last twenty years, comparatively small firms in these industries have evolved into industrial giants. Texas Instruments in electronics, Apple in computers, and MCI in telecommunications are three of many possible examples.

The Austrian perspective accents the folly in imposing impediments to the competitive process for the sake of increasing static efficiency. Regulations that deter competitive entry, such as those that are being dismantled in the transportation and telecommunications industries, or that require businesses to use particular technologies or techniques, such as environmental regulations that require particular pollution control devices or local building codes that require specified materials and technique, may, for example, increase static efficiency but only at the expense of decreasing the dynamic efficiencies possible from the perennial gale of entrepreneurial activity.

The next chapter will examine several theories of business formation, dissolution, and growth that integrate key aspects of the Austrian and classical schools. Before we develop these theories, however, it is useful to examine several key differences between larger and smaller firms.

Empirical Regularities Across Business Sizes

Businesses are remarkably varied even within the same industry. They come in different sizes, they earn different rates of return, their products are often differentiated from one another, they evolve in different ways over the business cycle, they vary in their relative use of capital and labor, and some have advantages—a unique location or special know-how—that others lack. Despite this diversity, economists have uncovered several relationships between business size and other business characteristics that appear to hold fairly systematically.

- In many industries, larger businesses have higher and more stable rates of return than smaller businesses.
- Smaller firms have higher and more variable rates of growth than larger firms.

- Smaller firms and younger firms are more likely to dissolve themselves during a given period of time than larger firms and older firms.
- The distribution of business sizes across industries and within industries often follows a lognormal distribution fairly closely.

These relationships have been documented in a number of studies for different countries and economic sectors. Although it is possible to quarrel with many aspects of these studies, the relationships listed above are useful working hypotheses. In addition to these relationships, recent research has found several other interesting differences between smaller and larger firms.

- Smaller and younger firms produce more innovations per employee than do older and larger firms.[68]
- Small firms create a disproportionate share of the nation's new jobs.[69]
- Small firms appear to act as shock absorbers for the economy, absorbing a disproportionate share of output fluctuations over the business cycle. Their ability to absorb shocks is partly due to their choice of more flexible, labor-intensive production techniques.[70]

It remains to be seen whether these differences will be confirmed by subsequent and more refined research. Because the last three relationships are less well documented than the first four, we concentrate our attention on the first four.

RATES OF RETURN

Table 2.13 shows the average after-tax rate of return on equity for six business size classes during four economic periods between 1963 and 1977.[71] The economy experienced normal growth between 1963 and 1965, rapid growth during the boom years of the Vietnam War, 1966–1969, sluggish growth between 1969 and 1971, and sluggish growth together with rapid inflation between 1975 and 1977 in the aftermath of the OPEC oil price rise. The economy was subjected to extensive wage and price controls that distorted market relationships between 1972 and 1974, so that these years are excluded from the data. Businesses with under $10 million of assets are often owned in whole or in large part by their manager. The owner-manager has many opportunities to take profits in the form of direct or indirect compensation, thereby biasing the profit figures. These companies are therefore excluded. Despite some anomalies, the data reported in the table show a fairly consistent positive relationship between size and profitability.

Several more refined statistical studies also suggest that the rate of return tends to increase with firm size. Hall and Weiss found a statistically significant positive relationship between the rate of return on assets and size after controlling for changes in demand and cost conditions among

TABLE 2.13
Average After-Tax Rate of Return on Equity for Manufacturing Corporations, 1963–1977

Corporation Asset Size (millions of dollars)	*Rate of Return (percentage)*			
	1963–65	*1966–69*	*1969–71*	*1975–77*
Over 1,000	13.5	12.7	10.3	13.2
250–1,000	11.0	12.1	10.4	13.0
100–250	11.2	12.0	9.7	12.1
50–100	10.4	11.2	8.6	12.0
25–50	10.0	11.0	7.9	12.4

SOURCE: Unweighted averages of quarterly rates of return derived from Federal Trade Commission, *Quarterly Financial Report for Manufacturing Corporations* (Washington, D.C.: Government Printing Office, various years). F. M. Scherer, *Industrial Market Structure and Economic Performance,* 2d ed. (Boston: Houghton Mifflin, 1980), table T4.1, p. 92.

NOTE: In order to reflect changes in the business cycle, the 1966–1969 period includes the first two quarters of 1969 and the 1969–1971 period includes the last two quarters of 1969.

companies listed on the Fortune 500.[72] The after-tax rate of return on assets was 30 percent higher for firms with assets of $2 billion or more than for firms with assets of between $50 million and $100 million. The positive relationship they found was stronger and statistically more significant than relationships found by earlier authors such as Alexander, Stekler, and Stigler.[73] The positive relationship between profitability and size is much less strong within narrowly defined industries. Marcus's study of three-digit industries found a statistically significant positive relationship between the after-tax rate of return on assets and size in 35 of 118 industries, no statistically significant relationship in 74 industries, and a statistically significantly positive relationship in 9 industries.[74]

None of the studies of the relationship between profitability and size, however, adjusts the rate of return for the risk borne by the firm. As shown below, the rate of return is much more variable for smaller than for larger businesses. Therefore, smaller businesses must receive a higher actual rate of return on investment than larger businesses in order to receive the same risk-adjusted rate of return on investment. Since virtually all studies show that the unadjusted rate of return on investment is a nondecreasing function of firm size, the risk-adjusted rate of return on investment may be an increasing function of firm size even within narrowly defined industries. Further research is needed to examine this possibility.

Alexander examined the variability of the rate of return for manufacturing firms between 1933 and 1947.[75] He found that the variability of the rate of return among smaller corporations is greater than that for larger corporations. He also found that the rate of return fluctuates more widely over time for smaller corporations than for larger ones. Subsequent cross-sectional studies have confirmed this finding.

GROWTH RATES

Hart and Prais's seminal study of companies listed on the London Stock Exchange between 1885 and 1950 found that the rate at which firms grew was roughly independent of their initial size.[76] Simon and Bonini examined the growth rates of companies listed on the Fortune 500 between 1955 and 1956.[77] They found that firm growth was proportionate to firm size on average. Hymer and Pashigian found that the growth rates of the largest thousand manufacturing firms were roughly independent of firm size between 1946 and 1955.[78]

This empirical regularity is known as Gibrat's Law of Proportionate Growth, after the statistician who first conjectured that the observed size distribution of firms could be explained as a consequence of the workings of this law. It has several implications. First, it implies that a small firm is just as likely to grow by a given percentage as a large firm. Second, it implies that the future growth rate of a firm is independent of the past growth rate of the firm.

Recent research indicates that Gibrat's Law is at best a crude approximation to the actual growth patterns of firms. Mansfield and Evans found that firm growth is much higher for smaller firms than for larger firms. Evans has also found that firm growth decreases with firm size for some samples of large firms. Some of his results are reported in Chapter 6.[79] One relationship that all of these studies find is that the variability of firm growth decreases with firm size.

BUSINESS FORMATIONS AND DISSOLUTION

Another extensively documented regularity is that smaller firms are more likely to fail than larger firms. Hart and Prais, Mansfield, and DuRietz found this relationship in their limited samples of corporations.[80] Birch found that same relationship in his extensive study of establishments listed on the Dun and Bradstreet Market Identifier File.[81] Table 2.14 shows the percentage of establishment dissolutions by size and age for the years 1969–1976. Establishments with fewer than twenty-one employees were more than two and a half times as likely to fail as establishments with more than five hundred employees (57.8 percent vs. 22.9 percent). The table shows a clear positive relationship between the number of employees and the probability of dissolution. It also shows that younger firms of all sizes are more likely to fail than older firms.

SIZE DISTRIBUTION OF BUSINESSES

Most of the early studies of size distribution of businesses focused on the size distribution of the largest businesses in the economy. For example,

TABLE 2.14
Probability of Establishment Dissolution, by Age and Employment Size, Between 1969 and 1976

Number of Employees	*Age (years)* 0–4	5–9	10+	Grand Average
0–20	64.8	56.9	54.1	57.8
21–50	50.4	38.0	29.2	35.1
51–100	47.4	37.9	27.7	32.8
101–500	46.3	37.6	25.7	30.9
501+	36.6	40.3	18.2	22.9
Grand average	63.6	55.6	51.5	55.8

SOURCE: David L. Birch, *The Job Generation Process* (Cambridge: Program on Neighborhood and Regional Change, MIT, 1979), table 4.4.

NOTE: A dissolution occurs when an establishment on the Dun and Bradstreet file in 1969 is not on the file in 1976. In some cases the establishment may have been acquired or merged with another establishment.

Simon and Bonini examined the size distribution of the Fortune 500 companies, and Hart and Prais examined the size distribution of companies listed on the London Stock Exchange.[82] These studies found that the size distribution of businesses followed a lognormal distribution (Hart and Prais) or the closely related Pareto distribution (Simon and Bonini).

Richard Quandt examined the size distribution of firms within particular industries.[83] He examined the size distribution of assets for firms listed on the 1963 Dun and Bradstreet's *Million Dollar Directory.* These data include far more small firms than the data sources used by Hart and Prais and Simon and Bonini, although many small firms remain excluded. He tested several alternative distributions of asset size.[84] Quandt used two criteria to determine whether a distribution provided a good fit. The first is how closely the estimated distribution fits the observed distribution (i.e., how closely the predicted frequencies match the observed frequencies between particular ranges). The second concerns the degree of randomness of the deviations between actual and predicted frequencies. Systematic deviations in predicted and observed frequencies suggest a poor fit. Based on these criteria, the lognormal distribution yielded good fits for twenty out of the thirty industries Quandt examined.[85]

We have seen that small businesses comprise an important sector of this country's economy. Most of the almost 17 million businesses in this country are small. Although these businesses contribute a disproportionately small share of our nation's output—the 98 percent of all businesses that have fewer than one hundred employees produce only 34 percent of the GNP—their share of output is by no means negligible. The importance of small businesses, however, lies not only in their numerousness and in their contribution to output. It lies as well in the competitive pressure they place on their larger rivals and in the often overlooked fact that the great corporations of tomorrow will spring from the small firms started today.

3

THEORIES OF BUSINESS FORMATION, DISSOLUTION, AND GROWTH

Despite the important role small businesses play in the American economy, little is known about the impact of federal policies on the formation, growth, and frequent dissolution of these businesses. To what extent do federal regulations stifle the formation of small businesses and affect the size distribution of businesses? What variables determine the *rates* of business formation, dissolution, and growth? To what extent would alternative taxes on small businesses, such as graduated income and capital gains taxes, value added taxes, and simplified payroll taxes, or reduced regulatory requirements, such as the tiered regulations encouraged by the Regulatory Flexibility Act, affect the formation, profitability, and competitive impact of small businesses?

Textbook economic theory sheds little light on these types of questions. This theory says that firms enter an industry until, at the equilibrium of industry supply and demand, potential entrants are unable to collect economic rents through entry.[1] Firms leave an industry when average variable cost exceeds price, which could happen if production costs rise or demand falls. In the simplest version of this theory, firms have identical cost curves. This version therefore does not identify which firms will enter or leave an industry. A more elaborate version of this theory assumes firms have different cost curves, perhaps because they have access to different technologies or to differing amounts of some specialized factor of production. The most efficient firms enter an expanding industry and the least efficient firms leave a contracting industry. The most efficient firms are those that have the lowest average *total* cost curves. Because sunk costs are irrelevant for rational decision making, the least efficient exiting firms are those that have the highest average *variable* cost curves.

As a tool for evaluating the impacts of federal policies, this theory is seriously deficient for three major reasons. First, it is a static equilibrium theory with virtually no implications for the rate of entry, exit, and growth or for the speed of adjustment of prices, quantities, profits, and the number of firms to long-run equilibrium levels. Policy makers are concerned as much with the short-term effects of their policies as with the long-term effects. Business formations and dissolutions take time. Entrepreneurs have to identify profit opportunities, raise financial capital, put physical capital in place, and develop skilled employees. When fixed costs are large relative to variable costs and capital is specific to the firm or industry, businesses may dissolve slowly in response to reductions in demand or increases in cost.

The policy importance of a theory that describes the speed of exit and entry is obvious. If the rate of entry is slow and capacity is fixed, tax remedies that reduce variable costs may not raise the entry rate substantially, may result in large profits for existing firms over the medium term, and may have little impact on innovation, prices, or quantities. On the other hand, accelerated depreciation of capital for small businesses may yield few tax benefits for existing small businesses but, by promoting rapid entry, may result in severe price competition, leaving existing firms with long-run *ex post* losses (i.e., a less than profitable rate of return on initial investment with hindsight). In these circumstances, policy makers might wish to couple accelerated depreciation for small businesses with a once-and-for-all tax credit for existing small businesses.

Second, the theory does not specify what determines the supply of entrepreneurs or managers. It implicitly assumes that supply is perfectly elastic in the sense that profit opportunities always elicit the appropriate number of entrepreneurs. This may not be the case. Would-be entrepreneurs weigh the risky stream of profits against certain wages from labor market employment. Different tax treatment of entrepreneurial income and wages may distort the process by which individuals sort themselves out as employers or employees.

Kihlstrom and Laffont have developed a simple general equilibrium model of firm formation in which production requires entrepreneurial as well as normal labor inputs.[2] Their model is largely a formalization of Knight's theory of the entrepreneur as a risk bearer. Relatively risk-averse individuals become employees. Lucas has also developed a simple general equilibrium model of firm formation in which individuals differ in their managerial abilities.[3] Individuals with relatively less managerial ability become workers. We review these theories below.

Policy makers could use a model of the impact of federal taxes on the supply of entrepreneurs to analyze a variety of options. Would a reduction in income taxes increase or decrease the supply of entrepreneurs? How would changes in double taxation of corporate income, liberalization of Subchapter S regulations, capital gains taxes, payroll taxes, or the creation of a separate small business tax entity affect the supply of entrepreneurs? Answers to these questions are important to policy makers concerned with promoting small businesses and encouraging innovation.

Third, the theory ignores the role of expectations in decisions to form or expand businesses. A potential entrant can count on many other entrepreneurs seeing the same profit opportunities as himself. He must guess how many other firms will enter the industry and how quickly they will do so. Considerations such as these will determine how quickly firms will form and how soon the new equilibrium will be attained in response to market or institutional changes. Models of economic behavior over time must take this role of expectations into account in order to be consistent with the underlying theory of rational profit-maximizing behavior. Consequently, it is necessary to determine the rate of business formation and dissolution and expectations of future profits simultaneously.[4]

Our purpose in this chapter is not to develop a model of business behavior that addresses these problems simultaneously. Rather we undertake the less ambitious but immediately more fruitful task of summarizing recent work by our colleagues on the determinants of business formation, dissolution, and growth. Although the theories we examine are abstract and somewhat removed from the realities of the business world, each sheds light on many interesting aspects of business behavior. In subsequent chapters we use these theories to study the impact of government regulations on smaller businesses and to guide the empirical analyses of business formation, dissolution, and growth. In order to ground our theories in the real world, we precede our survey of these theories with a review of what is known about the men and women who start businesses and a discussion of the aspects of business behavior that these theories fail to capture.

Characteristics of Entrepreneurs

Economists have largely suppressed the role of the entrepreneur in modern theory by relying on abstract production functions to describe the firm and by ignoring the process by which the economy evolves over time.[5] Because of this theoretical vacuum, economists have performed few empirical studies of entrepreneurship.[6] The major exceptions are Miller's studies of the background of 190 business leaders in the first decade of this century, Gregory and Neu's study of 247 business leaders in the 1870s, and Taussig and Joslyn's study of the origins of business leaders.[7] These studies found that business leaders come from a select portion of the population. Businessmen were often sons of professional men, often came from urban areas, were more highly educated than their countrymen, and were seldom immigrants. But these leaders were more often managers than founders. Only 14 percent of the leaders studied by Miller founded their own companies. Most managed large companies with many stockholders and bore little financial risk themselves. Thus these leaders were bureaucrats rather than entrepreneurs.

Dahmen's massive study of entrepreneurship in Sweden, although it did not examine the demographic characteristics of entrepreneurs, did discover some interesting patterns. The first generation of entrepreneurs in an industry usually came from a related industry—e.g., textile manufacturers evolved not from the tailor trade but from clothing merchants—whereas the second generation usually came from people who worked for the first-generation firms.[8]

Psychologists and sociologists have studied the personal characteristics of select groups of enterpreneurs. The studies by McClelland and Winter, Collins and Moore, and Shapero found that entrepreneurs have a number of common characteristics.[9]

- Entrepreneurs are often orphans or half-orphans or had fathers who were away for long periods of time. Entrepreneurs are often "on their own" as kids.
- Entrepreneurs are more likely to be immigrants or the sons of immigrants than nonentrepreneurs (note the contrast with the studies discussed above).
- Enterpreneurs are less able to submit to authority, push themselves more, and put less stock in getting ahead (in the sense of gaining approval from society) than nonentrepreneurs.[10]
- Entrepreneurs take calculated risks. They do not gamble. Because they are confident of their own abilities, they often discount risks.
- Entrepreneurs are much more likely to have fathers who were company owners, professionals, or otherwise self-employed than are nonentrepreneurs. Shapero found that more than 50 percent of the entrepreneurs he studied had self-employed fathers versus less than 10 percent for nonentrepreneurs.
- Entrepreneurs are often people who feel they have a great deal of influence over the course of events. They downplay luck.
- Entrepreneurs are relatively well educated. Douglas found that 37 percent of the entrepreneurs he studied had at least a college degree, compared with 14 percent of the population at large.[11]
- Most entrepreneurs are displaced persons whose niche in life has been upset and who are therefore outside the mainstream of society. Shapero found that, in 65 percent of the cases he examined, the primary influence on the entrepreneur was negative. The entrepreneur had lost a job, been divorced, or left the military.
- Once an entrepreneur always an entrepreneur. Shapero found that 72 percent of the entrepreneurs he surveyed would start a new company if their present one folded. Copulsky and McNulty also note that entrepreneurs often drift from one entrepreneurial pursuit to another. They note, "Some entrepreneurs have spent as much as twenty years in seemingly aimless drifting and dragon-tilting before they struck a successful deal."[12]
- People typically become entrepreneurs when they are young, between twenty-five and forty.

These studies suggest that entrepreneurs are intrinsically different from nonentrepreneurs and that there is a correlation between certain personality traits and entrepreneurial success. McClelland and Winter, Shapero, and Schrage emphasize that entrepreneurs receive much different scores than nonentrepreneurs on psychological tests. Several of the models we develop in the following section capture these intrinsic differences by assuming that individuals are endowed with a certain level of "entrepreneurial ability." Those with a high degree of such ability form businesses, and those with a low degree of such ability become workers. Profitability and growth are positively correlated with ability.

Theories of the Entrepreneur

The models we present below and rely upon in the remainder of this book are highly abstract. They do not capture the full flavor of the real business world. Before we present them, it is useful to provide an intuitive explanation of how these models, suitably extended and amplified, explain the coexistence of Safeway and corner grocers, MCI and AT&T, small specialty chemical companies and Dupont, Midway Airlines and TWA, and other large and small companies.

The models discussed below imply that small businesses are less efficient than big businesses but that policies that have a disparate impact on small businesses decrease social welfare. Let us explain. Big business B can produce 10 units of output for an average cost of $1. Small business S can produce 10 units of output for an average cost of $10. B can therefore produce 10 units of output more efficiently than S can. B can produce 100 units of output for an average cost of $10. B and S are therefore equally efficient when B produces 100 units and S "specializes" in producing 10 units. B can produce 110 units for an average cost of $11. S operating at 10 units is therefore more efficient than is B operating at 110 units. If the market were large enough to absorb only 110 units, society would gain by having one big business provide 100 units and one small business provide 10 units instead of having one big business produce everything. The same principle dictates that various-sized business should contribute to industry output.

These models assume that all businesses within an industry produce homogeneous products, e.g., that Sears, Marshall Fields, and K Mart provide comparable retail services; that MCI and AT&T provide comparable phone services; and that General Motors and Jaguar-Rover produce comparable cars. Although obviously silly, this assumption simplifies our analysis. It enables us to cut through the complexities of the real world and, we believe, obtain some understanding of the forces behind business formations, dissolutions, and growth.

The economics literature has devoted considerable attention to scale economies. Everyone is familiar with Adam Smith's description of scale economies in assembly lines for making standardized items like pins. The literature has given less attention to "specialization economies." In order to talk about economies of specialization we need to talk about measuring units of a good. Gasoline pumped by a friendly service station man at a station near your home at $1.45 per gallon is cheaper gasoline to you than gasoline you pump yourself for $1.19 a gallon at the U-Pump-It station five miles away. A suit that fits an average man is not the same good as a suit tailored to fit you. Adam Smith's suit factory can make suits of the first type at a lower cost per suit than a tailor can. But you receive more effective units of suit from a tailor. Hence, the main difference between the factory and the tailor is not that the factory can produce suits at lower cost than the tailor but that the tailor can produce effective units of suits more cheaply than the factory can, although only at a scale of operation that is small relative to that of the factory. Both the tailor and the factory can find a niche in the market. Many goods have these kinds of multidimensional characteristics when viewed closely.

Our basic observation is that for many goods and services a small enterprise can produce "effective units" at a lower average cost per "effective unit" than a large firm can. But the small firm can perform efficiently only at a small scale of output. Large firms can produce effective units at an average cost per effective unit that is relatively low at large scales of output. The moral is that large-scale technology is often efficient only at producing standardized items. Not all goods and services have this property. Giant enterprises will continue to produce automobiles and provide telephone service. But restaurant chains coexist with small eateries, supermarket chains with mom and pops, and clothing giants with tailors.

The trade-off between economies of scale and economies of specialization results from the trade-off between low-cost standardized goods and high-cost tailor-made goods. The true cost of consuming standardized goods is not only the dollar cost but also the diminished personal satisfaction when you consume goods tailored to the average when you are not average. Large-scale businesses cannot replicate the performance of small producers of specialized goods. Their technology destroys the personal enhancement characteristics of specialized customized goods. Therefore, policy makers should, under certain conditions we discuss in Chapter 4, avoid imposing fixed overhead costs that create artificial scale economies. We elaborate on this observation in the next chapter.

The trade-off between scale economies and specialization economies also manifests itself in the role of small "fringe" firms in disciplining monopoly elements. Suppose there is one extremely efficient entrepreneur along with many less efficient entrepreneurs. In this situation the large firm faces a residual demand curve (defined as the difference between market demand and supply from small competitors). Residual demand is highly elastic at prices high enough to induce entry by many small entrepreneurs. The elasticity of the residual demand restrains the price of the monopolist. Indeed, if the quantity of potential entrants is large at the price that just covers the minimum average cost of the monopolist, then the monopolist is forced to price at or near his minimum average cost. The antitrust literature has long recognized these benefits of potential entry.

By increasing fixed overhead costs, regulation may increase the minimum average cost much more to small enterprises than to the large monopolist. Therefore the monopolist can jack up his "limit price" to a much higher level without fear of attracting entry. This effect of regulation is particularly pernicious and may outweigh the benefits of some regulations to society. Indeed, it is probably this logic that has convinced some regulatory agencies to impose lighter regulatory burdens on smaller businesses.

Although the following theories do not capture all the nuances of the real business world, they do highlight several important aspects of business behavior. The stochastic theory emphasizes the role of luck in the growth of businesses over time. It is a mechanistic theory in which entrepreneurs are passive players in a game of chance. It ignores the differing abilities and preferences of the entrepreneur. Yet it explains observed patterns of business growth moderately well. Lucas's theory views the differing levels of business acumen among individuals as the major determinant of business formations, dissolutions, and growth. The Kihlstrom and Laffont theory views the differing tastes for risk among individuals as the major determinant of business formations, dissolutions, and growth. In focusing on different entrepreneurial characteristics, the Kihlstrom and Laffont and Lucas theories complement each other nicely. Finally, the Jovanovic theory synthesizes key elements of the stochastic theory and the Lucas theory. Individuals differ in their business abilities, which they cannot observe directly but rather must infer from their successes or failures at operating businesses in a risky environment.

STOCHASTIC THEORY

Perhaps because of the development of an innovative product such as the personal computer, a new industry comes into existence. How will this industry evolve over time as industry demand increases? The answer to this question depends upon the strategies adopted by the firms in this industry concerning pricing, advertising, and product differentiation, the technology for producing the product, government policies toward the industry, and the precise nature of the demand for the industry's product. But the answer may also depend on pure chance. The stochastic theory of market structure championed by Herbert Simon shows that the laws of luck can explain the observed evolution of market structures extremely well.

A primitive version of the stochastic theory assumes (1) that the population of firms is fixed so that over the time period under consideration there are no births or deaths of firms and (2) that the probability that a firm will grow at any particular rate is independent of a firm's size and its previous growth. An example based on these assumptions, developed by F. M. Scherer, illustrates this version of the stochastic theory.[13] An industry comes into existence with fifty firms, each with a 2 percent share of a $5 million market. The probability distribution of growth rates facing each firm is normal with a mean of 6 percent and a standard deviation of 16 percent.[14] Each firm takes a draw from this distribution each year.

The size of a firm at any point in time depends upon the sequence of growth rates the firm has drawn from the distribution of growth rates over time. Lucky firms grow rapidly and become large because they receive many draws exceeding the average draw of 6 percent. Unlucky firms languish because they receive many draws that fall short of the average draw of 6 percent.

Table 3.1 shows the evolution of this industry over time based on an average across sixteen separate simulations. It reports the share of sales made by the four largest firms at 20-year intervals over a 140-year period. The four largest firms begin with an 8 percent share of the market. After 140 years the four largest firms have a 57.4 percent share of the market. The largest firms are those that have received a long series of lucky draws.

The relative position of individual firms in the size distribution may change over time. The fourth-largest firm in year 2 may not be the fourth-largest firm in year 20. But over time it becomes increasingly unlikely that a large firm will be dislodged from its position. A large firm is as likely to grow by the industry average as a small firm. A large firm widens its lead over a small firm that grows at the same rate, however, because the growth applies to a larger initial base. For example, the leading firm in year 140 was also the leading firm in year 60 for four of the sixteen simulations performed and was among the four leading firms in ten of the sixteen simulations performed.

This primitive version of the stochastic theory is often identified with Gibrat's Law of Proportionate Growth. Gibrat's Law says that firm growth is independent of firm size or, equivalently, that the average change in firm size is proportionate to firm size. An important implication of Gibrat's Law under the assumptions made earlier is that the size distribution of firms—the percent of all sales made by firms of a particular size plotted against firm size—is lognormal. The lognormal distribution is skewed so that a few large firms make a disproportionately large share of sales and a great many small firms make a disproportionately small share of sales.

TABLE 3.1
Simulated Evolution of Four-Firm Concentration Ratio

Run	*Four-Firm Concentration Ratio at Year:*							
	1	*20*	*40*	*60*	*80*	*100*	*120*	*140*
1	8.0	19.5	29.3	36.3	40.7	44.9	38.8	41.3
2	8.0	20.3	21.4	28.1	37.5	41.6	50.8	55.6
3	8.0	18.8	28.9	44.6	43.1	47.1	56.5	45.0
4	8.0	20.9	26.7	31.8	41.9	41.0	64.5	59.8
5	8.0	23.5	33.2	43.8	60.5	60.5	71.9	63.6
6	8.0	21.3	26.6	29.7	35.8	51.2	59.1	72.9
7	8.0	21.1	31.4	29.0	42.8	52.8	50.3	53.1
8	8.0	21.6	23.5	42.2	47.3	64.4	73.1	76.6
9	8.0	18.4	29.3	38.0	45.3	42.5	43.9	52.4
10	8.0	20.0	29.7	43.7	40.1	43.1	42.9	42.9
11	8.0	23.9	29.1	29.5	43.2	50.1	57.1	71.7
12	8.0	15.7	23.3	24.1	34.5	41.1	42.9	53.1
13	8.0	23.8	31.3	44.8	43.5	42.8	57.3	65.2
14	8.0	17.8	23.3	29.3	54.2	51.4	56.0	64.7
15	8.0	21.8	18.3	23.9	31.9	33.5	43.9	65.7
16	8.0	17.5	27.1	28.3	30.7	39.9	37.7	35.3
Average	8.0	20.4	27.0	33.8	42.1	46.7	52.9	57.4

SOURCE: F. M. Scherer, *Industrial Market Structure and Economic Performance* (Boston: Houghton Mifflin, 1980), table T4.14, p. 146.

Early empirical studies found considerable empirical support for Gibrat's Law. Among the large firms studied by Gibrat, Hart and Prais, and Simon and Bonini, firm growth rates were roughly independent of firm size.[15] Many studies have found that the lognormal distribution provides a reasonable approximation to the actual size distribution for a large number of industries and for the economy as a whole.

Subsequent studies found that many of the assumptions and implications of Gibrat's Law are at odds with the facts. Three key assumptions of the primitive stochastic theory fail to hold. First, because many firms are born or die over time, the population of firms is not fixed, as assumed by Gibrat. Second, the variance of growth rates is not independent of firm size, as assumed above. Firm growth rates are more variable for smaller firms. Third, at least among firms that survive, growth rates are not independent of firm size. Tiny firms have higher growth rates than larger firms. The implication that the size distribution of firms is lognormal also fails to hold except as a crude approximation. Most empirical studies have found that the right-hand tails of actual size distributions are fatter than the right-hand tail of the lognormal distribution. There are more larger firms than the lognormal distribution would predict.

By making more realistic assumptions concerning the growth process, more complex versions of the stochastic theory rescue two key features of Gibrat's Law: the proportionate growth assumption, and the implication that the size distribution of firms is skewed. Simon has shown that skewed distributions similar to the lognormal distribution result when there is continual entry of new firms and when the variance of growth rates is not independent of firm size.[16] He has also shown that observed departures from the lognormal distribution can be explained by two phenomena.[17] The first is that the growth rates of individual firms are temporally correlated. A firm that has a high growth rate this year is likely to have a high growth rate next year. The second is that mergers and acquisitions also change the size distribution over time. Both phenomena tend to increase the share of sales made by larger firms. Mansfield has shown that tiny firms may have a higher average growth rate than larger firms because tiny firms with low average growth rates die and leave the sample. Indeed, the growth rates of firms that are larger than the minimum efficient firm size are independent of firm size for the industries examined by Mansfield.[18]

LUCAS MODEL

Lucas explores the implications of the assumption that individuals have differing endowments of what might be called business acumen or managerial ability.[19] He considers an economy in which there are N individuals and K units of capital. Each individual is indexed by his managerial ability a. The distribution of managerial ability across the population is G(a).[20] Each firm consists of a single manager and the labor and capital he controls.

A firm run by manager a can produce

$$q = af(l,k) \tag{3.1}$$

units of output, where f(l,k) exhibits diminishing returns to scale.[21]

The production function (3.1) implies cost functions of the form xc(q;r,w) where r is the rental rate of capital, w is the wage rate, x = 1/a denotes the manager's inefficiency level, and c(q;r,w) exhibits decreasing returns to scale. The average and marginal cost curves that correspond to q = f(l,k) for given factor prices r and w are drawn in Figure 3.1 for three different managerial inefficiency levels. Assuming there are a sufficient number of firms for perfect competition to arise, each firm produces at the point where price equals marginal cost. More efficient managers (lower x's and higher a's) produce more output (and employ more labor and capital) than less efficient managers (higher x's and lower a's). The best manager cannot achieve a monopoly because he has decreasing returns to scale.[22] For example, Figure 3.1 shows that the best manager x_l has higher mar-

Figure 3.1
Production Costs and Managerial Ability for the Lucas Model

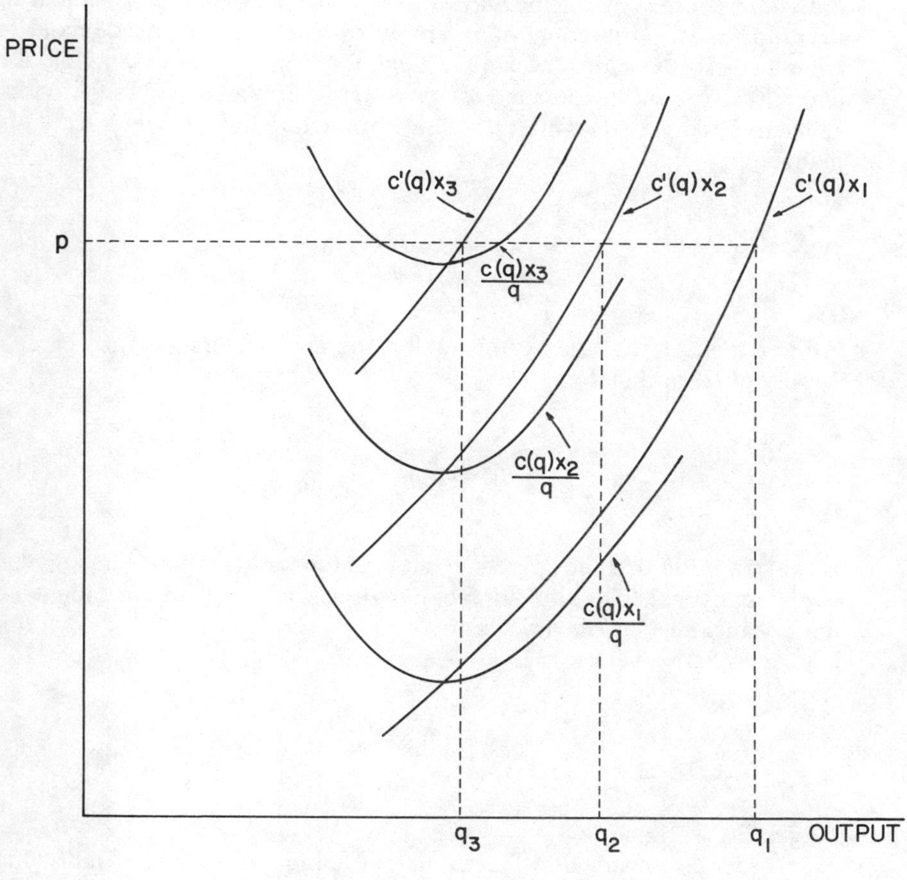

ginal costs for producing units greater than q_1 than has the poorest manager x_3 for producing units smaller than q_3. When industry price is p, the best manager will never expand past q_3 because poorer managers can always produce these units at a lower cost.

The equilibrium for this economy is characterized by an allocation of individuals across managing and working. This allocation is feasible if the demand for workers equals the supply of workers and the demand for capital equals the supply of capital. Let l(a) represent the demand for labor and k(a) represent the demand for capital by a firm managed by individual a. Then, if individuals with $0 < a < \mathit{a}$ work and individuals with $\mathit{a} \leq a < \infty$ manage,

$$(3.2) \qquad \int_{\mathit{a}}^{\infty} l(a)dG(a) = NG(\mathit{a})$$

is the condition that the aggregate demand for labor equals the aggregate supply of labor and[23]

$$(3.3) \qquad \int_{\mathit{a}}^{\infty} k(a)dG(a) = K$$

is the condition that the aggregate demand for capital equals the aggregate supply of capital. This allocation of individuals across working and managing is efficient if it maximizes the output produced by firms. Therefore $\mathit{a}, l(\,), \kappa(\,)$ must solve

$$(3.4) \qquad \underset{\mathit{a}}{\mathrm{Max}}\left\{\int_{\mathit{a}}^{\infty} af(l,k)dG(a)\right\}$$

subject to (3.2) and (3.3).

In order to ensure that there exists a unique allocation of individuals across managing and working that is both feasible and efficient, Lucas invokes Gibrat's Law, discussed earlier in this chapter.[24] He shows that when the growth rates of the capital and labor employed by a firm are independent of its size, the production function f(l,k) must have a particular form.[25] He then shows that when the production function has this particular form there is a unique *a* that solves the maximization problem (3.4).

This simple model of the size distribution of firms has an interesting implication for the change in average firm size over time. When the elasticity of substitution between capital and labor is less than unity, average firm size is an increasing function of the wealth of the economy.[26] The reason for this relationship is that when the elasticity of substitution is less than unity an increase in the capital stock increases the returns from working and decreases the returns from managing. Marginal managers find they can make more money working so they close down their firms. Since fewer firms employ more workers, average firm size increases.

Lucas tested this implication of his theory by regressing employees per firm (as a proxy for average firm size) against per capita gross national product (as a proxy for the per capita capital stock). He found a statistically significant positive relationship between average firm size and the capital stock. He estimated that a 1 percent increase in gross national product causes an approximately 1 percent increase in employees per firm.[27]

This relationship may explain the secular decline in the share of small businesses documented in Chapter 2. As our economy becomes wealthier, each worker has greater capital to work with, becomes more productive, and receives a higher wage. The gains from working fall relative to managing. Fewer individuals become entrepreneurs, but those who do form bigger firms.[28]

We now develop two simple variants of Lucas's model that apply to specific industries rather than to the economy as a whole. We shall use these variants of his model extensively in the following chapters. We assume that businesses have access to different technologies for producing the same homogeneous product. These technologies are summarized by the cost functions $c(q,x)$, where q denotes output and x indexes the technologies. The cost function is convex in q, $c_q > 0$, $c_{qq} > 0$, and is increasing in x, c_x, $c_{qx} > 0$. The last assumption implies that technologies with larger values of x have larger marginal costs at any given level of output.[29]

In order to place more structure on these cost functions, we appeal to two empirical regularities documented in Chapter 2. First, bigger businesses realize larger rates of return than smaller businesses. Between 1977 and 1980, for example, the average rate of return on assets increased monotonically from 6.1 percent for manufacturers with \$10–25 million in assets to 7.5 percent for manufacturers with more than \$1 billion worth of assets.[30] Second, entry and exit of businesses primarily involves smaller firms.[31] Between 1969 and 1976, firms with fewer than twenty employees were more than twice as likely to fail as firms with more than five hundred employees.[32] These regularities suggest that larger firms have lower average costs and realize larger rents than smaller businesses and that changes in costs or demand lead to the entry or exit of small, marginal businesses that earn small rents.[33] In order to make our cost function consistent with these regularities, we assume that average costs are higher for higher x's (who are less efficient managers).

(3.5) $$\partial[c(q,x)/x]/\partial x > 0$$

Businesses with larger values of x therefore have greater average and marginal costs at any given level of output. The cost functions implied by these regularities are the same as those implied by the Lucas model and illustrated in Figure 3.1.

In our model, x indexes the amount of some fixed factor held by actual or potential businesses. The fixed factor might be locational advantage, organization-specific capital such as the mores imparted by the founder of the business,[34] differential access to technological information, or managerial ability. For expositional simplicity we assume, following Lucas, that there is a manager-entrepreneur attached to each actual or potential firm and that x indexes the ability of this manager to operate some basic production technology. Better managers have smaller x's. The distribution of managerial ability across the population of actual and potential firms is H(x).

In the first version of the model outlined above, the supply of workers and managers to the industry in question is perfectly elastic at wage rate w. This version of the model is useful for studying industries where there is little industry-specific capital and where workers and managers can therefore move easily to other industries. The following assumptions characterize this version of the model:

1. Labor is homogeneous across industries.
2. The industry under consideration is small relative to the economy as a whole.
3. Each firm is small and acts as a price taker.
4. Managerial ability is uncorrelated across industries.[35]
5. Relative to the labor force, the number of managers in all industries is small.

Under these assumptions (1) the supply of labor to the industry under consideration is perfectly elastic at the economy-wide wage rate w, and (2) the opportunity cost of managing a business is w with virtual certainty. The constancy of the opportunity cost of managing across individuals ensures that business formations and dissolutions involve "marginal managers" characterized solely by their managerial ability parameter x.[36]

The assumptions that managerial ability is uncorrelated across industries and that all individuals have the same opportunity cost of managing capture the fact that many industries require managers who have industry-specific human capital that is costly to acquire. Chefs often become restauranteurs but seldom become steel magnates. Automobile executives usually rise from staff positions at automobile companies. They seldom come from unrelated industries.[37] The distribution of managerial ability for a given industry across the population at any given point in time reflects both the distribution of abilities for acquiring industry-specific human capital and past decisions by individuals concerning occupational choice and job tenure. We make no attempt, however, to model the long-run determinants of the managerial ability distribution and the sorting of individuals across occupations. This important but difficult problem would take us too far afield. We take H(x) as exogenous, an assumption that is reasonable for analyzing fairly aggregate industries over short periods of time.

We now derive the industry equilibrium. Given price p, manager x chooses q to maximize profit. Let q(x,p) denote his supply schedule and $\pi(x,p)$ his maximum profit function under the assumption he chooses to manage rather than work. He will manage if

$$\pi(x,p) = pq(x,p) - c(q(x,p),x) \geq w \tag{3.6}$$

and work otherwise. Let z denote the individual who is indifferent between working and managing, where z solves $\pi(z,p) = w$ so that $z = z(p,w)$. Industry output is

$$Q(z,p) = \int_0^z q(x,p)dH(x) \tag{3.7}$$

Demand is $p = D(Q)$, where $D' < 0$. Given wage rate w, industry equilibrium is characterized by the (p,z) that solve

$$p = D[Q(z,p)] \tag{3.8}$$

$$\pi(z,p) = w \tag{3.9}$$

It is easy to show that this equilibrium is unique if it exists. Figure 3.2 illustrates the equilibrium. The market clearing condition (3.8) is given by DD. This line is downward sloping because as z increases, the number of businesses and total output increase. For the market to clear, price must fall. The entry condition (3.9) is given by CC. This line is upward sloping because as price increases, the number of individuals whose profits will exceed their alternative opportunity cost w increases; thus z increases as p increases. Industry equilibrium occurs at that price p_e and managerial cutoff level z_e at which the market clears and at which there are no further incentives for workers to become managers. This equilibrium is given by

Figure 3.2
Market Equilibrium for the Lucas Model

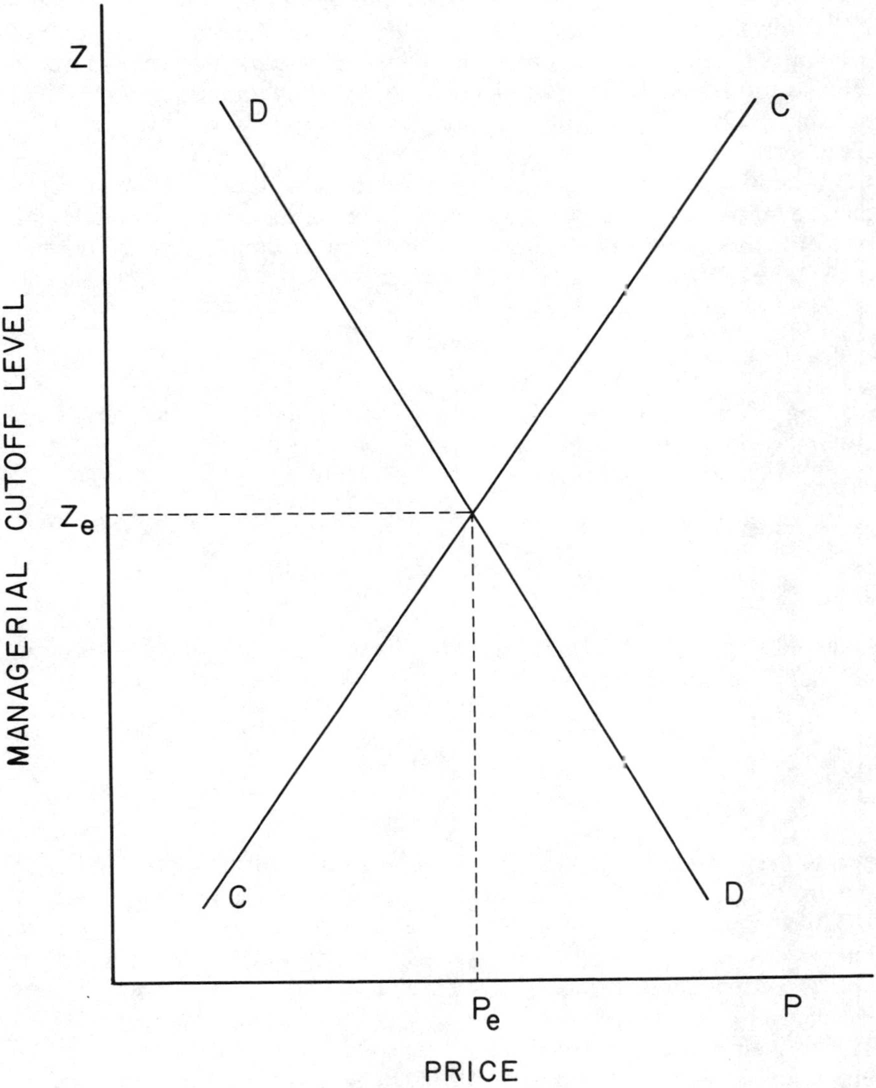

the point (which gives a unique combination of p and z) at which DD and CC cross.

For many industries, the assumption that there is no industry-specific human capital is clearly unrealistic. Workers laid off from the automobile and steel industries, for example, have had great difficulty finding comparably rewarding work. In the second version of our model the existence of industry-specific human capital is highlighted by making the extreme assumption that the supply of workers and managers to the industry in question is perfectly inelastic. The following assumptions characterize this version of the model.

First, the industry under consideration consists of N individuals who have the skills necessary to work or manage in this industry. People are free to change roles as entrepreneurs and workers but are unable to change industries. A chef can become a restauranteur, but he cannot become an autoworker or a chemical manufacturer. A chemist can become a chemical manufacturer, but he cannot become an economist or a retailer. This assumption may not be too unrealistic for highly aggregated industries over a short period of time. Some managers and entrepreneurs have industry-specific talents that they may not be able to transfer easily between industries. Skilled workers may also require extensive retraining in order to switch industries. Second, each firm is small and acts as a price taker.

Under these assumptions (1) the supply of labor and managers to the industry under consideration is perfectly inelastic and (2) the opportunity cost of managing a business is determined endogenously so as to equilibrate the demand and supply of labor by firms in this industry. The demand for labor by manager x is l(w,x). The fact that aggregate industry demand for labor equals aggregate industry supply implies

$$\int_0^z l(w,x)dH(x) = N\int_z^\infty dH(x) \tag{3.10}$$

The industry equilibrium is now characterized by the p, w, and z that solve equations 3.8 through 3.10.[38]

We shall use this second version of the model in the sequel to analyze the impact of regulation on an industry for which the alternative opportunities for workers and managers are limited. Alternative opportunities may be limited because workers and managers have industry-specific human capital that has little value elsewhere in the economy. Alternative opportunities may also be limited because the industry is isolated geographically—in a one-industry town such as Detroit, for example—so that the cost for workers and managers to move to another industry is high.

KIHLSTROM AND LAFFONT MODEL

There is no uncertainty in the models discussed above. Individuals are sure about demand and cost conditions as well as about their ability to run a business. They weigh a certain profit from running their own business against a certain wage from working for someone else. If the former is larger (smaller) than the latter, they become entrepreneurs (workers). Therefore, these individuals bear no risk.

Bearing risk, however, is an unavoidable aspect of running a business. Entrepreneurs are unsure of their own abilities, uncertain about the demand for their perhaps innovative product, and inexperienced at estimating production costs. The model we discuss in this section focuses on the implications of the fact that entrepreneurs bear more risk than workers.[39]

Individuals have access to the same technology for producing a product.[40] The technology is described by the production function

$$q = f(l,v) \tag{3.11}$$

where q is output, l is labor from workers hired by the entrepreneurs, and v is a random variable that varies from zero to infinity. This technology is risky. Entrepreneurs who draw a high value of v will produce more than entrepreneurs who draw a low value of v for any given input of labor l. All individuals face the same distribution of the random variable v, which may be correlated across firms, in which case all firms tend to get a good or bad draw at the same time.

Individuals maximize expected utility. Utility is given by

$$U = U(I,\rho) \tag{3.12}$$

where I is the income they receive from either working or managing and ρ is an index of how risk averse the individual is.[41] More risk-averse individuals have higher ρ's.[42] All individuals are either indifferent to risk or averse to risk. The assumption that individuals are never risk preferrers may seem contrary to the popular view of the entrepreneur as a gambler. But most entrepreneurs take calculated risks rather than outright gambles.[43]

Individuals can either work and earn a certain competitive wage of w or entrepreneur and earn a risky profit of

$$\pi(l,v) = f(l,v) - wl \tag{3.13}$$

An individual who becomes an entrepreneur will employ $l^*(w,\rho)$ workers, where $l^*(w,\rho)$ maximizes expected utility:[44]

(3.14) $$\underset{l}{\mathrm{Max}} E[U(A + f(l,v) - wl, \rho)]$$

An entrepreneur who hires l^* workers earns risky profits equal to

(3.15) $$\pi^* = \pi(l^*,v)$$

He will become an entrepreneur if the expected utility from running a business exceeds the certain wage he will receive as a worker

(3.16) $$E[U(A + \pi^*(w,\rho),\rho)] \geq U(A + w,\rho)$$

and work otherwise.

The equilibrium division of individuals between laborers and entrepreneurs occurs at that wage rate where the labor demanded by individuals who become entrepreneurs equals the labor supplied by individuals who become workers. Kihlstrom and Laffont show that a unique equilibrium exists. They then study the properties of this equilibrium, which we now summarize.

More risk-averse entrepreneurs run smaller firms. This result holds when the random variable v affects output and the marginal product of labor in the same way so that, for example, a lucky draw of v makes the marginal worker more productive and increases output.[45]

When all individuals become more risk averse, the equilibrium wage falls.[46] An economywide increase in risk aversion increases the supply of workers because more individuals prefer a riskless wage and decreases the demand for workers because entrepreneurs hire fewer workers in order to decrease their risk. The increase in the supply of workers together with the decrease in the demand for workers depresses the wage rate.[47]

The equilibrium allocation of individuals across working and entrepreneuring is inefficient.[48] There are several sources of inefficiency. First, less risk-averse firms produce more output than more risk-averse firms. But if all firms have access to the same technology, society would like all firms to produce the same level of output. To see this, suppose firm A produced more than firm B. Because there are diminishing returns to scale, firm A has higher marginal costs of production than firm B. Society could produce the combined output of these firms at a lower cost by shifting production from the high-cost firm A to the low-cost firm B until the marginal costs of these two firms were equalized. The desire by less risk-averse individuals to run larger firms therefore decreases social welfare. Second, only entrepreneurs bear risk in equilibrium. It is socially more efficient to diversify these risks across all individuals in the economy.[49] Third, in general there will be either too few or too many entrepreneurs. On the one hand, the fact that people are risk averse causes too few individuals to become entrepreneurs. On the other hand, the fact that risk-averse entrepreneurs hire too few workers depresses the wage rate and encourages too many individuals to become entrepreneurs. These offsetting effects would cancel each other out and lead to the correct number of entrepreneurs only under the most fortunate circumstances.[50]

Given the maldistribution of risk across individuals, the equilibrium is efficient. The maldistribution of risk discussed above causes too many or too few firms to form and leads these firms to hire too few workers. The maldistribution of risk in this model is due to the lack of a mechanism such as a stock market for sharing risks. If we accept this institutional lacuna as given, then it is not possible to improve social welfare by reassigning workers and entrepreneurs.

If we allow entrepreneurs to diversify risk through a stock market, then the resulting equilibrium is efficient. Kihlstrom and Laffont show that a stock market is required to achieve an efficient equilibrium if there is a fixed cost of setting up a firm and there is uncertainty and a large number of entrepreneurs are risk averse.[51] A stock market is not needed to achieve an efficient equilibrium if any of these features is absent. An important implication of the existence of a stock market is that entrepreneurship is no longer restricted to risk-averse individuals. An efficient stock market permits individuals to diversify their risk away. Consequently, an entrepreneur need not bear any more risk than a worker.[52]

JOVANOVIC MODEL

The models discussed above are static. They say little about how an industry and the firms within it will evolve over time. And they ignore the obvious fact that individuals can learn their business acumen by operating businesses for a period of time. Boyan Jovanovic has developed a model that addresses these deficiencies.[53] Jovanovic's model assumes that individuals differ in their entrepreneurial abilities (like Lucas's model) but that individuals are unsure of their abilities (unlike Lucas's model). His model assumes that the production technology is risky (like Kihlstrom and Laffont's model), partly because individuals are uncertain about their abilities and partly because production is inherently risky. His model also assumes that individuals learn about their business abilities over time by observing how well they perform in the rough and tumble business world. The fact that individuals gradually learn about their abilities changes their behavior over time and gives the Jovanovic model a realistic dynamic element that the Lucas and Kihlstrom and Laffont models lack.

Let us outline the Jovanovic model. Individuals decide each period whether to take a random profit π as a gizmo entrepreneur or to take a certain wage w as a worker in the gizmo or some other industry. Profits are random solely because costs are random. Costs depend upon quantity produced, managerial ability, and a random disturbance

$$C_i = C(q,a_i,e_i) \tag{3.17}$$

for individual i where q_i is the quantity produced by individual i, a_i is an index of entrepreneurial ability for individual i, and e_i is a random disturbance for individual i. Individuals do not know their true a_i's. Prior to operating a firm they assume $a_i = a_m$, which may be the population mean or some other common estimate. They revise their estimate of a_i from observations on costs and profits in previous periods in which they have operated.[54] We simplify the cost function, as we did for the Lucas model, by assuming that

$$C_i = C(q)x(a_i,e_i) \tag{3.18}$$

so that x may be viewed as a stochastic efficiency factor. Firms with larger x's have higher costs.

All individuals are risk neutral (in contrast to the Kihlstrom and Laffont model). They will base business formation, dissolution, and growth decisions on the stream of maximum profits they can expect to obtain given their estimates of their ability and of future industry prices. An individual will dissolve her business if her expected return from remaining an entrepreneur for at least one more period is less than her certain reward from pursuing some other line of work.

At the start of an industry individuals have the same estimates of their business abilities.[55] They all believe they have the same cost curve $c(q)x_1$, where $x_1 = x(a_m,e)$, because they all believe they have the average ability in the population. Each individual who forms a firm will produce the same quantity and expects to earn the same profit at any given industry price. In competitive equilibrium, prospective entrants must expect to make profits no greater than their alternative opportunity cost w. Businesses form until price is competed down to this level and the aggregate quantity supplied equals the aggregate quantity demanded at this price. If more businesses formed, price would fall below the minimum value consistent with zero expected net profits; some businesses would close, thereby competing price back up to p. If fewer businesses formed, price would exceed the minimum value consistent with zero expected net profits; the resulting high expected profits would attract more entrants, who would compete price down to p. As shown in Figure 3.3, period 1 price is p_1, each firm produces q_1, and aggregate output is Q_1.

Figure 3.3
Market Equilibrium for the First Period of the Jovanovic Model

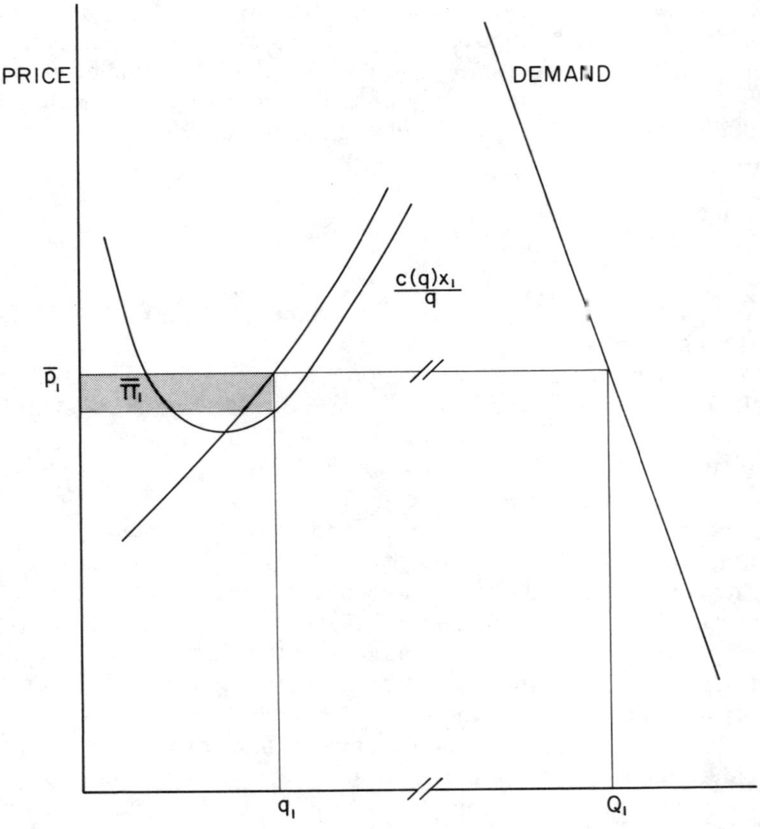

At the end of period 1, businesses that operated during this period calculate the profits they realized and the costs they incurred during this period. They can estimate their managerial ability from this information.[56] Suppose an entrepreneur estimates that his inefficiency level is $x_1 > \mathrm{x}_1$. The estimate x_1 reflects the individual's true inefficiency confounded by a random disturbance (all the uncontrollable factors that go into operating a business). This individual would be hasty to expand production under the assumption that x_1 is his true inefficiency since factors besides his innate ability affect this estimate. We assume instead that he forms a new estimate x_2 between x_1 and x_1.[57] The precise value of x_2 depends upon the population distribution of ability and the stochastic process that generates random (nonability-related) disturbances.

By assumption there is an infinite hoard of individuals who believe $\mathrm{x} = \mathrm{x}_1$ at all times. These individuals did not form businesses in period 1 because they were just indifferent between working and entrepreneuring. Had they formed businesses they would have depressed price so much they would have lost money. These individuals are always willing to form businesses that produce q_1 and charge p_1. Consequently, market price can never rise above p_1.[58] If price did rise above p_1, individuals who believe their $\mathrm{x} = \mathrm{x}_1$ would form businesses and compete price down. These individuals expect to break even in the long run when industry price is p_1.

Individuals with $\mathrm{x} > \mathrm{x}_1$ lose money at p_1. Those entrepreneurs who estimate $\mathrm{x}_2 > \mathrm{x}_1$ as a result of their period 1 experience expect to lose money in period 2. They therefore dissolve themselves. These individuals will never restart their businesses as long as price remains at p_1 or less.

Individuals who revise their inefficiency estimate downward (their ability estimate upward) produce more output in period 2 than they did in period 1 if they also believe that price in period 2 will be no lower than it was in period 1. These individuals expand output to the point where price equals marginal cost, $\mathrm{p}_2 = \mathrm{c}'(\mathrm{q})\mathrm{x}_2$. Under certain conditions, it is possible to show that the expansion by businesses that have $\mathrm{x}_2 < \mathrm{x}_1$ does not make up for the output lost from the closure of businesses with $\mathrm{x}_2 > \mathrm{x}_1$.[59] Aggregate output falls and price is bid up by demanders. Inexperienced individuals who believe $\mathrm{x} = \mathrm{x}_1$ form businesses until price is competed back down to p_1. Under other conditions, it is possible to show that the expansion by businesses that have $\mathrm{x}_2 < \mathrm{x}_1$ more than makes up for the output lost from business closures.[60] Aggregate output rises and price is bid down. Marginal managers—those with x_2 slightly greater than x_1, close down until aggregate supply equals aggregate demand at a price less than p_1. In the former case, price is always equal to p_1, and the least efficient manager is always given by $\mathrm{x} = \mathrm{x}_1$. In the latter case, price falls by successively smaller increments and the managerial cutoff level falls as well.

It is interesting to explore the implications of the Jovanovic model for the time path of a given individual's expected managerial ability as well as for the distribution of expected managerial ability within the population. Consider an individual whose expected ability never lies below the cutoff level x_1 and who therefore remains in business forever. It is possible to show that his expected managerial ability converges to his true managerial ability over time. He receives more and more observations on his managerial ability as he remains in business. Random disturbances tend to average out. And the informational value of these observations dominates the informational value of his prior belief that $x = x_1$. He also places greater reliance on the historical average value of his observed ability and less reliance on the ability estimated in any particular period. Occasional random shocks do not lead to substantial revisions of his estimated ability.

Managers who fail—whose estimated managerial ability falls below the cutoff point—never reopen their businesses under the assumptions made in this model. There is always an infinite hoard of inexperienced individuals who believe they are more efficient than failed experienced individuals. Inexperienced individuals believe $x = x_1$, whereas failed experienced managers believe $x > x_1$ (in the case where the price and cutoff levels are constant over time). Inexperienced managers (of whom there are infinitely many by assumption) are willing to sell output at a lower price than are failed experienced managers.

Failed managers never acquire additional information about their ability because they never have the opportunity to take more observations on their production costs. They generally have imprecise estimates of their ability because they tend to fail early in their business careers. Failures drop off rapidly for any cohort of entrepreneurs (that is, entrepreneurs who started their businesses at the same time).

Over the long run, business formations and dissolutions in this industry will dampen out to zero assuming demand is not growing. Surviving businesses will have very precise estimates of their abilities. Failed businesses will have fairly imprecise estimates of their abilities. These latter estimates will tend to be concentrated just below the ability cutoff level for two reasons. First, businesses fail as soon as their estimated ability falls below this cutoff level. Second, failed businesses never acquire additional information that would enable them to discover that they are particularly worse or better than they previously thought.

One implication of this equilibration and learning process is that there will be a substantial number of failed businesses whose true managerial ability is greater than the cutoff level. These businesses received bad draws from the distribution of random shocks. They interpreted these draws as evidence of poor managerial ability and withdrew. There will be relatively more efficient failed entrepreneurs in industries subject to highly variable shocks.

Our discussion thus far has assumed that the number of individuals in the population who believe $x = x_1$ is extremely large. The amount of output forthcoming from these prospective entrants is infinite at any permanent price above p_1. We now explore, in a heuristic fashion, the impact of relaxing this assumption on the model. Suppose at time zero there are N prospective entrants who believe $x = x_1$ and anticipate a self-fulfilling price sequence $p_1, p_2, \ldots$ Each prospective entrant is willing to produce $q(p_1, x_1)$ in period 1. Equilibrium price equals minimum average cost in order for anticipated net profits to equal zero. N_1 businesses form. Aggregate industry output is $N_1q(p_1, x_1)$, which must equal aggregate industry demand at price p_1. At the end of period 1 there are N_1 experienced managers and $N - N_1$ inexperienced managers. The N_1 experienced managers have observed their production costs and revise their estimated ability in light of these costs. Given the price sequence in periods 2 through ∞, these managers calculate their expected return from remaining in business at least one more period. Suppose n_1 inefficient managers leave and the expansion of output by remaining managers is less than the output lost from failed managers. There will be excess demand, price will be bid up, and new businesses will form. If the number of inexperienced managers $N - n_1$ is sufficiently large, price will be bid back down to p_1 and failed managers will still have no incentives to reopen their businesses. It is easy to see that price will remain constant at $p = p_1$ until there are too few inexperienced managers to make up the output lost by failed managers. If there are a large number of prospective entrants relative to market demand, it may take a long time for the supply of inexperienced managers to be exhausted. Notably the number of entrepreneurs who fail and the number of individuals who start businesses decline over time.

Suppose the supply of inexperienced managers eventually becomes exhausted. Price will be bid up above p_1, and some failed managers will have an incentive to reopen their businesses. The most efficient (based on their own expectations) failed managers will reopen their businesses. The cutoff level during this period will rise from x_1. In this industry there will be an initial period of lower prices during which inexperienced managers form businesses and either succeed or fail, a middle period of higher and possibly fluctuating prices during which failed managers have an incentive to reopen their businesses, and a final period—long-run equilibrium—during which the industry has stable prices and a stable group of entrepreneurs who have learned their true abilities.[61]

It is useful to show how the distribution of expected a's develops in this variation of the model (see Figure 3.4). Recall that $a = 1/x$ is the individual's ability level. In period 1, the distribution of a is a spike with N firms expecting $a = a_1$. N_1 firms form. At the end of period 1 these N_1 firms will revise their estimates of a, and as a result the population distribution of expected a's will spread out somewhat. $N - N_1$ inexperienced managers

Figure 3.4
Distribution of Managerial Ability with Finite Supply of Managers

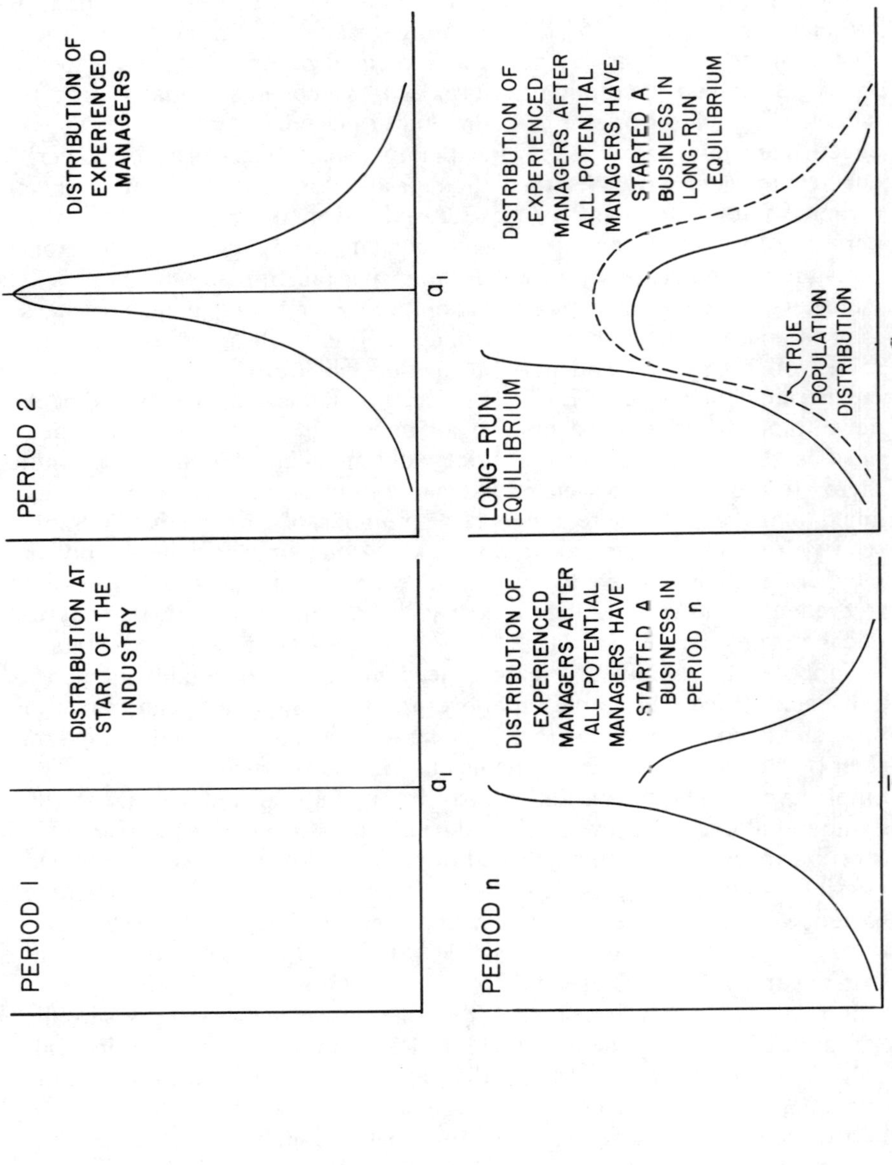

will continue to believe $a = a_1$. Eventually all N individuals will try their hands at running businesses, at which point the spike at $a = a_1$ will disappear. Until this happens the cutoff point will remain at $a = a_1$ and managers whose expected a's fall below this point will withdraw. The cutoff point may eventually fall below a_1, say to a_t, after all inexperienced managers have tried running businesses. Failed managers who left believing their ability was between a_t and a_1 will reopen their businesses, gather more information on their ability, and possibly survive for a long time.

Assuming the cutoff point does not change much from period to period, it is easy to show that the distribution of expected managerial ability will look like that shown in the lower right Figure 3.4. To the right of a_e, the distributions of expected and actual ability are roughly proportional to each other. This part of the distribution represents survivors who have precise estimates of their ability based on a large number of observations. The right side of the distribution of expected managerial ability represents fewer individuals (i.e., integrates to a smaller number) than the right side of the distribution of true managerial ability because some truly efficient firms failed. To the left of a_e, the distribution of expected a's is more concentrated about a_e than is the true distribution. The reason for this concentration is that managers represented in this portion of the graph have not had the opportunity to learn about their true a's. They were in business for a few periods, received information indicating that they were bad managers, and withdrew. This group can be decomposed into a group of individuals whose ability is in fact less than the cutoff level a_e and into a group of individuals whose true ability is in fact greater than the cutoff level a_e. We call the latter group efficient failures.

Jovanovic's model has a rich set of empirical implications. Young firms have accumulated less information than old firms about their managerial abilities. Consequently, younger firms have more variable growth rates than older firms because they have less precise estimates of their true abilities. Younger firms also grow faster than older firms.[62] How quickly the mean and variance of growth rates decline with age depends in part on the parameters of the stochastic process generating the disturbance and the distribution of ability across the population. Because younger firms are typically smaller firms, these predictions apply to smaller and larger firms as well.

Firms base growth decisions on this period's profit. If this period's profit is less than was expected, the firm will contract and possibly dissolve. We would expect growth rates to be positively correlated with deviations between realized and expected profits. We would also expect dissolution rates to be negatively correlated with deviations between realized and expected profits.

Price is determined at the margin in this model by smaller and generally younger firms. Larger, efficient firms receive rents for their exceptional abilities. The distribution of profits roughly follows the distribution of expected managerial efficiency in the population. The more dispersed these efficiencies, the more dispersed firms are in size and in profitability.

When the industry begins, all firms are the same size so the industry is at the minimum level of concentration.[63] As firms learn about their abilities, they expand or contract and concentration increases. Some firms become very large compared with other firms.

Although the concentration of profits is positively correlated with the size distribution of firms, we have not determined any necessary relationship between average industry profits and industry concentration. Jovanovic shows, however, that for each cohort of firms average profits and concentration increase with age so that average cohort profits and concentration are positively correlated.

Applications

Government regulations and taxes affect virtually every business decision, from the young entrepreneur s plans for starting a company to the small businessman's plan for closing his company and working for someone else, to the large corporation's plans to build a new plant. Moreover, according to a presidential report on small business,

> [Federal policies] are rarely neutral in their effect on small business. The availability of equity capital and credit is affected dramatically by Federal tax, securities, and banking policies. The ability of small businesses to utilize labor and capital and to produce goods and service is regulated extensively by an agglomeration of agencies, often with overlapping or conflicting mandates.[64]

Some federal policies clearly benefit small businesses. An obvious example is the progressive corporate income tax. Other federal policies may place small businesses at a competitive disadvantage. Pension regulations are often cited as examples because they impose administrative costs that larger businesses can average down over a larger quantity of output.

By highlighting a number of important but often neglected aspects of business behavior, the models we have described in this chapter are useful tools for analyzing the impact of government policies on business formation, dissolution, and growth and for assessing the differential impact of government policies across business sizes. In order to illustrate the relevance of these models to policy analysis, this section uses these models to examine the economic impact of regulations and taxes on businesses.

REGULATION

Many of the regulations imposed during the late 1960s and early 1970s were designed to alter economic behavior in ways that, advocates of these regulations believed, would benefit society as a whole. Environmental regulations were imposed to deter businesses from emitting effluents that diminish the quality of the air breathed and water used by the public at large. The Occupational Safety and Health Act was intended to reduce the health risk of employment. The Food and Drug Act, the Consumer Product Safety Act, and the Toxic Substances Control Act were designed to screen products that might have deleterious effects on their users or on the general public.

Economists have used the concept of "externality cost" to rationalize these forms of government intervention. An externality cost is incurred by society but not by the party who created the externality. Some firms create pollutants that degrade our air and water. Without regulation these firms would have insufficient incentives for reducing their pollution or compensating society for the costs of their pollution. Chemical firms may create substances that harm society. To the extent our legal system shields these firms from the financial liabilities resulting from toxic substances, these firms have insufficient incentives to prevent the distribution, consumption, or disposal of toxic substances.[65] Regulations can protect society from the excessive production of toxic materials.[66]

In recent years policy makers have expressed considerable concern that there are scale economies in complying with regulations and that these scale economies confer an artificial advantage on larger businesses.[67] There are scale economies in regulatory compliance if the average cost of complying with regulations—measured by the total cost of complying with regulations divided by firm size (as measured by the number of employees or sales)—decreases with firm size. Scale economies in regulatory compliance give larger businesses a greater cost advantage over smaller businesses than larger businesses would have in the absence of regulation.

In order to analyze scale economies in regulatory compliance it is useful to differentiate between two kinds of regulatory costs. First are costs that do not vary with output. Examples of fixed costs include the cost of hiring lawyers to interpret the regulations and the cost of installing a pollution control device that must be the same for all plant sizes. Second are costs that vary with output. Examples of variable costs are the cost of providing safety gear for workers and the cost of installing pollution control devices that are more expensive for larger plant sizes.[68]

Let total regulatory costs be $T(q) = F + V(q)$, where q is the size of the firm (its output, for example). Then average regulatory costs are

$$ARC(q) = F/q + V(q)/q \tag{3.19}$$

If average variable costs ($V(q)/q$) do not increase with firm size, then the existence of fixed costs causes average total costs ($ARC(q)$) to decrease with firm size and therefore gives rise to scale economies in regulatory compliance.

In order to highlight the impact of fixed costs, it is useful to consider the case where regulations impose fixed costs but no variable costs. We use the two versions of the Lucas model and the Jovanovic model to analyze the differential impact of fixed regulatory costs across firm size. For these models each firm has nonregulatory costs given by c(q)x for an individual with managerial efficiency x. Average nonregulatory costs are

$$ANC = c(q)x/q \tag{3.20}$$

The average nonregulatory cost curve is shown in Figure 3.5. Total regulatory costs are equal to fixed regulatory costs F so that average regulatory costs are given by

$$ARC = F/q \tag{3.21}$$

Total costs are c(q)x + F. Average costs are equal to average regulatory costs plus average nonregulatory costs

$$\begin{aligned} ATC &= ARC + ANC \\ &= c(q)x/q + F/q \end{aligned} \tag{3.22}$$

The average total cost curve is also shown in Figure 3.5.

The imposition of fixed regulatory costs increases average cost at all levels of output and increases minimum average cost, the lowest price at which a firm can break even. Marginal cost remains the same because the imposition of fixed regulatory costs does not change the cost of producing an additional unit. We now look at the impact of fixed regulatory costs more closely using the models discussed above. We shall see that each model enables us to focus on different aspects of the impact of fixed regulatory costs on business formation, dissolution, and growth.

We begin with the second variant of Lucas's model, where the supply of workers and managers is perfectly inelastic. The initial impact of the regulation is to force managers whose minimum average cost is above the market price p to close down. These managers become workers. The resulting excess supply of labor at prevailing wage rates forces the wage rate down, and the resulting excess demand for output at the prevailing product price will force the product price up. The decrease in the wage rate and the increase in the product price will enable some businesses that would have closed down at the old wage rate and product price to remain

Figure 3.5
The Impact of Regulatory Fixed Costs

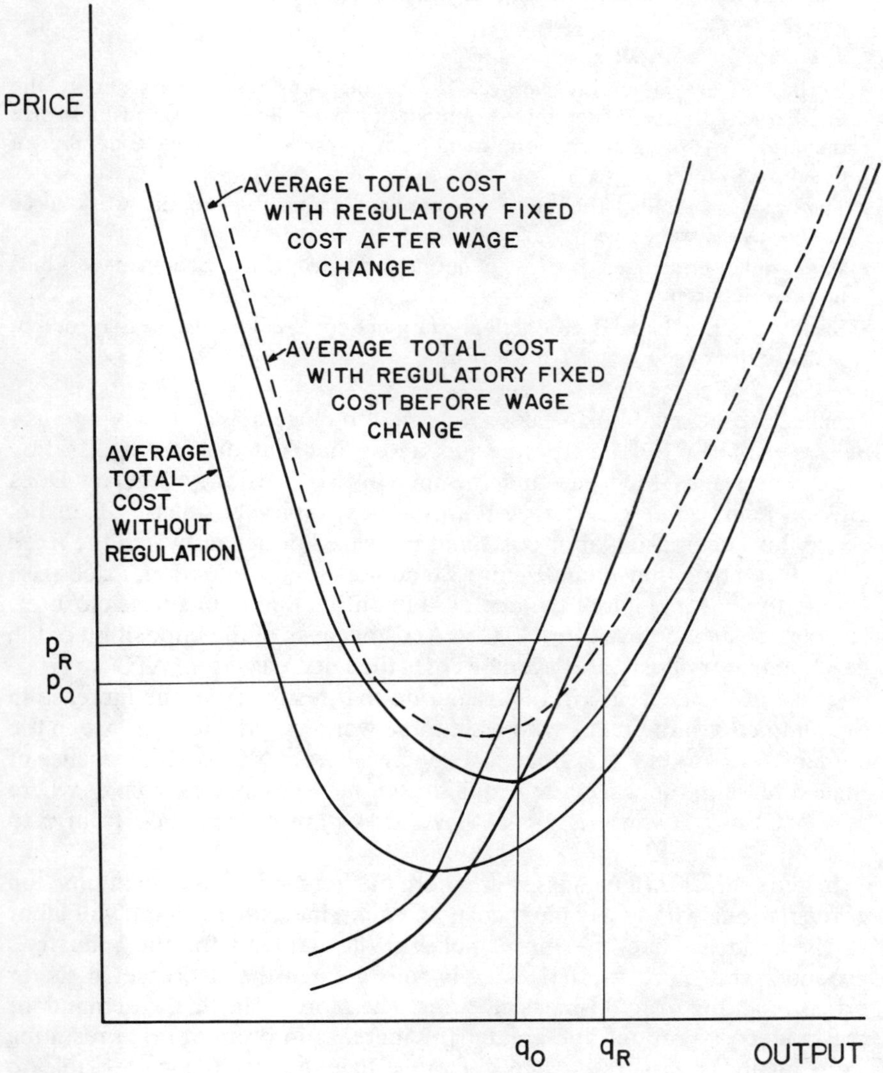

in operation. Thus the decrease in the wage rate and the increase in the product price cushion the impact of the fixed regulatory costs on business dissolutions.

In equilibrium it is easy to see that

- There are fewer businesses. Marginal businesses close down and their managers join the work force.
- There are more workers.
- Businesses are larger on average. The average business size is simply the number of workers divided by the number of businesses. Average business size rises from q_o to q_R because the number of workers rises and the number of businesses falls.
- The wage rate falls. The influx of marginal managers into the work force depresses the wage rate.
- The product price rises. The loss of output produced by marginal managers bids up the price from p_o to p_R.
- Surviving firms expand production. Marginal costs fall at all levels of output because the wage rate falls. Price rises.

Who loses? Small businesses are forced to close down. Surviving businesses each lose F dollars per period, a loss that is at least partly offset by the lower wages they pay and the increased prices they receive. Does anyone gain? Under certain circumstances, larger businesses gain because their decreased labor costs and increased prices outweigh the fixed regulatory costs they incur. Figure 3.6 depicts such a situation. Prices rise from p to p″ as a result of the decrease in output due to business closures. Average costs increase from ATC to ATC′ because of the imposition of the fixed regulatory costs. But average costs then decrease from ATC′ to ATC″ because of the decrease in the wage rate that results from the increase in the number of individuals who want to be workers and the decrease in the demand for workers. Marginal costs decrease from MC to MC″ because of the decrease in the wage rate. Equilibrium output increases from q (where p = MC) to q″ (where p″ = MC″). As drawn, profits increase from π to π''.[69]

In general, larger businesses are more likely to gain from the imposition of regulations with heavy fixed costs the more inelastic the supply of labor to the industry and the more inelastic the demand for the industry's product. The more inelastic supply, the greater the decrease in factor prices resulting from business closures. The more inelastic the demand for the industry's product, the greater the increase in product price resulting from business closures. Also, if more efficient firms are better able to average down fixed regulatory costs than are less efficient firms, then the largest firms are even more likely to benefit from regulations that impose heavy fixed costs.

Figure 3.6
An Example Where Big Business Gains from Regulation

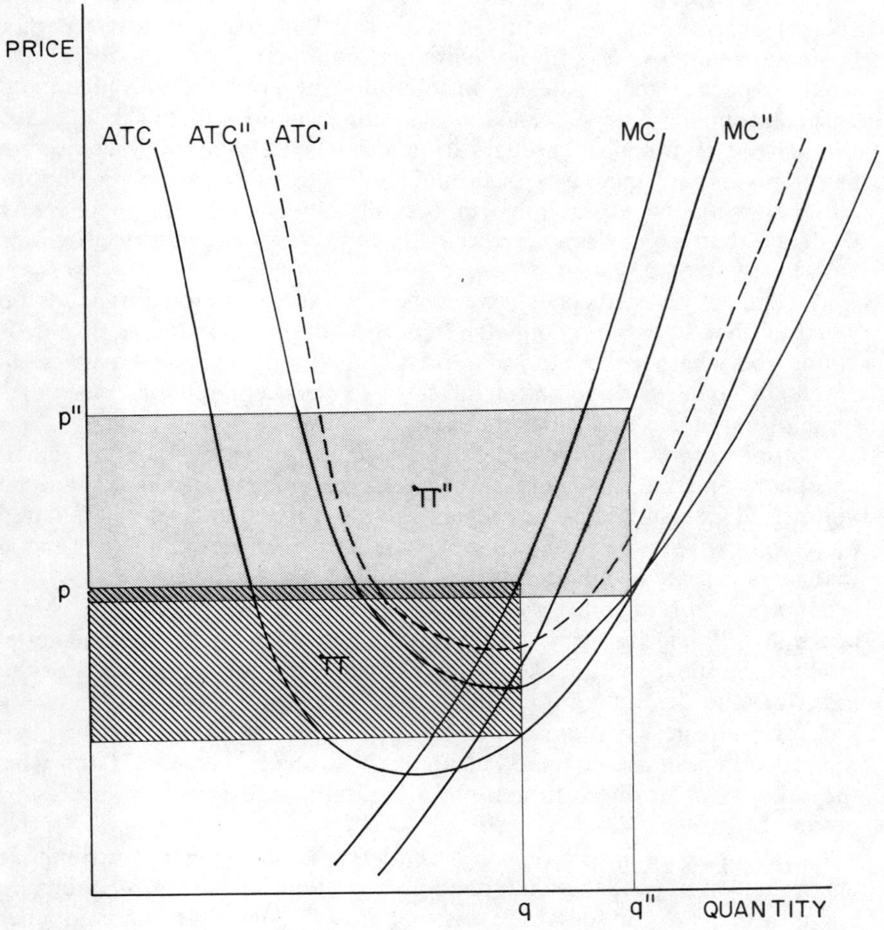

The fact that regulatory programs with heavy fixed costs may actually benefit the larger firms in an industry is an interesting finding. It suggests that larger firms may lobby for regulations that impose heavy fixed costs and thereby place their smaller rivals at a competitive disadvantage. There is an important corollary to our finding. Consider two alternative regulatory programs that impose the same total regulatory cost on an industry. The first program entails high fixed costs and low variable costs. The second program entails low fixed costs and high variable costs. Larger businesses will lose less from the first program than from the second. We would expect larger businesses to lobby for the program with high fixed costs and smaller businesses to lobby for the program with low fixed costs. We leave it to other researchers to determine whether the decreases in factor prices and increases in product prices resulting from regulations with heavy fixed costs are important empirically and whether there is any evidence that larger firms have actually lobbied for regulatory programs with heavy fixed costs.

The impact of fixed regulatory costs in Jovanovic's model depends on whether these costs are initially imposed when the industry is old or young and whether the supply of managers who believe their managerial efficiency equals the population mean (or some other common estimate) is finite or infinite. We consider these cases in turn.

Old industry. If we impose the fixed regulatory cost on a mature industry where existing managers have precise estimates of their managerial abilities, the least efficient managers will close down, output will fall, and price will rise. These results will hold whether the supply of inexperienced managers is finite or infinite.

Infinite supply of inexperienced managers and young industry. Managers in a young industry have imprecise estimates of their managerial abilities. Suppose we impose the fixed regulatory cost at the start of the industry. The common minimum price at which inexperienced managers will form businesses increases as a result of the regulation. Fewer businesses form because demand is satiated at a smaller quantity. Otherwise the process of business formation, dissolution, and growth proceeds as before.

Finite supply of inexperienced managers and young industry. Suppose again that we impose the fixed regulatory cost at the start of the industry. As in the case discussed above, inexperienced managers require a higher price to come into the market. Because demand will be satiated at a smaller level of output, fewer managers will form businesses. Consequently, it will take longer for the supply of inexperienced managers to become exhausted. Consequently, the period during which price remains constant becomes longer. After this period, price will rise for at least some time, and some failed managers will reopen their businesses. Eventually, the industry will settle down to an equilibrium price that is higher with regulation than it would be without regulation.

Now suppose we eliminate the fixed regulatory cost. In all the cases discussed above new businesses will form, output will expand, and price will fall. However, in the case where the regulation was originally imposed on a young industry with a finite supply of inexperienced managers, eliminating the fixed regulatory cost will induce a large spurt of entry. As shown in Figure 3.4, the distribution of expected managerial ability is asymmetric around the cutoff point. There is a large concentration of failed managers who believe their managerial ability is just below the minimum level required for them to break even (at prevailing and future prices). Eliminating the regulatory fixed cost lowers the marginal cutoff point and induces this group of failed managers to reenter the industry. Some of these failed managers will fail once again. But many of those we have called "efficient failures" will survive. Thus deregulation may cause rapid entry, increases in output, and decrease in price in industries that were subjected to heavy fixed regulatory costs early in their existence.

TAXES

We now examine the impact of alternative kinds of profit taxes on smaller businesses. It is useful to divide profits into normal profits and excess profits. Normal profit is simply the opportunity cost of operating a business. The opportunity cost of operating a business is what the business gives up by devoting its resources to its business rather than to the next best alternative available for its resources. For the models we have developed, the opportunity cost of operating a business is the wage income w the manager forgoes by managing rather than working. Thus, normal profit is simply w.[70] Excess profit is the difference between profit and normal profit, that is, the amount by which profit exceeds the alternative opportunity cost of the business. For the models we have developed, excess profit is the difference between profit and the wage rate.

The first tax we consider is a constant tax on all profits, whether normal or excess. Consider the second variant of Lucas's model, where the supply of workers and managers is perfectly inelastic.[71] Suppose the market was in equilibrium at price p and wage w before the tax was imposed. The marginal manager operates at the point where price equals the least average cost of production inclusive of his opportunity cost w. He earns a normal profit of w. Now impose the tax of t. He earns an after-tax profit of $(1 - t)w$. Because his profit is less than his opportunity, he would dissolve his business if p and w remained unchanged. Other more efficient managers whose after-tax profits also fall below their opportunity costs withdraw as well.[72] Managers who remain in business, however, do not alter their production decisions assuming p and w remain the same. It is easy to see why this must be so. Managers produce out to the point where price equals marginal cost. The marginal unit, by definition, adds as much to profit as it does to cost. The profit on the marginal unit, and therefore the tax on the marginal unit, is therefore zero. Inframarginal units add to profits. They will add less to after-tax profits than they will to before-tax profits. But, because they add to profits either way, the manager will continue to produce these units. We conclude that managers who remain in business at an unchanged price p and wage w will continue to produce the same level of output after the imposition of the tax as they produced prior to the imposition of the tax.

The product price and wage rate, however, must change. Failed managers become workers and depress the wage rate. The output lost from these failed managers creates excess demand and forces product price up. Some businesses that would have dissolved themselves after the imposition of the tax at the prevailing product price p and wage rate w will remain in business. Surviving businesses will expand output in response to the lower production costs and higher product price. As with the regulatory fixed cost discussed above, the largest firms in the industry may actually benefit from the tax. They are more likely to benefit the more inelastic the demand, the more inelastic the supply of labor, and the larger the proportion of marginal managers.

Now consider a tax on excess profits. Marginal firms earn only a normal profit. These firms therefore obviously do not have to pay any tax. Inframarginal firms do earn excess profits and consequently pay a tax. But because the excess profits tax does not alter a business's marginal costs or marginal revenues it does not alter a business's production decisions. Therefore, all firms remain in business and all firms continue to produce the same level of output. Product price stays the same because industry output remains unchanged. The wage rate does not change because neither the demand nor the supply of workers changes. All that changes is that inframarginal firms earn less profit.

Similar results hold in the Jovanovic model when the excess profits tax is imposed on a mature industry. But the situation is quite different when the excess profits tax is imposed on a new industry. The inexperienced managers who believe their managerial efficiency is equal to the average in the population expect to just break even by entering an industry.[73] But they realize that their true managerial ability may be quite high, enabling them to earn excess profits over a long period of time, or quite low, in which case they will lose money for one or more periods and eventually dissolve themselves. It is easy to see that newer firms lose money on average during the first few periods of their existence. They are willing to lose money during the first few years of their existence because they are gambling that they are exceptionally able managers who will survive to old age and earn excess profits. For some the gamble will pay off. For others it will not.

The policy implication of the fact that younger firms lose money on average is that a tax on excess profits reduces the willingness of inexperienced managers to test their business abilities. Although they do not incur a tax liability if they lose money, the excess profits tax decreases their ability to recoup their losses later in their existence. Therefore an excess profits tax reduces entry by inexperienced managers and, by creating excess demand, makes industry output lower and price higher than it would otherwise be.

Qualifications

The models we have described in this chapter are useful for describing the process of business formation, dissolution, and growth in many industries where entry is relatively easy because of the absence of natural barriers to entry such as scale economies and artificial barriers to entry such as those often imposed by public utility regulations.[74] Economists often equate the lack of barriers to entry with competition and competition with a large number of small firms. This equation overlooks the fact that many industries in which barriers to entry are high and in which price competition may not prevail are dominated by small businesses. Real estate, building construction, and the professions (doctors, lawyers, dentists, and opticians) are but a few examples. Although these industries are populated nationally by a large number of small firms, they have succeeded in restricting entry into local markets (local building codes do this for the building industry, real estate boards do this for the real estate industry, and hospital boards do this for the medical profession) or in artificially reducing the number of businesses or practitioners (real estate licensing boards and licensing boards for the professions limit entry).[75]

The next chapter analyzes the circumstances under which policy makers may increase social welfare by giving the little guy a break. This analysis applies only to truly competitive industries, where barriers to entry are minimal.

4

TIERING REGULATIONS

Many regulatory requirements are tiered according to the specific circumstances of the regulated firm. Some firms face lighter regulatory requirements than other firms, and some are exempted from regulatory requirements altogether. Tiering may occur in any of the major aspects of a regulatory program: in the substantive requirements; in reporting and recordkeeping requirements; or in enforcement and monitoring efforts. Tiering may entail less frequent inspections, lighter fines for noncompliance, exemptions, waivers, reduced requirements, or simpler reporting requirements for certain types of firms. Criteria for tiering include business size indicators such as sales, employment, assets, and market share and other indicators such as the risk imposed on society, ability to comply with regulatory requirements, and location.[1]

The classic example of tiering by size is the "Mrs. Murphy" exemption to the Civil Rights Act of 1968. Owner-occupied apartment buildings with four or fewer units—such as the rooming house owned by Mrs. Murphy, an imaginary constituent—are exempted from the nondiscrimination provisions of this act.[2] There are many other examples. The Toxic Substances Control Act of 1976 exempts small chemical companies from various testing and reporting requirements. The Office of Federal Contract Compliance exempts businesses with fewer than fifty employees from filing affirmative action plans. The Occupational Safety and Health Administration exempts firms with fewer than twenty employees from routine inspections. The civil penalties assessed by the Environmental Protection Agency under the Federal Insecticide, Fungicide, and Rodenticide Act vary with firm size. Larger firms are assessed larger penalties than smaller firms for comparable violations. The Securities Exchange Commission tiers reporting requirements for security issues according to the size of the issue.[3]

Tiering of businesses according to size may become even more prevalent due to the enactment of the 1980 Regulatory Flexibility Act.[4] The RFA encourages regulatory agencies to minimize the disproportionate impact of regulatory requirements on small businesses by using devices such as tiering.[5] Although the RFA does not require regulatory agencies to impose lighter regulatory requirements on smaller businesses, it makes it more troublesome for agencies to impose or continue rules that have significant adverse effects on smaller businesses.[6]

This chapter presents a framework for analyzing tiering. The most frequent justification for tiering is that imposing uniform regulatory requirements across all types of businesses has a disparate impact on smaller businesses because there are scale economies in regulatory compliance. Scale economies arise because regulations impose fixed costs. Larger businesses can average these fixed costs over a larger quantity of output and thereby achieve a competitive advantage over their smaller rivals.[7]

There is evidence that scale economies in compliance are quite extensive for some regulatory requirements. The Federal Home Loan Bank Board found that savings and loan institutions with less than $10 million in assets have thirteen times the regulatory cost per million dollars of assets as institutions with $100–200 million in assets.[8] Arthur Andersen & Co. found that the ten smallest employers in its sample of forty-eight large businesses incurred almost seven times the average ERISA (Employee Retirement Income Security Act) cost per employee incurred by the ten largest employers.[9] The prevalence of tiering by size also suggests that regulators have found that the uniform application of certain rules would have a disparate impact on smaller businesses.[10]

In order to concentrate on the salient aspects of tiering, we make four simplifying assumptions. (1) Regulators use taxes to control the amount of noxious substances emitted by firms. In order to show how our framework can be extended to nontax-based schemes, we also analyze the tiering of performance requirements and marketable permits. (2) The collection of taxes imposes administrative costs on both the taxed firm and the regulatory agency. We capture scale economies in regulatory compliance by assuming that administrative costs are independent of the size of the regulated firm. (3) Firms comply fully with the regulations, and monitoring and enforcement costs are zero. (4) The size distribution of businesses is generated according to the model developed in Chapter 3.[11] Specifically, firms differ in size because they differ in their access to a scarce factor. Firms that have more of the scarce factor are bigger and earn larger rents. As in Chapter 3, for expositional simplicity, we assume that there is an entrepreneur associated with each firm, that entrepreneurial ability is a scarce factor, and that there is a known distribution of entrepreneurial ability across the population of potential entrepreneurs.

Before getting into detailed derivations, it is useful to begin with a simple numerical example. There are ten entrepreneurs who have the background and knowledge to produce gizmos. Each entrepreneur can either produce gizmos and earn some profit or work as a laborer in another industry and earn a wage of w. Assume the wage is \$10. Each entrepreneur has managerial ability indexed by x_i and costs given by

$$C_i = 40 + 2x_i q_i^2 \qquad (4.1)$$

where q_i is the output produced by entrepreneur i. Demand is perfectly elastic at price p so that consumers are willing to buy as many units as the entrepreneurs are willing to produce for a price of p per unit.

Simple economics tells us that businesses produce out to the point where price equals marginal cost. Using this relationship together with some simple calculus, it is easy to show that entrepreneur i will produce

$$q_i = p/4x_i \qquad (4.2)$$

if his profits inclusive of foregone wages are positive, and zero otherwise. Profits are

$$\begin{aligned} P_i &= pq_i - C_i - w \\ &= p^2/(8x_i) - 50 \end{aligned} \qquad (4.3)$$

after inserting (4.1) and (4.2) into the first line of (4.3) and simplifying the resulting expression.

Social surplus, a welfare measure commonly used by economists, equals the value consumers place on output less the cost of producing this output. When demand is perfectly elastic at price p, consumers place a value of p on each unit. Therefore consumers place a value of pq_i on the output produced by business i. Then social surplus is given by

$$\begin{aligned} W_i &= pq_i - C_i - w \\ &= p^2/8x_i - 50 \end{aligned} \qquad (4.4)$$

In this particular example, the social surplus created by the business equals the profit earned by the business. W_i would exceed P_i if consumers valued units more highly the fewer the units produced, as they would if demand were less than perfectly elastic.

An entrepreneur will produce gizmos if his profits are positive. Therefore, only individuals who have

$$x_i \leq \frac{p^2}{400} \qquad (4.5)$$

will produce gizmos. When p is \$20, individuals with x_i less than or equal to one will produce gizmos, and individuals with x_i greater than one will work for someone else. Since $W_i = P_i > 0$, all entrepreneurs ($x_i \leq 1$) contribute to social surplus. The equivalence of P_i and W_i is important. It implies that the profit system induces only entrepreneurs whose contribution to social surplus is positive to produce gizmos and thereby discourages the formation of small, inefficient businesses.

Now suppose gizmo factories emit one unit of pollution for each gizmo produced. Also suppose that each unit of pollution "costs" society s dollars. In other words, society would be willing to pay s dollars to reduce pollution by one unit. Private profit—the profit pocketed by each entrepreneur—is still

$$P_i = \frac{p^2}{8x_i} - 50 \tag{4.6}$$

But social surplus is reduced by the cost of the effluent

$$\begin{aligned} W_i &= pq_i - C_i - w - sq_i \\ &= p^2/8x_i - sp/4x_i - 50 \\ &= P_i - sp/4x_i \end{aligned} \tag{4.7}$$

Obviously, P_i exceds W_i so that entrepreneurs are induced by the possibility of private profit to open socially wasteful gizmo factories. To see this result, assume s is \$2 and p is \$20. Then social surplus is zero when

$$\begin{aligned} W_i &= 400/8x_i - 40/4x_i - 50 = 0 \\ &= 40/x_i - 50 = 0 \end{aligned} \tag{4.8}$$

which implies x_i must be less than or equal to 0.8. Let our ten entrepreneurs be indexed, in order of decreasing efficiency, by x = 1.0, 0.9, 0.8, 0.7, 0.6, 0.5, 0.4, 0.3, 0.2, and 0.1. Then entrepreneurs with x = 1.0 and x = 0.9 actually reduce social welfare by operating gizmo factories. Entrepreneurs with $x \leq 0.8$ do not contribute as much to social surplus as they could. It is easy to show that social surplus would increase if these entrepreneurs decreased output.[12]

The standard economic solution to the pollution problem is to impose a tax, equal to the social cost of the pollution, on each unit of output. This tax forces the entrepreneur to consider the social cost of the pollution in her private cost calculations. Let us see what happens when we impose this tax. The cost of producing q_i becomes

(4.9) $$C_i = 40 + 2x_iq_i^2 + tq_i$$

Output is

(4.10) $$q_i = (p - t)/4x_i$$

Profit is

(4.11) $$\begin{aligned} P_i &= p(p - t)/4x_i - 2x_i(p - t)^2/4x_i^2 \\ &\quad - w - 40 - t(p - t)/4x_i \\ &= (p - t)^2/8x_i - 50 \end{aligned}$$

after substituting the value of 10 for w. Let $t = s = \$2$. Then P_i is greater than or equal to zero when x_i is less than or equal to .80. The profit system together with the regulatory tax system induces entrepreneurs whose output would decrease social welfare to stay out of the gizmo business and efficient entrepreneurs to produce the optimal number of gizmos. It is possible to show that, when regulations can be enforced and administered costlessly, imposing an effluent tax equal to the social cost of the pollution maximizes social welfare as measured by social surplus.

Unfortunately, the collection of most taxes imposes administrative costs on firms. Firms must maintain records, complete forms, and keep abreast of the tax codes.[13] Since paperwork requirements may be stiffer for more onerous taxes, these administrative costs may increase with the tax rate t and the tax burden tq_i. In order to capture administrative costs, let us assume that these costs are ten times the size of the tax rate.[14] If the tax rate is $2 per unit, administrative costs are $20 per taxed firm. These administrative costs reduce social welfare. Profits after administrative costs earned by firm i are

(4.12) $$P_i = (p - t)^2/8x_i - 50 - 10t$$

If $t = 2$ and $p = 20$ then

(4.13) $$P_i = 324/8x_i - 70$$

It is easy to verify (by setting $P_i = 0$ and solving for x_i) that only entrepreneurs with x_i less than or equal to 0.58 produce gizmos. Entrepreneurs with $x = 0.8$, 0.7, or 0.6 close down because of the administrative costs. But these entrepreneurs added to social surplus even when they were allowed to produce to their hearts' content. We found earlier that only entrepreneurs with $x = 0.9$ and 1.0 reduced social surplus. From (4.7) it is easy to show that an entrepreneur with $x = 0.8$ adds almost nothing to social surplus, with 0.7 adds roughly $7, and with 0.6 adds roughly $17. At a minimum, society could do better by exempting these businesses from taxation.

This finding suggests, for this particular example, that the tax should depend on business size and that small businesses should bear a lighter regulatory burden than larger businesses. In order to derive the tax rate that maximizes social surplus, we let the tax rate depend on business size and make the following observation. Social surplus contributed by this industry equals the sum of the social surplus contributed by each firm in this industry. Therefore, in order to maximize social surplus, we need to maximize the social surplus contributed by each firm in the industry.

Social surplus contributed by business i is

$$(4.14)\quad \begin{aligned} W_i &= p(p - t_i)/4x_i - 2x_i(p - t_i)^2/4x_i^2 \\ &\quad - w - ft_i - s(p - t_i)/4x_i \\ &= (p - s)(p - t_i)/4x_i - (p - t_i)^2/8x_i - ft_i - w - 40 \end{aligned}$$

when administrative costs are f times the tax rate. Using simple calculus, it is easy to show that the tax schedule that maximizes social surplus is

$$(4.15)\quad t_i = \begin{cases} s - 4fx_i, & x_i \leq s/4f \\ 0, & x_i > s/4f \end{cases}$$

Since smaller businesses have larger x's, t_i is smaller for smaller businesses. Table 4.1 shows the tax schedule for the ten entrepreneurs in our example for alternative values of s and f.[15] When $s = \$2$ and $f = .5$, all the entrepreneurs in our example should be exempted since $s/4f = .05$. Fewer firms are exempted as, moving horizontally across the table, we increase the ratio of externality cost to the fixed cost. When the externality cost is $10 and the fixed cost is equal to the tax, it is not desirable to exempt any firm.

Unfortunately, this tax scheme induces some inefficient entrepreneurs to form businesses. We found earlier that when $s = \$2$ entrepreneurs with $x = 1.0$ or $x = 0.9$ reduce social surplus. But because these entrepreneurs are exempted from the tax they will find it privately profitable to operate businesses. There are several methods for discouraging inefficient firms from forming. One method discussed below involves charging all firms a license fee to operate in the industry. When set at an appropriate level, the license fee discourages inefficent firms from operating in the industry. A license fee of $25 would discourage entrepreneurs with x = 1.0 or x = 0.9 from establishing businesses in the example above since these entrepreneurs can expect a private profit of less than $25. This license fee would not discourage entrepreneurs with x ≤ 0.8 from establishing firms because these entrepreneurs can expect a private after-tax profit of $25 or more. The entries preceded by asterisks in Table 4.1 indicate those entrepreneurs whose entry society would like to discourage.

The major problem with implementing the tax scheme described above is that regulators cannot observe the entrepreneurial ability level.[16] The tax schedule they issue must depend upon unobservable characteristics of the firm—such as output, employment, or profit—rather than upon unobservable entrepreneurial ability. We show below how to design a tax schedule that is a function of output. We assume that regulators know the distribution of entrepreneurial ability across the population of potential managers but that they do not know the entrepreneurial ability for any particular manager.[17] The tax schedule we design addresses a problem known as self-selection that generally afflicts the design of incentive mechanisms in the face of imperfect information.[18] Let us briefly illustrate this problem.

TABLE 4.1

Relationship among Optimal Tax, Externality Cost, and Fixed Regulatory Cost

	Externality Cost (s) and Regulatory Cost (f)				
Ability Level (x=)	*s=$2* *f= 5*	*$4* *4*	*$6* *3*	*$8* *2*	*$10* *1*
0.1	0.00	$2.40	$4.80	$7.20	$9.60
0.2	0.00	0.80	3.60	6.40	9.20
0.3	0.00	0.00	2.40	5.60	8.80
0.4	0.00	0.00	1.20	4.80	8.40
0.5	0.00	0.00	*0.00	4.00	8.00
0.6	0.00	*0.00	*0.00	3.20	7.60
0.7	0.00	*0.00	*0.00	2.40	7.20
0.8	*0.00	*0.00	*0.00	1.60	6.80
0.9	*0.00	*0.00	*0.00	0.80	6.40
1.0	*0.00	*0.00	*0.00	*0.00	6.00

NOTE: Entries are calculated from the formula t = s − 4fx, where s is the externality cost per unit of output and f is a measure of administrative costs such that ft equals the total administrative cost imposed on the firm. A tax of 0.00 implies that the firm is effectively exempted from the program. A tax of *0.00 implies that society would like to prevent this firm operating at all, perhaps by imposing a license fee on all firms that would discourage entry by inefficient firms. Calculations based on a price of $20, a wage of $40, and non-regulatory fixed costs of $10. Asterisks indicate entrepreneurs whose entry society would like to discourage.

Suppose s = \$6, p = \$20, and f = 10. Consider an entrepreneur with x = 0.1. According to (4.15), social surplus contributed by this entrepreneur is maximized when he pays a tax of \$2 per unit of output. According to (4.10), he produces 45 units of output at this tax rate. Since regulators cannot discern that he has x = 0.1, they might consider imposing a tax of \$2 per unit of output on all firms that produce 45 units of output instead of imposing a tax of \$2 per unit of output on all firms with x = 0.1. Now consider an entrepreneur with x = 0.2. It is easy to verify from (4.15) that regulators would like to exempt him from the tax. Since they cannot discern that he has x = 0.2, they might consider exempting businesses that produce less than 33 units of output.[19] The entrepreneur with x = 0.2 produces 25 units of output and therefore gains the exemption.

The problem with this approach is that entrepreneurs now have an incentive to decrease their production in order to obtain lower tax rates or an outright exemption. Consider entrepreneur x = 0.1. Facing a tax rate of \$2 and producing 45 units of output he earns an after-tax profit (from (4.11) of \$335. By producing 33 units of output he obtains an exemption from the tax and earns a profit of \$392.[20] He therefore gains \$57 profit by reducing his output from 45 units to 33 units. He "acts as if" his entrepreneurial ability level is x = 0.15, when in fact it is x = 0.1.[21] He therefore deceives his regulators. Regulators must take these perverse incentives into account when they design a tax schedule that varies with output rather than with ability.[22]

We address this problem below. We derive the optimal tax schedule under the assumption that regulators cannot observe entrepreneurial ability. This schedule minimizes the impact of the perverse incentives described above on social welfare.

This chapter has five remaining sections. The second section presents a model of the size distribution of businesses patterned after the Lucas and Kihlstrom and Laffont models discussed in Chapter 2. Firm heterogeneity arises because individuals who operate firms have differential access to some scarce factor. The scarce factor might be locational advantage, organization-specific capital such as the mores imparted by the founder of the business, or differential access to technological information. For expositional simplicity we assume that the scarce factor is entrepreneurial ability. The product price and the wage rate (the opportunity cost of managing) are treated as exogenous so that the model focuses on partial equilibrium. This section then formulates the basic problem addressed in the remainder of the chapter. Firms use inputs whose prices do not fully reflect social costs and that therefore generate externalities. Society would like to devise regulations for alleviating these externalities. But these regulations necessarily impose administrative costs on both regulated firms and regulatory agencies. Administrative costs are nondecreasing in the tax rate and the tax burden imposed on a firm. Society's problem is to devise optimal regulations in the presence of firm heterogeneity and administrative costs.

The third section derives the optimal relationship between the flat-rate tax and entrepreneurial ability when regulators can observe ability.[23] It yields our basic result: the optimal regulatory tax schedule consists of a tax rate for businesses together with a license fee to discourage the formation of inefficient businesses. The tax rate may be zero for businesses below some size threshold. Such businesses are effectively exempted from further regulation after paying a license fee to operate in the industry. The tax rate may also vary with ability for nonexempt firms. We investigate the circumstances under which this tax rate is neutral, progressive, or regressive. This section also derives an explicit optimal tax schedule for the case of linear-quadratic costs and administrative costs that are a linear function of the tax rate.

The fourth section considers the more general problem of designing an optimal multipart externality tax schedule when regulators cannot observe entrepreneurial ability. The multipart externality tax schedule is solely a function of externality emissions. This imperfect information problem is solved using a technique developed by Spulber.[24] Section four then discusses informally the shape of the optimal multipart tax schedule that emerges from this framework.

The fifth section considers four extensions and applications of our framework. (1) It shows how our framework can be used to design optimal performance requirements. (2) It incorporates imperfect compliance and costly monitoring into our framework and it shows that when there are scale economies in monitoring efforts it may be optimal to skew enforcement efforts toward larger firms. (3) It shows how our framework can be used to design optimal marketable permit programs when these programs impose administrative costs. (4) It relates the tiering schemes we propose to those used in practice and discusses the circumstances under which existing tiered regulations are likely to be preferable over untiered regulations.

The final section summarizes our major results.[25]

Basic Model

Individuals can either work for someone else or manage their own business. An individual who works receives a wage of w per unit of time. An individual who manages forgoes a wage of w per unit of time. Individuals differ in their endowments of characteristics that make successful entrepreneurs. The one-dimensional index a summarizes an individual's entrepreneurial ability.[26] An individual with ability a can produce a single product according to the concave differentiable production function f(l,e,a), where l denotes the quantity of labor input and e denotes the quantity of inputs that the private market cannot price without government intervention and that therefore gives rise to production externalities. The distribution of entrepreneurial ability across the population of potential workers or entrepreneurs is given by

$$G(a) = \int_0^a g(x)dx$$

where g(a) is the density of individuals with ability a.

Under modest regularity assumptions, a central planner maximizes social surplus by choosing an ability cutoff level *a*, assigning all individuals with ability level a < *a* to work, assigning all individuals with a ≥*a* to entrepreneurship, assigning l(a) workers to a ≥ *a,* and allowing a ≥ *a* to emit e(a) units of externality. That is, *a*, l( ), e( ) solve the problem

$$\text{(4.16)} \qquad \underset{a,l(\ ),e(\ )}{\text{Maximize}} \int_a^\infty \{pf(l(x),e(x),x) - wl(x) - se\,(x) - w\}g(x)dx$$

where p denotes the price of the good and s denotes the social cost of the externality. The prices p, w, and s are given exogenously. The case where p and w are determined endogenously in a general equilibrium framework can be analyzed by methods similar to those developed here.

The first-order necessary conditions for a maximum are

$$\text{(4.17a)} \qquad \kappa(a) = 0,$$

$$\text{(4.17b)} \qquad \kappa(a)_a = pf_a > 0,$$

$$\text{(4.17c)} \qquad \kappa(a) \equiv \max_{l,e}(pf(l,e,a) - wl - se - w),$$

$$\text{(4.17d)} \qquad pf_l = w,$$

$$\text{(4.17e)} \qquad pf_e = s.$$

Subscripts denote partial derivatives. The necessary conditions have the standard economic interpretations. The second-order necessary conditions for a maximum with respect to l and e hold because of the assumed concavity of f in l and e. The concavity of

$$W(a) \equiv \int_a^\infty \kappa(x)dG$$

follows from

$$W' = -\kappa g,$$

$$W'' = -\kappa_a g - \kappa g'$$

which in turn follows from our definition of ability provided that $\kappa_a g + \kappa g' > 0$, which we assume. Notice that $\kappa_a = pf_a > 0$, which in turn follows from our definition of ability.

Private markets do not price the externality e. Hence, unregulated firms will employ e out to the point where $f_e = 0$ and therefore use too much of the externality-generating inputs. The standard remedy for this market failure is to place a "Pigouvian" tax on the effluent at rate s, thereby forcing firms to internalize their externalities and obey the necessary condition (4.17e). But levying this tax will ordinarily impose administrative costs on both the firms that pay the tax and the government agency that collects the tax. The flat-tax rate of s is suboptimal in the presence of these administrative costs.[27]

Denote the administrative cost borne by the firm by F(t(a),t(a)e(a)) and the administrative cost borne by the regulatory agency by R(t(a),t(a)e(a)). We make the following assumption concerning administrative costs.[28]

> *Assumption 4.1:* The functions F and R are convex in (t,T), take global minima at (0,0), and are nondecreasing in $|t|$, $|T|$, where $|y|$ denotes the absolute value of the real number y and $T = t(a)e(a)$.

This section analyzes two related problems concerning the optimal design of regulation when there are administrative costs of the form assumed above and when firms are heterogeneous. First, we shall treat the regulator as a discriminating monopolist owner of the environment who can observe ability a and levy a flat externality tax of t(a) per unit. The proceeds of the tax are distributed back to the public in a lump sum non-distorting manner. Second, we assume that the regulator cannot observe the underlying ability parameter a although he can observe the amount of externality e(a) emitted by a firm. We discuss the optimal multipart externality tariff schedule in the face of this imperfect information.

Optimal Regulation with Perfect Information

Given an emission tax schedule t = t(a), an individual with entrepreneurial ability a solves

$$J(t,a) = \max_{l,e}(pf(1,e,a) - wl - te\ F(t,te) - w) \tag{4.18}$$

He works if $J(t,a) < 0$ and entrepreneurs if $J(t,a) \geq 0$. Denote the a that solves $J(t,a) = 0$ by a′. Then social surplus is

$$(4.19) \qquad W(t) \equiv \int_{a'}^{\infty}\{J(t(a),a) + (t(a) - s)e(t(a),a) - R(t(a),t(a)e^*(t(a),a)\}$$

$$\equiv \int_{a'}^{\infty}\Gamma(t(a),a)dG.$$

where $e^*(t(a),a)$ is the emission level that solves (4.18).

We are now in a position to state our first problem.

Problem 1: Let t be chosen to maximize

$$W(t) = \int_{a'}^{\infty}\Gamma(t(a),a)dG.$$

Then locate sufficient conditions on Γ such that the optimal tax rate t(a) is progressive, i.e., $dt^*/da > 0$.[29] Here t^* defines the optimal tax.

The optimal tax schedule must provide the proper incentives for the entry and exit of firms. We show that in order to achieve the optimal entrepreneurial cutoff level a^* regulators may have to impose a lump-sum tax or subsidy, which does not vary with the ability level of the firm, on all firms that enter an industry.[30]

Assuming a maximum over t exists for each a, Problem 1 involves a simple pointwise maximization of a sum of independent terms for all forms of $\Gamma(t,a)$. It is socially optimal for individual a to entrepreneur if $\max\Gamma(t,a) \equiv H(a) > 0$ and to work otherwise. The optimal set of entrepreneurs has the form $[a^*,\infty)$ under the following assumption.[31]

Assumption 4.2: H(a) increases in a.

Assumption 4.2 states that the maximum social surplus that the regulator can get out of ability type a increases as ability increases. This assumption is modest.

We begin by analyzing the optimal tax schedule when the entrepreneurial cutoff level a′ is fixed exogenously. Let $T = te$.

Proposition 4.1. If F and R are increasing in t and T for $t \geq 0$, if $e_t < 0$, if $dT/dt > 0$, and if $t > 0$, then $t^* \leq s$ where t^* is the optimal tax schedule.[32]

We now investigate the circumstances under which the optimal tax schedule is progressive, i.e., $t^*_a > 0$. The optimal tax schedule t^*_a satisfies

$$(4.20) \qquad \Gamma_t(t^*(a),a) = 0$$

Hence

(4.21) $$\Gamma_{tt}t^*_a + \Gamma_{ta} = 0$$

But $\Gamma_{tt} < 0$ at a regular maximum. Therefore,

Proposition 4.2: If $\Gamma_{ta} > 0$, then $t_a > 0$.

It is straightforward to derive an expression for Γ_{ta} in terms of more primitive data such as π, s, F, and R. But the expression is messy and not very edifying. It is possible to gain more insights into the forces that cause the tax schedule to be progressive by examining specific examples. An interesting case is where F and R are both constant in T. In this case it is possible to establish the following proposition.

Proposition 4.3: If F and R are constant in T and increasing in t, if π_e is convex in e, if $\pi_{ea} > 0$, and if $\pi_{eea} > 0$, then $\Gamma_{ta} > 0$.[33] Therefore, $t^*_a > 0$.

Let us now consider the optimal managerial cutoff level. Society would like the borderline entrepreneurs to be those a* for which $H(a^*) \equiv \Gamma(t(a^*),a^*) = 0$. Since

(4.22) $$\Gamma = J + (t - s)e^* - R \equiv J + A$$

$J^* = -A^*$ at a*. If the conditions stated in Proposition 4.1 hold, $t^* < s$ at a*, so that

(4.23) $$J^* = -A^* = (s - t(a^*))e^* + R^* > 0$$

at a*. But if $J^* > 0$, there are incentives for individuals with ability less than a* to enter. That is, in general the a′ that solves $J(t,a) = 0$ is less than the a* that solves $H(a^*) = 0$. Society can deter this socially inefficient entry by imposing a license fee of $L = J(t(a^*),a^*)$ on all firms. We therefore have the following proposition.[34]

Proposition 4.4: If J(t(a),a) is increasing in a, if the optimal set of entrepreneurs has the form $[a,\infty)$, and if the optimal tax satisfies $t^* < s$ at a*, then inefficient firms will form. A license fee of $L = J(t(a^*),a^*)$ levied on all firms will discourage the formation of inefficient firms.

Two remarks are in order here. First, there may not be an optimal tax schedule in the class $M \equiv (M|M(e,a) = t(a)e)$. The class M may need to be broadened to the class $M' \partial (M'|M'(e,a) = L + t(a)e)$. Second, the license fee L adds a regressive component to a possibly progressive marginal tax schedule t(a).

A major theme of this chapter is that administrative costs induce situations in which it is socially efficient to regulate smaller businesses even though these businesses are not as efficient at complying with socially desirable regulations as larger businesses. This result is obviously true when regulation imposes a fixed cost on a business that is large relative to the value of the pollution eliminated by this business as a result of regulation. For example, if there is a fixed cost R_0 to the government for administering the tax-cum-license fee regulation in addition to the administrative cost F(t,te) and if R_0 is large relative to the social gain from regulation, $D(a) = \Gamma(t^*(a),a) - \Gamma(0,a)$, then it is sometimes desirable to exempt smaller firms altogether from the regulation.[35] That is to say, the scheme (L,t*( )) should be implemented only for those a that have $D(a) - R_0 > 0$. What is more subtle is that there may be circumstances under which it may be desirable to impose a lighter regulatory burden on smaller businesses even when there are no pure fixed costs, as established in Propositions 4.2 and 4.3.

At this point, it is useful to work through an example for a particular production technology in order to express the optimum regulatory schedule as a function of a few key parameters. We shall consider a technology characterized by the following cost function

(4.24) $$c(q,x) = b + cxq^2$$

where q denotes output, b is the fixed cost per period of running a business, and x = 1/a is the entrepreneur's incompetence level. Note that larger x's are less able and run smaller businesses. We assume that the administrative costs to the government are zero, R = 0, and that the administrative costs to the firm are an increasing function of the tax rate F = ft where f is a constant. The externality is produced in fixed proportions with output so that the externality cost is sq. Profits are given by

(4.25) $$J = pq - (b + cxq^2 + ft + tq) - w$$

The optimum output is

(4.26) $$q(x,t) = (p - t)/2cx$$

The marginal manager, who satisfied J = 0, is given by

(4.27) $$z(t) = (p - t)^2/\{4c[ft + b + w]\}$$

maximum profits to firm x facing tax rate t are

$$J(t,x) = (p - t)^2/4cx - ft - b - w \tag{4.28}$$

Total welfare generated by tax function t(x) is

$$W(t) = \int \Gamma(t(x),x)dG \tag{4.29}$$

where

$$\Gamma(t,x) = (p - s)(p - t)/2cx - (p - t)^2/4cx - ft - b - w \tag{4.30}$$

We may now state

Proposition 4.5: The optimal tax function t and exemption level x are

$$t(x) = s - 2fcx,\ x < x^* \tag{4.31a}$$

$$t(x) = 0,\ x \geq x^* \tag{4.31b}$$

$$x^* = s/2fc \tag{4.32}$$

Figure 4.1 shows the optimal regulatory design across firm sizes.

Notice that it is optimal to exempt small firms from the variable tax t(x) (but not the license fee) when $z > x^*$. Also notice that the administrative cost drives a wedge between price and social marginal cost at the optimum. This result is consistent with the finding by Heller and Shell that divergences from production efficiency may be optimal when there are taxes that impose administrative costs.[36] The mathematically inclined reader may work out the value of x^* that satisfies $\Gamma(t(x^*,x^*) = 0$ where t(x) is given by (4.31a) and (4.31b). This value of x^* is the socially optimal cutoff level. Society can prevent entry of firms with $x > x^*$ by imposing a license fee on all operating firms.

Optimal Regulation with Imperfect Information

It is clearly unrealistic to assume that regulators can observe the entrepreneurial ability level a for each firm. A more realistic assumption is that regulators can observe the pollution emitted by the firm.[37] Regulators then search for an optimum multipart externality tariff schedule $m(e) \equiv dM/de$, where M(e) is the total charge levied on a firm that emits *e* units of externality. Formally, we have

Figure 4.1
Economics of Tiering

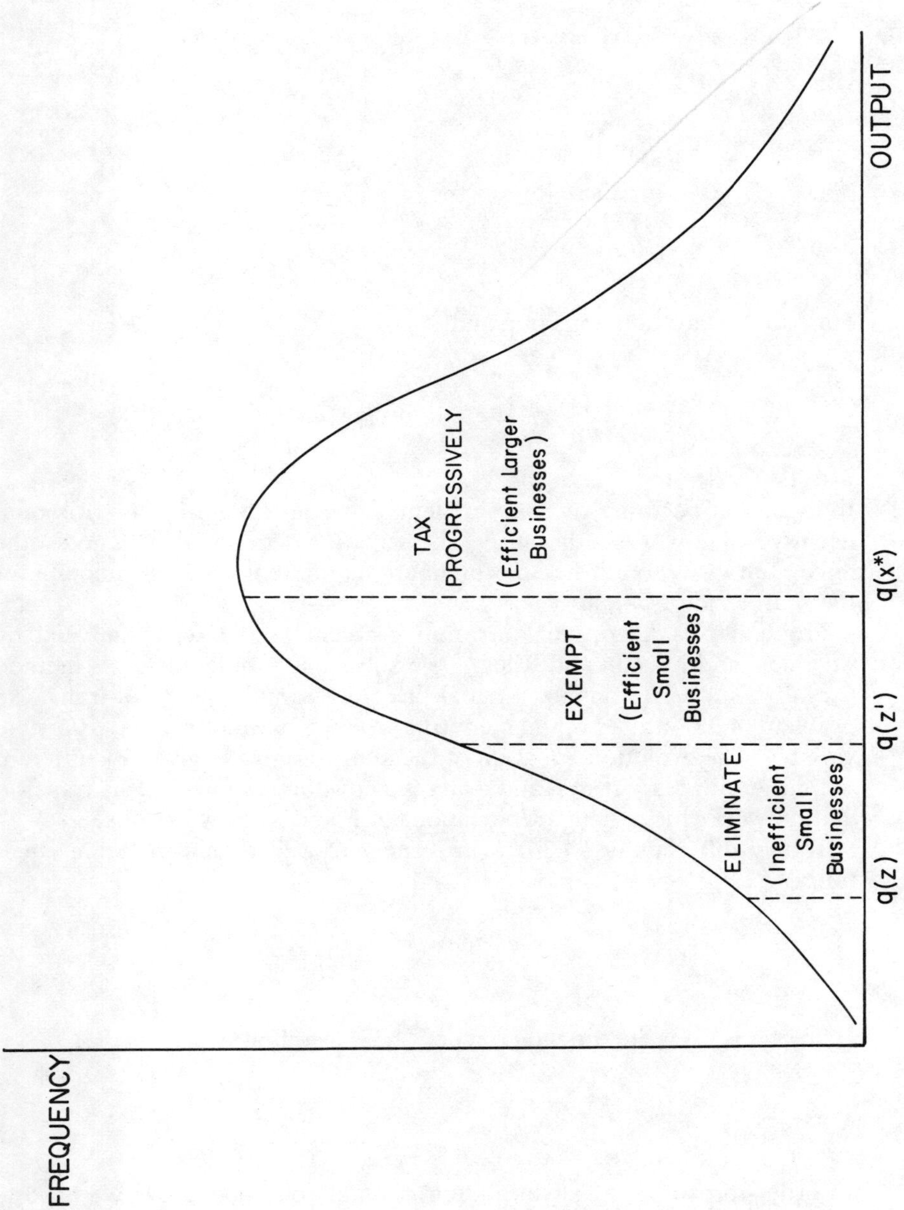

Problem 2: Find an optimal multipart externality tariff schedule m(e) that solves

(4.33) $$\underset{m,l,e}{\text{maximize}} \int_a^\infty [pf - wl - w - se - F - R]dG$$

subject to

(l,e) solve

(4.34) $$\underset{l,e}{\text{maximize}}[pf - wl - M - F - w] \equiv V(a)$$

(4.35) $$V(a) \geq 0$$

Here m, l, e are functions of a and

$$M(e) = \int_0^e m(y)dy$$

Individual a becomes an entrepreneur if the maximum in (4.34) is nonnegative and works otherwise. The function V(a), which denotes the maximum value to a if he entrepreneurs, is the rent gradient function for the scarce factor "ability."

Problem 2 is an optimal taxation problem of the type analyzed by Mirrlees, and Maskin and Riley.[38] We solve this problem using a method used by Spulber to analyze spatial price discrimination.[39] We transform problem (4.33) into an optimal control problem by treating V(a) as a state variable. The evolution equation of the state variable is given by differentiating V with respect to a and using the envelope theorem. This transformation works for certain specifications of F and R, as we shall see.

Totally differentiate (4.34) with respect to a to obtain the state equation[40]

(4.36) $$dV/da = V' = pf_a$$

Using (4.34), rewrite the integrand of (4.33) as follows

(4.37) $$pf - wl - se - F - R - w = V + M - se - R$$

In order to use the "transformation method" outlined above we need to formulate the problem so that we maximize equation (4.38) below to solve for M in terms of V, e, l, a

(4.38) $$pf(l,e,a) - wl - M - F - w = V$$

Obviously if F is a function of $M' \equiv m$ we cannot solve for M in terms of (V,e,l,a). Therefore, we shall asume that both F and R are functions of total taxes and the average tax rate M/e. Notice that this formulation squares with that used in Problem 1, where F and R were functions of total taxes te and the average tax rate t.

Let

(4.39) $$M = \theta(V,e,l,a)$$

solve (4.38). Insert the solution (4.39) into the right-hand side of (4.37) and call the result N(V,e,l,a). We have now transformed problem two into the control problem

(4.40) $$\underset{l,e,a'}{\text{maximize}} \int_{a'}^{\infty} N(V,e,l,a)dG$$

subject to

(4.41) $$V' = pf_a(l,e,a),\ V \geq 0$$

Notice that this is a free "time," free endpoint problem with the state variable bounded away from zero.

The actual analytical solution of this problem is difficult and technical. It would take us far afield into the realm of abstract mathematics to work out the solution here.[41] Nevertheless, the statement of Problem 2 offers an excellent schematic which can be used to organize a heuristic discussion of regulatory tiering under imperfect information.

There are two main cases. The first case is where the regulator can costlessly administer a lump-sum license fee that is the same for all firms. The second case concerns costly administration of the license fee. We are going to devote the most attention to the first case. But before turning to the first case let us treat the second case briefly.

Regulators may exempt on the basis of sales q because it is costly to observe emissions, if administrative costs of the license fee are large relative to the potential social damage done by a firm selling q under no regulation and if it is privately costly for other firms selling $10,000 per firm regulating an externality of maximum social cost of $500 per firm.

A delicate tradeoff emerges when firms have an incentive to cut back harmful emissions dramatically in response to a small amount of emission taxation or emission regulation. The fact that emissions are privately costless provides firms with incentives to emit to the point where an extra unit of emission does not lower their cost or raise their profit at all. This kind of incentive may lead to large amounts of extra emissions that generate small extra private profits at large extra social cost. Furthermore, socially conscious operators may be forced by cost-cutting competition from socially unconscious operators to emit more and more in order to get costs down to avoid being undercut by socially unconscious operators. Such private cost *reducing* but social cost *increasing* competition forces everyone down to the lowest common denominator of behavior toward the environment.

Typically it is easier for a regulator to observe and measure variables such as sales, employment, or other measures of size rather than emissions. Hence it is natural for a regulator to exempt all firms from regulation if, for example, sales fall below some cutoff level q. The regulator faces a delicate tradeoff in choosing q. On the one hand he saves society administrative costs for all firms with q < q, but on the other hand he generates perverse incentives. In industries where technologies are such that increased emissions lead to a lot of reduction in costs, such exemption may cause a lot of damage. Larger firms may contract output to get the exemption. New firms that are socially inefficient may form because they are exempt so long as q < q. The combined effects of price undercutting by these unregulated firms may put a lot of pressure on large firms that must comply with the regulations. They in turn may shrink output in order to get relief from regulation.

The wise regulator must balance this trade-off in designing an exemption level. Much like the college professor searching for a gap in the grade distribution for a cutoff level between an A and a B, the regulator must search for a gap in the output distribution to set q where it is privately costly for firms with sales greater than q to shrink themselves to q. He must also take into account the incentive of large firms to divest smaller pollution-intensive subsidiaries in order to gain the exemption.

If it is costless to impose a "license fee" L on all firms, the regulator can use this tool to deter the formation of new socially inefficient firms and to deter the spinning off of pollution-intensive subsidiaries from old firms. In practice, the regulator must temper the license fee L to respect risk aversion on the part of smaller firms in a world of imperfect capital markets. This is so because the fee L is a lump-sum up-front operating cost that is independent of the actual profits produced by a firm in a risky world.

If profits are volatile the presence of a fixed operating cost may deter many socially desirable small businesses from operating. This is a commonplace objection to the fixed costs of regulation: they increase socially undesirable risk aversion as well as socially undesirable scale economies among average smaller firms. The regulator could make the license fee L contingent on actual IRS-reported operating profits, but this solution may lead to additional distortions.

Even if the risk aversion problem is solved, we still face the problem of how to design the socially optimal regulatory schedule m( ) once we decide to regulate. Suppose that we have set up the administrative apparatus to measure e. We can imagine its being funded by revenues from the fee L imposed on all operating firms. Let us use the statement of Problem 2 as a schematic to organize our discussion of the trade-offs that the regulator faces.

The regulator knows that administrative costs at the firm level increase with the average tax rate and the total taxes taken in. He wishes to regulate smaller firms more lightly in order to avoid creating socially undesirable artificial scale economies. He also wishes to economize on administrative costs at the government level. These costs also increase with the amount of taxes taken in as well as with the average tax rate. Yet the regulator knows that regulating smaller firms lightly will cause bigger firms to masquerade as smaller firms in order to get more favorable treatment.

Suppose the regulator knows the distribution of firm types and the technology of each type, can observe the emissions of each type, but cannot observe the type itself. Also suppose that the marginal product of emissions increases with ability and marginal cost of production falls with ability. Then the regulator knows that emissions, output, and ability all tend to be positively related.

We can imagine him attempting to find a regulatory schedule m( ) that maximizes social surplus. The regulator can control type a's choice of inputs only indirectly because he cannot observe the type. By assumption, he can observe only the emissions. We may view the regulator's constraint that he cannot observe each type as forcing him to design a schedule m( ) that will induce each type a to act as if he were type a and not some other type a′. This "truth telling" or "incentive compatibility" constraint may or may not be a tight constraint on the regulator's freedom to design a workable schedule of regulation. In any event we may view the regulator's problem as choosing input and emission levels for each type and the schedule m( ) so as to maximize the sum of social welfare generated subject to the constraint that, facing the schedule m( ), each type "a" has an incentive to choose that input level and emission level "assigned" to him by the regulator. Viewing the problem this way captures the constraints on a regulator who knows the distribution of types and technology in an industry but cannot observe each type directly although each emission level may be observed directly.

Without doing any mathematics let us reason our way toward an understanding of the solution to this problem. Ideally the regulator wants to induce each type to emit the socially optimal level of emissions for that type. If there were only one type "a" and e(a) is the socially optimal amount of pollution emitted by type a, then the regulator could design a schedule that penalized a sharply for emitting more than e(a) but did not penalize him at all for emissions less than a. In this way few taxes are collected at the *actual* level of emissions. Hence administrative costs due to tax collection would be small. If administrative costs depend on the average tax rate as well as total taxes actually collected, it may be possible to design the schedule to deter emissions beyond e(a) in such a way that the *actual* tax rate is small.

Suppose now that there are two types $a_1 < a_2$. If the types are far apart so that a_1 is much smaller than a_2, then it would be very costly to the high ability a_2 to masquerade as the low ability a_1 to obtain the preferential treatment for a_1. In this case the regulator could design a schedule that severely penalizes all emissions above the socially optimal level of pollution $e(a_2)$ for type a_2, freely allowing all emissions below $e(a_2)$. Taking into account administrative costs, this solution may be optimal if the fraction of type a_1 is small and the type a_1 technology does not allow much substitution of cheap emissions for other inputs in cost reduction. In any event some general properties of an optimal regulatory schedule are: First, a license fee is generally needed to discourage the formation of inefficient firms. Second, the variable tax schedule m( ), unlike the case in which ability is observable, depends on characteristics such as the dispersion of the type distribution as well as the technology.

Extensions and Applications

The framework developed in this chapter illustrates the trade-off between artificial economies of scale created by administrative costs and the social benefits of regulation. If we wanted only to develop a framework where the disproportionate burden of administrative costs on small firms could be illustrated, we would not need such a fancy apparatus. A minor adaptation of the industry equilibrium model developed in freshman economics textbooks would do. But such a model does not have a useful theory of the size distribution of business firms as we have here. Such a model does not allow us to efficiently formalize the optimal trade-off among distortions in the size distribution of business firms, administrative costs of regulation, and the level of regulation across firms as we are able to do here. Another benefit of our framework is that it can be extended easily. We discuss four extensions.

The first extension concerns performance requirements. Suppose that regulators can observe the ability level of each entrepreneur and can require firm a to clean up fraction $\lambda(a)$ of its pollution where the cost of cleanup and compliance is $K(e,\lambda,a)$. In this case private profits are $pf(l,e,a) - wl - w - K(e,\lambda,a)$. Social welfare generated by a is $pf - wl - w - se - K(e,\lambda,a)$. The problem is to choose the function $\lambda(a)$ to maximize the sum of welfare generated by all operating firms. This is the same type of problem that we solved in the perfect information case with $\lambda(a)$ playing the role of t(a). A license fee of L will typically be required to deter the formation of inefficient firms. The optimal function $\lambda(\ )$ will depend on technology. Small firms may receive lower standards than larger firms.

The standard λ may be set on the basis of some observable index of firm activity such as output in the case where ability is not observable. In this case the problem setup is exactly the same as that of designing a regulatory tax schedule t(q) as a function of output q. The standard may be broadly interpreted to include the degree of compliance with regulations such as safety rules, civil rights laws, pension regulations, and so forth. Here "e" could be interpreted as privately profitable but socially damaging behavior.

A second application is the determination of the optimal frequency and intensity of tax audits across business sizes by a regulator such as the IRS. Frequent and intensive tax audits may create artificial scale economies that involve socially undesirable discrimination against small businesses that cannot afford to retain a staff of fancy lawyers and accountants to deal with the IRS. This problem has the same analytical structure as our basic problem.

A third application concerns transferable discharge permits. Transferable discharge permits (TDPs) help minimize the cost of achieving a given level of emission by allowing firms that are less efficient at controlling emissions to purchase discharge permits from firms that are more efficient at controlling emissions. TDPs provide stronger incentives for the development of more cost-effective emission-control devices than do the standards usually imposed by regulators.[42]

The solution to Problem 1 may be viewed as an optimal TDP scheme where the administrative costs (for both the firm and government) for each type of firm depend upon the total value of permits purchased by firm type a (t(a)e*(t(a),a)), and the permit price t(a) for firm type a. To see this, notice that there is a functional relationship between the price t of permits and the number e*(t,a) of permits through the equilibration of supply and demand. That is, given t,e*(t,a) solves

$$\pi_e(e,a) = t(1 + F_M(te,t)) \tag{4.42}$$

and given e there is a t that solves (4.42). If TDP administrative costs for each a can be represented by F(te,t), R(te,t), then we can obtain an optimal TDP scheme as follows: First, solve Problem 1. Let t(a)e*(t(a), a) denote the solution for each a. Assign t(a)e*(t(a),a) as the total allowed emissions for the group (or cluster) of type a's. Second, allow free trading of permits within cluster a. A market clearing price will emerge that solves (4.42) with e fixed at e*(t(a),a). Here t(a) solves (4.42) with e fixed at e*(t(a),a). The license fee L is set in the same way as in Problem 1.

Although we grant that this approach to designing optimal TDP systems is rather abstract, it provides a useful framework for designing workable TDP systems. Viewing TDP systems this way shows us that when there are administrative costs, there may be sizable social gains from "social price discrimination" by setting different allowable emissions for different firm types even when emissions are homogeneous, when firm types are highly heterogeneous. We can see this by examining the example of an optimal flat-tax schedule in the section on optimal regulation with perfect information. In this example, clusters of small firms (high x's and therefore low a's) receive proportionately smaller reduction quotas or, equivalently, larger emission allowances. Some clusters of firms will receive unlimited emission rights after they pay their entry fee into the industry. TDPs will trade at a zero price for such clusters.

The fourth application concerns the desirability of existing tiering schemes. The tiering schemes derived in this chapter have three common features. (1) A license fee that all firms must pay to operate in the industry. This fee encourages the dissolution of inefficient small firms. (2) An exemption from regulatory requirements that discourages the dissolution of efficient small firms. (3) Lighter regulatory requirements for smaller nonexempt firms under certain circumstances.[43]

The tiering schemes used in practice generally (1) either exempt all firms below some size threshold from regulatory requirements or impose lighter regulatory requirements on firms below some size threshold and (2) impose the same regulatory requirements on firms above this size threshold.[44] Table 4.2 reports the key features of twenty-nine federal tiering schemes.[45] Of these twenty-nine schemes, fifteen exempt businesses below some threshold, fourteen impose lighter requirements on businesses below some threshold (but do not exempt these businesses), twelve exempt or impose lighter *substantive* requirements on smaller entities, and seventeen exempt or impose lighter reporting, recordkeeping, inspection, or other administrative requirements on smaller entities.

If the tiering schemes we have derived are as feasible and as inexpensive to administer and enforce as the tiering schemes used in practice, then our proposed schemes can achieve a given reduction of emissions at a lower social cost than existing schemes.[46] But this is a big if. It may be expensive to administer the licensing scheme we proposed. It also may be politically unfeasible, at least in some industries, to force inefficient small firms to close down. Multitiered regulations where regulatory requirements vary across narrowly defined business types may entail huge administrative expenses.[47]

Unfortunately, once we depart from the optimal tiering schemes derived above it becomes a delicate question whether tiered regulations are supe-

TABLE 4.2
Summary of Tiered Federal Regulations

Program (Department)	*Tiering Criteria*	*Number of Tiers*	*Type of Tiering*
Federal Grain Inspection Service (Energy)	output per year	1	inspection exemption
Handicap Discrimination Regulations (Education)	employees	1	administrative requirements exemption
Natural Gas Regulations (Energy)	number and type of pipeline customers	NA	special allocations
Day Care Regulations (Health and Human Services)	amount of federal funding	1	substantive exemption
Medical Device Regulations (Food and Drug Administration)	health risk	3	recordkeeping exemption
Medical Device Regulations (Food and Drug Administration)	employment	1	inspection exemption
Home Health Agency Regulations (Health Care Financing Administration)	amount of federal funding	1	lighter recordkeeping requirements
Mineral Mining Regulations (Bureau of Land Management)	degree of environmental disturbance	3	reporting requirements (exemption for first tier)
Employee Pension Plans (Labor)	number of participants	1	reporting requirements exemption
Health and Safety Regulations (OSHA)	employment and risk	1	reporting and recordkeeping exemption
Health and Safety Regulations (OSHA)		NA	fewer inspections for lower risk (usually smaller) firms
Cotton Dust Standard (OSHA)	technologies	NA	substantive requirements
Mine Safety Training (Mine	employment	1	lighter

TABLE 4.2 (Cont'd)

Summary of Tiered Federal Regulations

Program (Department)	*Tiering Criteria*	*Number of Tiers*	*Type of Tiering*
Safety and Health Administration)			substantive requirements
Aircraft Safety Regulation (FAA)	aircraft size	1	lighter substantive requirements
Motor Carrier Safety Regulations (Federal Highway Administration)	risk	NA	substantive requirement exemptions
Bank Regulation (Office of the Comptroller of the Currency)	value of debt or equity security sold	2	substantive requirement exemption or reduced burden
Bank Regulation (Office of the Comptroller of the Currency)	number of shareholders	1	reduced substantive requirements
Hazardous Waste Regulations for Generators (EPA)	output	1	reporting requirement exemption
Noise Standards on Tractors (EPA)	risk and type of tractor	NA	lighter substantive requirements
Federal Insecticide,Fungicide, and Rodenticide Act Regulations (EPA)	operating revenues and gravity of violation	5	smaller fines for smaller firms and less serious offenses
Equal Employment (EEOC)	employment	1	recordkeeping exemption
Credit Union Reserve Requirements (National Credit Union Administration)	asset size	1	substantive exemption
Airline Regulations (CAB)	gross revenue and aircraft size	3	lighter and less frequent reporting and recordkeeping requirements for smaller airlines

TABLE 4.2 (Cont'd)
Summary of Tiered Federal Regulations

Program (Department)	*Tiering Criteria*	*Number of Tiers*	*Type of Tiering*
Federal Deposit Insurance Corporation Regulations	asset size	1	lighter reporting requirements for small banks
Maritime Tariffs (Federal Maritime Commission)	cargo capacity and horsepower	1	substantive exemption
Bank Reserve Requirements (Federal Reserve System)	size of deposits	2	substantive exemption for first tier and lighter reporting requirements for second tier
Merger and Acquisition Regulations (FTC)	size	NA	premerger notification
Trucking Regulations (ICC)	gross operating revenue	1	lighter reporting requirements
Security Regulations (SEC)	size of issue	1	lighter substantive requirements

SOURCE: U.S. Regulatory Council, *Tiering Regulations: A Practical Guide* (Washington, D.C.: U.S. Regulatory Council, March 1981), pp. 31–52. This report lists forty-three regulatory programs that either were tiered or for which tiering was being considered. Only regulations actually in force as of 1981 are included in this list.

rior to untiered regulations. In order to address this question we compare two alternative regulatory schemes that correspond roughly to the schemes currently used. The first scheme imposes the same regulatory requirements on all firms that are larger than some size threshold and exempts all firms that are below this threshold. We can characterize this scheme by a tax rate t^1 that applies to all firms that are larger than the exemption level q^*. The second scheme imposes the same regulatory requirements on all firms regardless of size. We can characterize this scheme by a tax rate t^2 that applies to all firms. The second scheme is a special case of the first scheme with $q^* = 0$. We are interested in the circumstances under which the optimal exemption level for the first scheme is $q^* = 0$ so that the first scheme reduces to the second scheme and untiered regulations are therefore optimal.

The choice of an exemption level for the first scheme must take two factors into account. First, some businesses will contract themselves in order to gain the exemption even though they could operate more efficiently at a larger size. Society loses social surplus from this suboptimal reduction in output.

The Department of Energy's Crude Oil Entitlements Program provides a good example of this perverse impact of the exemption scheme. This program

> enabled smaller refineries to purchase crude oil at subsidized prices. An unintended consequence of this program was that although the minimum technologically efficient refinery size is 175,000 barrels a day, 37 of the 38 refineries built in the United States between January 1974 and September 1977 were designed to process less than 40,000 barrels a day in order to take advantage of the subsidy.[48]

The second factor that dictates the choice of an exemption level is that the exemption applies to small inefficient businesses as well as to small efficient businesses. Society would like to eliminate businesses with $x > x^*$, where x^* is defined in (4.32), because these businesses decrease social surplus. The tiered regulations described in Table 4.2 have no mechanism for eliminating small inefficient businesses. Exemptions therefore preserve "bad" small businesses as well as "good" small businesses.

The optimal exemption level and tax rate must balance the social loss from inducing inefficient business contractions and saving small inefficient businesses against the social gain from preserving small efficient businesses and inducing larger businesses to reduce their pollution.[49] When the exemption preserves a large number of small inefficient businesses and when there are strong incentives for businesses to contract in order to gain the exemption, the optimal exemption may well be zero.

Regulators could lessen the potentially adverse consequences of tiering by mimicking more closely the schemes we have devised. Regulators might consider incorporating a mechanism for eliminating small inefficient firms, perhaps by using exemptions that are based not on firm characteristics that distinguish efficient firms from inefficient firms as well as small firms from large firms. They might also consider increasing regulatory requirements gradually for firms that are past the exemption level. Such gradual tightening of regulatory requirements would lessen inefficient business contraction.

Regulators could also mimic more closely the schemes we have devised by using a suitable distribution of enforcement and monitoring efforts across firms. They could capture the spirit of the regulatory scheme presented in Proposition 4.5 by using a U-shaped enforcement plan. Small inefficient businesses would face stiff enforcement. Small efficient businesses would face light enforcement. Larger firms would face increasingly stiffer enforcement.

Summary

Our results all assume that firms are heterogeneous and that regulations impose administrative costs along the lines discussed in the section on our basic model:

1. When there is perfect information and regulators impose ability-specific flat taxes, the optimal scheme generally entails a tax rate that varies with business size and a license fee that applies to all operating firms. The tax rate may be zero for some small businesses. These businesses are exempted from all further regulatory requirements after they pay a license fee and are licensed to operate.
2. When there is imperfect information and regulators impose multipart regulatory tariff schedules, the optimal scheme generally entails a license fee that all businesses must pay. It may include an exemption from the tariff schedule but not the license fee for small businesses. The optimal marginal tax rate may not be progressive.
3. In an ideal world, where regulators have perfect information and can impose multipart tariffs tailor-made for each type of firm, regulators can achieve the first-best level of externality production at virtually zero administrative cost. Regulators do this by imposing a high average tax rate on emissions above some level, a low average tax rate on emissions below this level, and a high marginal tax rate on the first unit of emissions that regulators would like to deter. Administrative costs will be almost nil because the total tax burden and the marginal tax rate will be almost zero.[50]
4. When the workers and managers in an industry have few alternative employment opportunities, it is difficult to substitute away from inputs that cause externalities, and there are few spillover effects from the industry (perhaps because there is only one industry in a region of the country), regulation of externality emissions may not be desirable.[51]
5. Existing tiered regulations have two adverse consequences. They encourage some efficient large businesses to contract in order to gain an exemption from regulatory requirements. They encourage the formation (and discourage the dissolution) of small inefficient businesses. These adverse consequences may outweigh the benefits of tiering under certain circumstances. Regulators could lessen these adverse impacts by avoiding abrupt increases in regulatory requirements and by discouraging the operation of small inefficient firms.

We end this chapter with an important caveat. The conclusion that it may be desirable to exempt smaller firms may not apply to industries that have high barriers to price competition even if these industries are highly deconcentrated with many small businesses. In some industries such as real estate and professional practices there is evidence that existing firms have erected institutional barriers to price competition (such as licensing boards) that stimulate socially undesirable "service" competition, prevent entry and may keep businesses artificially small. Policy makers concerned with advancing economic efficiency by maintaining a strong small business sector should be certain to focus their attention on industries where small businesses help rather than impede competition.[52]

5

THE DIFFERENTIAL IMPACT OF REGULATIONS ACROSS BUSINESS SIZES: A SURVEY OF THE LITERATURE

Policy makers have expressed increasing concern that federal regulations have a disparate impact on smaller businesses. Supposedly many regulations impose fixed costs that create artificial scale economies and thereby place smaller business at a competitive disadvantage. Weidenbaum says, "Government regulation . . . hits small business disproportionately hard."[1] Berney argues that regulations impose fixed costs, which larger firms can average over larger outputs.[2] A recent presidential report on small business notes, "Small business has repeatedly claimed that the uniform application of the same requirements to them and to larger entities produces economic inequity."[3] These regulations have allegedly forced many small business closures, have reduced the share of output produced by smaller businesses, and have increased industrial concentration.[4] Reflecting these concerns, in 1980 Congress passed the Regulatory Flexibility Act, which encourages federal agencies to impose lighter regulatory burdens on smaller businesses.[5]

There are many plausible reasons for suspecting that federal regulations hit smaller businesses especially hard. First, stiff paperwork requirements accompany many regulations. The Small Business Administration estimates that "paperwork burdens alone cost small business $12.7 billion per year."[6] These paperwork requirements probably increase less than proportionately with firm size. Second, bigger businesses can spread the administrative costs of complying with regulations over a larger sales volume than smaller businesses can. These administrative costs include the time lawyers and managers must spend keeping abreast of regulatory requirements and dealing with regulatory agencies. Pashigian finds some evidence that there are scale economies in legal costs.[7] Third, many regulations require businesses to adopt certain procedures or install certain equipment. These requirements may impose fixed costs that bigger businesses can average over a larger quantity of production. Finally, regulation of the various public utility and transportation industries has erected entry barriers that have prevented some smaller firms from capturing market niches in these industries. This disparate impact on smaller businesses is exemplified by the rapid formation of small specialized firms upon the deregulation of the airline, telecommunication, and trucking industries.[9]

A number of studies have been prepared in the last ten years concerning the differential impact of regulations across firm or establishment sizes. These studies adopt one of three possible approaches. The first approach uses data on the regulation and on the industry to estimate the costs of compliance. Compliance costs are usually divided into fixed and variable costs. Studies based on this approach are often prepared prior to the implementation of the regulations and are submitted by the regulatory agency or affected parties in the hearings concerning the proposed regulations. These studies often fail to estimate the actual costs of regulation accurately, either because many firms do not comply fully with the regulatory requirements or because the regulatory requirements change between the time the study is prepared and the requirements are imposed. Examples of such *ex ante* studies are Arthur D. Little's study of the impact of toxic substance regulations on chemical firms and Charles River Associates' study of the impact of OSHA regulations on the lead industry.[10] Because studies based on this approach are highly conjectural, this chapter does not review them.

The second approach examines changes in industry strcture and performance after the imposition of regulations. Studies based on this approach try to determine whether regulations have altered the size distribution of profits, output, or employment or have increased business failures or average business size. These studies face extraordinary problems of measurement and inference. They often lack reliable data on smaller firms. They also have trouble distinguishing the impact of regulations from the impact of other economic changes. Finally, they have difficulty determining whether the estimated impact of regulations is due to scale economies in regulating compliance. It is therefore not possible to place a great deal of confidence in the results of these studies.

The third approach asks firms how much they spend in order to comply with regulations. Studies based on this approach usually ask firms to respond to questionnaires concerning regulatory costs. Unfortunately, responding businesses have weak incentives to provide accurate information and strong incentives to exaggerate regulatory costs. The reliability of regulatory cost estimates based on survey data is therefore somewhat questionable. It is hoped that studies based on these three approaches will provide a useful check on each other.

The studies reviewed in this chapter vary in coverage. The next section reviews studies based on the second and third approaches that examine the impact of a broad set of regulations on a broad set of industries. The following section reviews studies of particular regulations or specific industries. The final section summarizes our findings. The next chapter reports our own study of the differential impact of regulations across firm size.

Economy-wide Studies

There are three major studies available as of this writing that examine the impact of regulations on the economy. The Booz-Allen and Hamilton (hereafter, Booz-Allen) study examines the change in market shares for large firms, the change in market shares for small firms, and changes in business formations and dissolutions for twenty-seven industries heavily affected by environmental regulations and twenty industries affected only lightly by environmental regulations.[11] The Pashigian study examines the impact of environmental and safety regulations on average plant size, the coefficient of variation of plant size, and the market shares of small and large plants for heavily and lightly regulated industries.[12] The Cole and Sommers studies use survey data from a sample of businesses to determine whether average regulatory costs decrease with firm size.[13]

BOOZ-ALLEN AND HAMILTON STUDY

Booz-Allen chose twenty-seven four-digit SIC code industries that were subject to extensive environmental regulations and twenty four-digit SIC code industries that were only lightly affected by environmental regulations. The twenty-seven heavily regulated industries were chosen in the following manner: Booz-Allen scanned the *Federal Register* for the promulgation of environmental regulations and identified all industries affected by these regulations. They then collected information on projected compliance costs for the regulations from EPA economic impact reports and data on total investment in pollution control expenditures from the Pollution Abatement Costs and Expenditures (PACE) series of the Census Bureau. They compiled a list of industries "whose projected compliance costs from EPA information and actual investments from PACE data were high relative to the size of the industry."[14] Finally, they chose twenty-seven industries for which complete information was available. The twenty lightly regulated industries were chosen from a list of industries that were not affected or only lightly affected by EPA regulations. Booz-Allen then chose from this list "twenty industries whose general characteristics best matched those of the highly regulated industries.[15] Table 5.1 lists the industries examined by Booz-Allen.[16]

TABLE 5.1
Sample of Industries Examined by Booz-Allen and Hamilton

SIC Code	*Heavily Regulated Industries*	*SIC Code*	*Lightly Regulated Industries*
2046	Wet corn milling	2259	Knitting mills
2231	Weaving and finishing mills, wool	2279	Carpets and rugs
2295	Coated fabrics	2292	Lace goods
2421	Saw mills and planing mills	2329	Men's and boys clothing
2611	Pulpmills	2519	Household furniture
2621	Papermills	2645	Die cut paper and board
2631	Paperboard mills	2655	Fiber cans, drums
2661	Building paper and board mills	2739	Bookbinding and related work
2819	Industrial inorganic chemicals	2794	Electrotyping and stereotyping
2821	Plastics materials and resins	2831	Biological products
2822	Synthetic rubber	3031	Reclaimed rubber
2851	Paints and allied products	3142	House slippers
2879	Agricultural chemicals N.E.C.	3151	Leather gloves and mittens
2911	Petroleum refining	3161	Luggage
3011	Tires and inner tubes	3271	Concrete block and brick
3069	Fabricated rubber products	3565	Industrial patterns
3079	Miscellaneous plastics products	3572	Typewriters
3241	Cement hydraulic	3576	Scales and balances
3292	Asbestos products	3582	Commercial laundry equipment
3293	Gaskets, packing, and sealing devices	3586	Measuring and dispensing pumps
3296	Mineral wool		
3312	Blast furnaces and steel mills		
3315	Steel wire and related products		
3321	Gray iron foundries		
3341	Secondary nonferrous metals		
3471	Plating and polishing		
3479	Metal coating and allied services		

SOURCE: Booz-Allen & Hamilton, *Impact of Environmental Regulations on Small Business* (Bethesda, Md.: Booz-Allen & Hamilton, May 24, 1982), exhibits III-1, III-2.

In order to determine whether environmental regulations have affected small firms "in a disproportionate manner," Booz-Allen used data from Dun and Bradstreet's Market Identifier Files for 1970, 1974, and 1980. These data, which include information on the sales and employment of individual establishments, were used to calculate changes in the market shares of smaller establishments and changes in the number of establishment formations and dissolutions between 1970 and 1974 and 1980.

Table 5.2 reports the average shares of total industry sales obtained by establishments with less than twenty, fifty, and one hundred employees for the heavily and lightly regulated industries separately in 1970, 1974, and 1980. Table 5.3 reports the average percentage change in the shares for the periods 1970–1974, 1974–1980, and 1970–1980. The market shares for small establishments fell between 1970 and 1974 and between 1974 and 1980 for both heavily regulated and lightly regulated industries. The percentage decrease was much greater for lightly regulated than for heavily regulated industries between 1970 and 1974—17.8 percent vs. 9.2 percent for the smallest establishments—but was much greater for heavily regulated than for lightly regulated industries between 1974 and 1980—33.4 percent vs. 12.8 percent. Since many federal environmental regulations took effect in the latter period, Booz-Allen concluded that environmental regulations caused a decrease in the market shares of small establishments. In fact, investment in pollution abatement capital decreased from the former to the latter period. The growth rate of the real pollution abatement capital stock was 16.3 percent between 1967 and 1970, 16.1 percent between 1970 and 1975, and 8.3 percent between 1975 and 1981.[17] Thus, Booz-Allen's inference that regulations "caused" a decrease in the small business share is highly suspect.

Closer inspection of the data in Tables 5.2 and 5.3 reveals that it was primarily establishments with fewer than twenty employees that lost market share between 1974 and 1980. The market share of establishments with 20–49 employees decreased modestly in the heavily regulated industries and increased modestly in the lightly regulated industries. The market share of establishments with 50–99 employees increased modestly for the heavily regulated industries and dropped precipitously for the lightly regulated industries.

There are two further difficulties with the Booz-Allen analysis. First, they do not perform a statistical test of the hypothesis that market shares of small establishments have decreased to a greater extent in heavily than in lightly regulated industries. The market shares reported in Table 5.2 are averages across twenty-seven heavily regulated industries and twenty lightly regulated industries. Although the difference in the average for these two samples is large, if the variability of changes in market shares across industries is large the difference might not be statistically significant. Booz-Allen do not report such a statistical test, nor do they report sufficient data for other researchers to perform such a statistical test.

Second, environmental regulation is by no means the only factor affecting changes in the size distribution of establishments during the 1970s. This fact is clear from 5.2 and 5.3. Market shares of small establishments decline for both heavily and lightly regulated industries for both 1970–1974

TABLE 5.2
Average Market Shares for Heavily and Lightly Regulated Industries, by Size
(percent)

Number of Employees	*1970*		*1974*		*1980*	
	HR	*LR*	*HR*	*LR*	*HR*	*LR*
1–19	12.5	28.6	10.5	23.6	7.5	20.5
1–49	16.8	41.8	17.9	41.8	14.5	39.5
1–99	28.1	58.4	25.7	59.3	22.9	52.9

SOURCE: Booz-Allen & Hamilton, *Impact of Environmental Regulations on Small Business* (Bethesda, Md.: Booz-Allen & Hamilton, May 24, 1982), exhibits IV-2.

NOTE: Market shares are the percent of total industry sales made by establishments in a particular size category. HR denotes heavily regulated industries, of which there are twenty-seven; LR denotes lightly regulated industries, of which there are twenty.

TABLE 5.3
Average Changes in Market Shares for Heavily and Lightly Regulated Industries, by Size
(percent)

Number of Employees	*1970–1974*		*1974–1978*		*1970–1980*	
	HR	*LR*	*HR*	*LR*	*HR*	*LR*
1–19	−9.2	−17.8	−33.4	−12.8	−35.4	−28.2
1–49	6.9	0	−19.2	−5.7	−13.6	−5.7
1–99	−8.4	1.5	−10.9	−10.6	−18.4	−9.4

SOURCE: Booz-Allen & Hamilton, *Impact of Environmental Regulations on Small Business* (Bethesda, Md.: Booz-Allen & Hamilton, May 24, 1982), exhibits IV-2.

NOTE: Market shares are the percent of total industry sales made by establishments in a particular size category. HR denotes heavily regulated industries, of which there are twenty-seven; LR denotes lightly regulated industries, of which there are twenty.

and 1974–1980. It is simply impossible to separate the impact of environmental regulations from the impact of these other factors, at least from the data reported by Booz-Allen. A major factor may have been the differential growth in demand for the heavily and lightly regulated industries. The value of sales in constant dollars grew for both sets of industries: between 1970 and 1974, 18 percent for the heavily regulated industries and 12 percent for the lightly regulated industries; between 1974 and 1980, 28 percent for the heavily regulated industries and 17 percent for the lightly regulated industries. This growth in demand explains the general decline in market shares for small establishments. As industry demand increases, all establishments expand by increasing employment and output. This general increase skews the distribution of sales toward larger establishments. Although new establishments will form, increases in demand are met in great part by the expansion of existing establishments. Because of these two problems, Booz-Allen's conclusion that environmental regulations have reduced the market shares of small businesses must be viewed with a good deal of skepticism.

Table 5.4 reports the number of business formations, migrations, and dissolutions for heavily and lightly regulated industries in the periods 1970–1974 and 1974–1980. Business formations, migrations, and dissolutions have decreased for both sets of industries between these periods. The percentage changes were roughly the same for heavily regulated industries as for lightly regulated industries. Table 5.5 reports the distribution of business dissolutions and migrations for several business size categories measured by sales. Most dropouts are small. Notably, however, the distribution of dissolutions across size categories is virtually the same for heavily regulated industries as for lightly regulated industries. A slightly greater fraction of small establishments were dissolved in the lightly regulated industries than in the heavily regulated industries during both periods. The same holds true for migrations. These data therefore are not consistent with the hypothesis that regulations have caused small business failures. Given these results, we do not believe that Booz-Allen's conclusion that environmental regulations made it more difficult for small businesses to survive is supported.[18]

The Booz-Allen study provides two key findings. First, the market share of establishments with fewer than twenty employees decreased more dra-

TABLE 5.4

Number of Annual Business Dissolutions, Migrations, and Formations in Heavily and Lightly Regulated Industries

	Heavily Regulated Industries		
	1970–1974	*1974–1980*	*Percent Change*
Annual dissolutions	2,346	2,250	−4.1
Annual migrations	632	318	−49.7
Annual formations	4,037	3,143	−22.2

	Lightly Regulated Industries		
	1970–1974	*1974–1980*	*Percent Change*
Annual dissolutions	556	525	−5.6
Annual migrations	182	93	−48.9
Annual formations	721	596	−17.3

SOURCE: Booz-Allen & Hamilton, *Impact of Environmental Regulations on Small Business* (Bethesda, Md.: Booz-Allen & Hamilton, May 24, 1982), exhibit IV-6.

matically in heavily regulated industries than in lightly regulated industries between the period 1970–1974, when regulations were light, and the period 1974–1978, when regulations were heavy. This difference may not be statistically significant and may be due to the differential growth of heavily versus lightly regulated industries between these two periods. Second, the percentage of business dissolutions and migrations involving small establishments (those with less than $1 million of sales) was roughly the same for heavily as for lightly regulated industries. Environmental regulations have not increased the small business failure rate according to the data produced by Booz-Allen.

The second finding sheds light on the first finding. Regulations will reduce the market share of small business if there are fixed compliance costs that force small businesses to close down. Tables 5.4 and 5.5 suggest that environmental regulations did not increase small business failures. The decreased market share of small firms reported in Table 5.2 must therefore be due to the movement of small establishments into larger size categories. The movement was probably due to industry expansion.

PASHIGIAN STUDY

Pashigian collected data on 319 four-digit manufacturing industries for 1958, 1963, 1967, 1972, and 1977. He used these data to estimate two types of regression equations. The first type of equation examined changes in the number of establishments and average establishment size for all 319 industries. The second type of equation examined the market shares of small and large establishments before and after the imposition of regulation for 20 heavily regulated industries and 20 lightly regulated industries.[19] Since the second type of regression equation provides the more direct test of the hypothesis that environmental and safety regulations impose scale economies that force small establishments to close down, we examine this equation first.

Pashigian examined the changes in the size distribution of plants before and after the imposition of regulations in 20 heavily regulated and 20 lightly regulated industries listed in Table 5.6.[20] He calculated the percent change in the market shares of small and large plants between 1958 and 1972 and between 1972 and 1977. Table 5.7 reports summary data. He then regressed these growth rates against a dummy variable equal to one if the observation was for a heavily regulated industry during the regulated period and zero otherwise and against several control variables which were generally statistically insignificant.[21] He found that regulations led to a statistically significant decrease in the market share of small establishments and a statistically insignificant increase in the market share of large establishments.[22] Table 5.8 reports the regression estimates.

There are three problems with this regression analysis. First, it is not possible to categorize the 1958–1972 and 1972–1977 periods neatly as "lightly regulated" and "heavily regulated." The growth rate of the real pollution abatement capital stock between 1967 and 1970 and between 1970 and 1975 were almost the same—16.3 and 16.1 percent respectively. The growth rate between 1960 and 1967 and between 1975 and 1981 were also similar—9.9 and 8.3 percent respectively.[23] State and federal environmental regulations were becoming increasingly burdensome in the late 1960s. But it appears that much of the investment necessary for complying with these regulations was completed by the mid 1970s.

The second problem with this analysis is that it assumes that the disturbance term in the regression is homoskedastic. If the disturbance term for the growth rates of heavily regulated industries in the regulated period has a different variance than the disturbance term for the other growth rates, then the estimated standard errors and test statistics obtained from ordinary least squares regression are biased. Data reported in Table 5.9 indicate that the growth rates are much more variable in the heavily regulated industries during the regulated period than either the growth rates of heavily regulated industries before the imposition of reg-

TABLE 5.5

Distribution of Dropouts and Migrants in Heavily and Lightly Regulated Industries, by Size Interval (percent)

	Highly Regulated Industries			
	1970–1974		*1974–1980*	
Size (millions)	*Dropouts*	*Migrants*	*Dropouts*	*Migrants*
0–1	87.3	79.3	86.2	64.9
1–5	10.2	18.4	10.4	19.8
Over 5	2.5	2.3	3.4	15.3

	Lightly Regulated Industries			
	1970–1974		*1974–1980*	
Size (millions)	*Dropouts*	*Migrants*	*Dropouts*	*Migrants*
0–1	90.7	85.1	88.9	67.7
1–5	8.3	12.4	9.3	24.0
Over 5	0.1	2.5	1.8	8.3

SOURCE: Booz-Allen & Hamilton, *Impact of Environmental Regulations on Small Business* (Bethesda, Md.: Booz-Allen & Hamilton, May 24, 1982), exhibit IV-7.

TABLE 5.6

Industries with the Twenty Highest and Twenty Lowest Ratios of Pollution Abatement Costs to Value Added

Twenty Highest			*Twenty Lowest*		
Industry	*SIC Code*	*PACVA (percent)*	*Industry*	*SIC Code*	*PACVA (percent)*
Primary copper	3331	8.72	Lace goods	2292	
Primary zinc	3333	7.14	Periodicals	2721	.02
Petroleum refining	2911	5.87	Miscellaneous publishing	2741	.02
Electrometallurgical products	3313	5.75	Typesetting	2791	.04
Inorganic pigment	2816	5.58	Book publishing	2731	.05
Primary lead	3332	5.42	Special dyes, tools, and jigs	3544	.06
Pulp mills	2611	4.74	Industrial patterns	3565	.06
Lime	3274	4.74	Newspapers	2711	.06
Phosphatic fertilizers	2874	4.71	Jewelry, precious metals	3911	.06
Explosives	2892	4.68	Hoists, cranes, and monorails	3536	.06
Carbon black	2895	4.65	Industrial furnaces and ovens	3567	.07
Hydraulic cement	3241	4.55	Set-up paperboard boxes	2652	.07
Paper board mills	2631	4.27	Blankbooks and looseleaf binders	2782	.08
Cyclic crudes and intermediates	2865	4.02	Jewelers' materials and lapidary	3915	.08
Paper mills excl. building paper	2621	3.63	Women's handbags and purses	3171	.08
Minerals, ground or treated	3295	3.38	Signs and advertising displays	3993	.08
Primary aluminum	3334	3.13	Luggage	3161	.09
Blast furnaces and steel mills	3312	2.99	Conveyers and conveying equipment	3535	.09
Mineral wool	3296	2.76	Fabricated structural metal	3441	.09
Wet corn milling	2046	2.73	Fabricated pipe and fittings	3498	.09
Average		4.67	Average		.06
Standard deviation		1.47	Standard deviation		.08

SOURCE: B. Peter Pashigian, "The Effect of Environmental Regulation on Optimal Size and Factor Shares," Working Paper no. 025 (Chicago: Center for the Study of the Economy and the State, University of Chicago, April 1983), table 5.

NOTE: Average for all 319 manufacturing industries examined was .74 with a standard deviation of 1.19.

TABLE 5.7
Changes in the Size Distribution of Plants, 1958–1977
(percent)

	Plant Size of Twenty Industries with Highest Value of Relative Pollution Costs			*Plant Size of Twenty Industries with Lowest Value of Relative Pollution Costs*		
	Small	*Medium*	*Large*	*Small*	*Medium*	*Large*
Market share						
1958	25	50	25	25	50	25
1963	27.5	47.6	25.1	27.1	47.8	25.1
	(6.0)	(5.0)	(4.3)	(6.6)	(4.8)	(3.9)
1967	29.5	45.3	25.2	26.6	45.1	28.3
	(8.7)	(5.9)	(9.2)	(5.7)	(4.6)	(5.3)
1972	30.2	42.8	26.9	25.5	47.0	27.5
	(11.9)	(7.6)	(7.7)	(6.4)	(4.6)	(5.6)
1977	25.0	45.4	29.7	27.4	46.1	26.6
	(12.9)	(9.1)	(10.1)	(6.7)	(4.9)	(5.2)
Mean of the annual percent change in market share						
1958–1972	.81	−1.00	.12	.02	−.46	.55
	(3.1)	(1.3)	(2.7)	(1.6)	(.7)	(1.6)
1972–1977	−3.51	1.22	1.32	1.43	−.30	−.55
	(11.1)	(4.7)	(7.2)	(3.1)	(1.5)	(2.5)
Number of industries with decreases in market share						
1958–1972	7	16	8	11	15	7
1972–1977	12	10	6	6	9	13

SOURCE: B. Peter Pashigian, "The Effect of Environmental Regulation on Optimal Size and Factor Shares," *Journal of Law and Economics* (April 1984), table 10.

NOTE: Standard deviations are in brackets. Market shares may not add to 100 because of rounding.

ulation or in lightly regulated industries before or after the imposition of regulations.

It is possible to take the different variances of growth rates into account in testing whether the growth rates are different. Most of the control variables in Pashigian's regressions were statistically insignificant. Moreover, the inclusion of these variables has only a minor impact on the estimated coefficient and standard error of the regulatory dummy. Thus

TABLE 5.8
Determinants of the Annual Growth Rate of Market Share

	Size of Plant					
Variable	*Small*			*Large*		
Constant	.740	.393	.843	.040	.335	.483
	(1.0)	(.4)	(1.0)	(.1)	(.5)	(.8)
Pollution abatement dummy (D)	−4.245	−4.940	−4.040	1.280	1.869	2.165
	(2.8)	(2.6)	(2.4)	(1.2)	(1.5)	(1.9)
Time dummy (T)		1.042	.592		−.884	−1.032
		(.6)	(.4)		(.8)	(1.1)
Industry dummy variable						
Lime			−17.989			8.446
			(4.7)			(3.3)
Cyclic crudes						−8.504
						(3.3)
Phosphatic fertilizers						−5.864
						(2.3)
R^2 (adjusted)	.077	.070	.220	.006	.001	.2481
Standard deviation of residuals	5.97	6.00	5.31	4.07	4.08	3.54

SOURCE: B. Peter Pashigian, "The Effect of Environmental Regulation on Optimal Size and Factor Shares," *Journal of Law and Economics* (April 1984), table 11.
NOTE: Total of 80 observations; t = statistics in parentheses.

his regression amounts to regressing growth rates against a constant term and a dummy variable equal to one for heavily regulated industries during the regulated period and zero otherwise. The t-statistic on the estimated coefficient of the dummy variable is equivalent to the t-statistic for the test of the difference in the mean m_R of the growth rates of the heavily regulated industries during the regulated period and the mean m_U of the growth rates for the remaining industries, under the assumption that these growth rates are drawn from two normal distributions with means μ_R and μ_u and common variance σ^2. If we relax the assumption that the growth rates are drawn from distributions with common variance, we must use a different testing procedure. A conservative procedure relies on the following statistic[24]:

$$\xi = [m_R - m_U]/V^{1/2} \tag{5.1}$$

where

(5.2) $$V = [(t_R{}^2 s_R{}^2)/n_R + t_U{}^2 s_U{}^2/n_U]$$

where the subscript R denotes the heavily regulated industries in the regulated period and the subscript U denotes the heavily regulated industries in the preregulatory period, m_R and m_U denote the sample means of the growth rates for the categories R and U, $s_R{}^2$ and $s_U{}^2$ denote the sample variances of the growth rates for the categories R and U, and t_R and t_U denote the upper 0.025 points of Student's t-distribution with n_R and n_U degrees of freedom respectively. Under the null hypothesis that the means

TABLE 5.9
Mean Percent Changes in Market Share of Small Plants

	Number of Establishments Method	
Mean Annual Percent Change in Market Share	*20 Heavily Regulated Industries*	*20 Lightly Regulated Industries*
1952–1972	0.81 (3.10)	0.02 (1.60)
1972–1977	3.51 (11.10)	1.43 (3.10)
$s_U^2 = 7.4$	$m_U = 0.75$	$n_U = 60$
$s_R^2 = 123.2$	$m_R = -3.51$	$n_R = 20$
	Value Added Method	
Mean Annual Percent Change in Market Share	*20 Heavily Regulated Industries*	*20 Lightly Regulated Industries*
1952–1972	1.41* (2.90)	−0.86 (2.30)
1972–1977	−4.29 (12.90)	−1.50 (4.70)
$s_U^2 = 8.1$	$m_U = -0.95$	$n_U = 58$
$s_R^2 = 166.4$	$m_R = -4.29$	$n_R = 20$

SOURCE: B. Peter Pashigian, "Effect of Environmental Regulation on Optimal Plant Size and Factor Shares," Working Paper no. 025 (Chicago: Center for the Study of the Economy and the State, University of Chicago, April 1983).

*Based on eighteen observations.

are equal, $\mu_R = \mu_U$, the probability that ξ is greater than 1.0 is .05. The values of the relevant quantities are reported in Table 5.9.

Pashigian uses two methods to calculate the share of small businesses.[25] The first method uses number of establishments. For this method, $\xi = .87$. The second method uses value added. For this method $\xi = .53$. Therefore, it is not possible to reject the null hypothesis that the mean growth rates are the same for both categories for either small business definition used by Pashigian.[26] Small plants in heavily regulated industries have not fared significantly differently than small plants in lightly regulated industries for the sample of industries considered by Pashigian.

The third problem with this approach is that, aside from pollution abatement costs, the "lightly regulated" and "heavily regulated" industries are very different from each other. The heavily regulated industries have a small number of large establishments while the lightly regulated industries have a large number of small establishments. The difference in the number of establishments and average establishment size is more than tenfold.[27] The fact that the "heavily regulated" industries are dominated by large establishments and that the "lightly regulated" industries are dominated by small establishments is not consistent with Pashigian's conclusion that "While both large and small companies may have suffered losses from environmental regulation, the available evidence suggests that small business has suffered relatively more."[28]

Pashigian also regressed the change in average establishment size and the change in the number of establishments (both between 1972 and 1977) against (a) a measure of the cost of complying with environmental regulations during these years (the ratio of gross pollution abatement operating costs reported by the industry to industry value added for 1974–1978), (b) a measure of the cost of OSHA regulations (average annual penalties for violations per dollar of industry value added, or alternatively, per plant in the industry), and (c) other variables which measure the change in industry conditions between 1972 and 1977 (change in industry value added as a measure of change in market size, change in energy cost per dollar of value added, and change in the ratio of wage payments to value added, between 1972 and 1977). All variables were measured in logs. His regression results are reported in Table 5.10.[29]

The negative and statistically significant coefficient of the environmental regulation variable in the number of establishments regression suggests that environmental regulations have reduced the number of establishments. Industries that have higher costs of complying with environmental regulations have experienced a greater reduction in the number of establishments, holding industry size and relative energy costs constant. The positive and statistically significant coefficient of the environmental regulation variable in the plant size regression suggests that environmental regulations have increased average plant size. Industries that have higher costs of complying with environmental regulations have experienced a greater increase in average plant size, holding energy costs constant.[30] The coefficients of the OSHA variables are statistically insignificant in both regressions and have a nonsensical sign in the number of establishment regressions. OSHA regulations have not apparently affected the number of establishments or average plant size.

It is not clear how to interpret these results. Pashigian regresses *changes* in the number and average size of establishments between 1972 and 1977 against *levels* of average pollution abatement costs between 1974 and 1978.[31] It is difficult to see what economic model of industry behavior

TABLE 5.10

Changes in Labor's Shares of Value Added, Number of Plants, and Plant Size, 1972–1977

Independent Variables	*Dependent Variables*					
	Change in Labor Share DLL_7		*Change in Establishments* DLN_7		*Change in Plant Size* DLS_7	
Constant	−.362 (9.8)	−.349 (9.6)	−.372 (5.4)	−.297 (4.3)	.888 (10.8)	.509 (6.2)
Change in market size			.336 (8.3)	.425 (9.3)		
Environmental regulation	−.023 (4.2)	−.026 (4.8)	−.045 (5.0)	−.038 (4.2)	.068 (5.6)	.040 (3.6)
OSHA regulation	.0081 (2.9)	.0060 (2.4)	.0015 (5.0)	.0016 (4.2)	.0032 (5.6)	.0098 (3.6)
OSHA regulation	−.011 (1.8)					
Change in energy	.283 (11.4)	.279 (11.3)	.053 (1.2)	−.028 (.6)	−.305 (5.4)	−.011 (.2)
Change in labor share				.412 (3.9)		−1.086 (9.6)
R^2 (adjusted)	.287	.282	.224	.256	.123	.320
Standard deviation of residuals	.101	.101	.170	.166	.231	.203

SOURCE: B. Peter Pashigian, "The Effect of Environmental Regulation on Optimal Size and Factor Shares," *Journal of Law and Economics* (April 1984), table 6.

NOTE: 319 observations; t-statistics reported in parentheses.

would give rise to such a specification. After all, it is presumably differential increases in regulatory costs across industries that "cause" the differential impacts on the size distribution of businesses across industries claimed by Pashigian.[32] Moreover, the simple industry model proposed by Pashigian himself posits a relationship between *changes* in pollution abatement costs and *changes* in the size distribution of plants.[33] Using a data set similar to that used by Pashigian, the next chapter examines the relationship between changes in federal regulation between 1967 and 1977 in greater detail.

Pashigian concludes that "Environmental regulation has not only reduced the number of plants in affected manufacturing industries but has placed the greater burdens on small than on large plants."[34] This conclusion is dubious for two reasons. First, it is not possible to reject the null hypothesis that the growth rates of market shares for small businesses have been the same in heavily as in lightly regulated industries. Second, his regression analysis of the impact of regulations on the number of establishments and average establishment size needs to be refined before we can be confident that environmental regulations have actually increased average plant size or decreased the number of establishments.

ARTHUR ANDERSEN

The Business Roundtable commissioned Arthur Andersen & Co. to measure the cost of complying with certain federal regulations during 1977 for forty-eight companies that are members of the Business Roundtable. The regulatory requirements of six federal agencies and programs were examined: the Environmental Protection Agency (EPA), Occupational Safety and Health Administration (OSHA), Department of Energy (DOE), Federal Trade Commission (FTC), Equal Employment Opportunity (EEO) regulations, and Employee Retirement Income Security Act (ERISA). The forty-eight companies accounted for 5 percent of civilian employment, 8 percent of all sales, and 19 percent of private capital expenditures for plant and equipment in 1977.

Arthur Andersen developed a methodology for calculating regulatory costs. It then trained employees of the participating companies to collect the data identified by this methodology. Finally, it reviewed the results to make sure that "each company had properly interpreted and applied the methodology, and that its results were both supported by adequate documentation and reasonable in relation to those of other companies within the same industry classification.[35] The methodology attempted to identify "the cost of an action taken to comply with a regulation that would not have been taken in the absence of that regulation."[36] Thus the cost of minority training programs that companies would have undertaken even without being specifically required to do so was excluded. Secondary costs such as changes in productivity and regulatory-caused delays were also excluded.

Arthur Andersen used the cost data collected from the participating companies to calculate the cost per dollar of complying with federal regulations for several establishment-size categories. This work was commissioned by the Small Business Administration after the completion of the Business Roundtable study. Table 5.11 reports the results for EPA and OSHA regulation in the electrical machinery industry. Table 5.12 reports the results for the EPA and OSHA regulations in the chemical industry. Table 5.13 reports the results for EEO regulations in the communications industry. These regulations were the most important for each respective industry. No clear pattern emerges from these tables. These data are certainly not consistent with the hypothesis that there are scale economies in regulatory compliance.

It would be hasty, however, to conclude from the data reported by Arthur Andersen that there are no scale economies in regulatory compliance. All the companies that participated in this survey were extremely large, as were most of the establishments owned by these companies. No establishment had fewer than five hundred employees. Therefore, even the smallest of these companies may have been able to average the fixed costs

TABLE 5.11

Average Cost of Compliance with EPA and OSHA Regulations in the Electrical Machinery Industry

Establishment Size (sales in millions of dollars)	*Number in Group*	*Regulatory Costs per Thousand Dollars of Sales*					
		EPA			*OSHA*		
		Total	*Capital*	*Operating*	*Total*	*Capital*	*Operating*
0–75	5	2.50	0.90	1.50	2.20	1.50	1.20
75–100	5	2.10	0.10	0.50	2.50	0.70	0.40
100–150	5	1.30	0.20	0.40	0.90	1.10	1.00
150–175	3	1.70	0.90	0.70	1.00	3.00	0.20
175–200	3	1.20	0.40	0.70	3.20	0.50	1.20
200–250	2	1.80	0.70	1.00	2.10	0.90	1.00
250–525	5	0.60	0.40	0.30	1.30	0.50	0.30
525–1,000	0	—	—	—	—	—	—
1,000–2,000	4	1.80	0.70	0.70	0.90	0.50	0.30

SOURCE: Arthur Andersen & Co., *Analysis of Regulatory Costs on Establishment Size for the Small Business Administration* (Chicago: Arthur Andersen & Co., October 1979), pp. 20–21.

TABLE 5.12
Average Cost of Compliance with EPA and OSHA Regulations in the Chemical Industry

*Establishment Size**	*Number in Group*	*Regulatory Costs per Thousand Dollars of Sales*					
		EPA			OSHA		
		Total	*Capital*	*Operating*	*Total*	*Capital*	*Operating*
100–225	4	7.20	1.00	5.90	0.90	26.90	1.30
225–475	4	33.40	23.20	13.40	5.20	3.90	1.80
475–800	3	11.70	7.00	5.20	2.50	1.60	0.90
800–2,000	4	16.90	14.30	6.80	1.10	0.50	0.40
2,000–6,500	3	32.10	12.70	5.10	2.70	0.50	1.20

SOURCE: Arthur Andersen & Co., *Analysis of Regulatory Costs on Establishment Size for the Small Business Administration* (Chicago: Arthur Andersen & Co., October 1979), pp. A10–A11.
*We have not reported data for establishments with sales under $100 million because of inconsistencies in the Arthur Andersen data for these firms.

of regulation down to a negligible amount. Also, the industries examined by Arthur Andersen were extremely broad. Establishments in different size classes may have operated in different markets and faced different regulatory requirements.

COLE AND SOMMERS STUDIES

Cole and Sommers have prepared two studies of the differential impact of regulations across business sizes. Their first study analyzed data on regulatory costs obtained from a mail survey of 3,500 businesses in Washington State with fewer than five hundred employees.[37] Usable questionnaires were received from 361 of these businesses. They obtained data on twenty-one measures of compliance costs. They found that average costs of compliance were higher for all twenty-one measures and that the differences were statistically significant for all but one measure. Their results are shown in Table 5.14. They also regressed each average cost measure against a constant and the number of employees for the firm. They allowed the coefficient in the number of employees to differ for firms with fewer than fifty employees and for firms with fifty employees or more. They found that the small firm coefficient was significantly different from zero at the 5 percent level in about a quarter of the regression equations and that the moderate-size firm coefficient was not significantly different from zero at the 5 percent level in any equation. The cost measures with statistically significant coefficients were: whether there were any changes in work routines; number of facilities changes; any EED impact (they do not say what this is); number of disciplinary fines; and number of challenges to regulatory rulings. There is no straightforward correspondence between these measures and actual cost. The coefficients for more relevant measures such as the cost of facilities changes were not statistically significant. Finally, when Cole and Sommers controlled for the industry in which a firm operated, none of the coefficients was significantly different from zero. Their regression analysis therefore fails to reject the hypothesis that average regulatory costs are constant across firm sizes. It is hard to reconcile the results of their regression analysis with the results of their tests of the differences in means.

Cole and Sommers's analysis is afflicted with a statistical problem. Their theoretical analysis suggests and their empirical results confirm that the variance of average compliance costs is much greater for smaller firms than for larger firms. Consequently, their means test is invalid since this test is performed under the assumption of constant variances across size classes.[38] The difference in means remains statistically significant, however, when the correct test is used. The standard errors of their estimated regression coefficients are biased because they failed to control for the heteroskedasticity of the disturbances. The direction of the bias is unknown.

Based on the differences in means, Cole and Sommers's analysis suggests that smaller firms do indeed incur higher average regulatory costs than larger firms. Had Cole and Sommers performed these tests separately

TABLE 5.13

Average Cost of Compliance with EEO Regulations in the Communications Industry

Establishment Size (sales in millions of dollars)	*Number in Group*	*Regulatory Costs per Thousand Dollars of Sales*		
		Total	*Capital*	*Operating*
0–35	1	1.40	0.00	1.00
35–245	2	1.70	0.00	1.70
245–575	3	2.30	0.10	2.20
575–1,600	6	2.50	0.20	2.40
1,600–2,000	4	2.90	0.50	2.70
2,000–3,010	3	3.00	0.10	3.30
3,010–4,154	3	3.80	0.20	3.00

SOURCE: Arthur Andersen & Co., *Analysis of Regulatory Costs on Establishment Size for the Small Business Administration* (Chicago: Arthur Andersen & Co., October 1979), pp. A12–A13.

TABLE 5.14

Means and Standard Deviations of Cost Variables for Two Employment Size Categories

Variable	*< 50 Employees* *N*	*Mean*	*Standard Deviation*	*≥50 Employees* *N*	*Mean*	*Standard Deviation*	*Difference of Means t-statistic*	*Difference of Variance F-statistic*
Number of areas checked	262	0.025	0.043	78	0.003	0.003	8.215	205
Number of heavy impacts—Areas	176	0.010	0.026	59	0.001	0.001	4.582	676
Number of moderate impacts—Areas	209	0.008	0.012	73	0.001	0.002	8.117	169
Number of federal agencies checked	209	0.007	0.015	75	0.001	0.001	5.747	225
Number of state agencies checked	238	0.011	0.022	77	0.001	0.001	6.990	484
Number of local agencies checked	205	0.007	0.011	67	0.001	0.002	7.442	30
Number of moderate impacts—agencies	166	0.007	0.014	63	0.001	0.001	5.485	196
Annual cost, licenses—permits—filings	194	3.376	18.552	39	0.595	1.093	4.370	287
Any changes in work routines?	263	0.027	0.051	77	0.002	0.003	7.903	289
Number of facilities changes—how many?	258	0.029	0.057	80	0.002	0.003	7.575	361
Total cost of facilities changes	88	1.119	3.365	40	0.168	0.224	2.638	225
Any EED impact (none—moderate—large)?	279	0.025	0.051	82	0.002	0.004	7.455	162
Any disciplinary fines—how many times?	261	0.030	0.053	79	0.002	0.004	8.456	175
Hours per year—inspections	137	0.131	0.864	51	0.021	0.041	1.486*	444
Hours per year—reporting and applications	207	0.575	2.057	66	0.134	0.319	2.974	41
Hours per year—recordkeeping	162	1.174	3.841	56	0.107	0.184	3.524	435
Percent of owner-manager time	104	0.035	0.105	46	0.003	0.003	3.897	1225
Percent of administrative costs	279	0.159	0.345	82	0.012	0.032	7.015	116
Miscellaneous administrative costs	134	2.887	9.367	42	0.648	1.318	2.684	50
How often do you need a lawyer?	256	0.009	0.015	76	0.001	0.001	8.470	225
Any challenges—how many?	259	0.026	0.055	79	0.001	0.002	7.299	756

SOURCE: Roland J. Cole and Paul Sommers, *Costs of Compliance in Small and Moderate-Size Businesses* (Seattle: Battelle Human Affairs Research Center, February 1980), table A4.

NOTE: All variables deflated by gross revenues. All t-statistics are significant at the 5 percent level (one-tailed test) except the one indicated by single asterisk. All F-statistics are significant at the 5 percent level.

for each industry, it would be possible to place greater confidence in this finding. Without controlling for industry, however, it is impossible to know whether average regulatory costs are higher for smaller businesses or whether the smaller businesses in their sample were concentrated in heavily regulated industries. Finally, the Cole and Sommers study provides interesting information on the cost of all government requirements on businesses. This strength is also a weakness. Their data fail to separate the cost of federal requirements such as environmental and safety regulations from state and local requirements such as building codes and business licensing. Their data also fail to separate the cost of regulations from the cost of tax programs.

In a more comprehensive study, Cole and Sommers collected data from a stratified random sample of businesses in Georgia and Massachusetts.[39] They obtained usable responses from 129 of 497 Georgia firms (a 30 percent response rate) and 126 of 526 Massachusetts firms (a 24 percent response rate). The firms operated in a wide range of industries. They obtained information on three sets of cost measures: (1) overall cost measures that give the number of local, state, or federal agencies having light, medium, and heavy impacts; (2) direct cost measures including the cost of licenses and the cost of changes to physical facilities; and (3) administrative cost measures such as the number of staff days spent on government inspections.

They regressed the log of each of these cost variables against the log of the number of employees, several other control variables, and a series of dummy variables indicating the industry in which the firm operates. The coefficient of the employment variable was positive and statistically significantly different from zero for twenty-two of twenty-four cost measures. R^2's average around .25, varying from a low of .07 to a high of .45. They used these regression results to calculate the difference in costs per one thousand dollars of sales for the median small firm (twenty or fewer employees) and the median large firm (more than twenty employees) in the sample. The results are reported in Table 5.15. The cost penalty is positive—indicating that average costs are higher for smaller firms—in sixteen out of twenty-one instances. They also calculated the difference in costs per thousand dollars of sales for a twenty-employee firm and a median larger firm. These results are also reported in Table 5.15.

There are two problems with these results. First, Cole and Sommers do not report significance tests. It is impossible to determine whether the differences reported in Table 5.15 are statistically significantly different from zero. Second, it is hard to relate many of the cost measures to actual monetary costs incurred by firms. The following discussion illustrates some of the problems with interpreting their results.

Cole and Sommers found that, ignoring industry differences, the average cost of changes in physical facilities required by regulation was

TABLE 5.15

Small Business Cost Penalty per Thousand Dollars of Sales

Cost Variable	Georgia: Median Firm Comparison	Georgia: Twenty-Employee vs. Median Larger Firm	Massachusetts: Median Firm	Massachusetts: Twenty-Employee vs. Median Larger Firm
Number of areas of government requirements	.00447	.00397	.00626	.00378
Number of federal agencies with heavy impacts	−.00267	.00273	−.00457	.00278
Number of federal agencies with medium impacts	.00104	.00126	.00121	.00127
Number of federal agencies with light impacts	.00267	.00143	.00374	.00142
Number of state agencies with heavy impacts	−.00439	.00156	−.00579	.00157
Number of state agencies with medium impacts	−.00263	.00228	−.00257	.00225
Number of state agencies with light impacts	.00106	.00180	.00224	.00176
Number of local agencies with heavy impacts	.00100	.00224	.00143	.00224
Number of local agencies with medium impacts	.00102	.00225	.00144	.00225
Number of local agencies with light impacts	.00112	.00188	.00174	.00187
Approximate annual costs to business for licenses, permits, registrations, and filings (dollars)	.01378	.00986	.01564	.00995
Number of changes in work routines to comply with government requirements	−.01162	.00231	−.01602	.00235
Costs of major changes to physical facilities (dollars)	.02496	.01285	.02962	.01298
Number of times business required to pay civil or criminal fines for violations of government requirements	.00119	.00118	.00179	.00117
Average number of staff days spent on government inspection	−.00715	.00706	−.00938	.00706
Average number of staff days spent on filling out government reports	−.00085	.00618	−.00061	.00616
Average number of staff days spent on filling out licenses, permits, registrations and filings	−.00063	.00452	−.00204	.00457

Average number of staff days spent on recordkeeping for primarily government purposes	.00071	.00490	−.00006	.00494
Average number of staff days spent on other administrative activity related to government requirements	.00233	.00099	.00255	.00101
Approximate percent of owner's time spent on government reporting	.00219	.00406	.00250	.00408
Approximate percent of total administrative costs attributable to government reporting and recordkeeping	.00130	.00065	.00158	.00066
Business participated in effort to influence government requirements before it was passed	.00054	.00101	.00063	.00101
Business got information regarding government requirements obtained from business or trade association	.00032	.00101	.00078	.00100
Number of times business challenged or appealed government rulings or proposed requirements	−.00895	.00537	−.01136	.00536

SOURCE: Roland J. Cole and Paul Sommers, *Costs of Compliance in Small and Moderate-Size Businesses* (Seattle: Battelle Human Affairs Research Center, February 1980), table A5.

$$\ln C = \underset{(4.6)}{5.2} + \underset{(0.37)}{0.89} \ln E \qquad (5.3)$$

where E is the number of employees, C is cost, and standard errors appear in parentheses. Two points are noteworthy about this regression. First, the intercept can be interpreted as the fixed cost of changes required by regulation (i.e., $\ln C = 5.2$ if $E = 1$). But this intercept is not significantly different from zero. Thus, we cannot reject the hypothesis that fixed costs are zero. Second, the coefficient of lnE is the proportionate change in cost due to a proportionate change in employment. This coefficient is not significantly different from one. Therefore, we cannot reject the hypothesis that regulatory costs rise proportionately with employment size. This finding argues against the authors' conclusion that small businesses pay a disproportionate share of regulatory costs.

Cole and Sommers found that smaller businesses spend proportionately more staff days on regulatory activities than larger businesses. But smaller businesses usually pay lower wages. Their finding, therefore, does not necessarily imply that smaller businesses spend proportionately more money in order to comply with regulations. They also found that, ignoring industry differences, the average percent of administrative costs attributable to government recordkeeping was 0.65 percent plus 0.04 percent per employee. They calculated that smaller businesses spend roughly thirteen cents more on administrative costs than larger businesses for each $100,000 of sales. It is difficult to interpret this finding without more information on how administrative costs vary with size. If administrative costs rise more than proportionately with size, their finding suggests smaller businesses incur a proportionately smaller regulatory burden than bigger businesses and conversely if administrative costs rise less than proportionately with size.

Regulation-Specific Studies

This section reviews five studies that examine the differential impact across business sizes of specific regulations for affected industries. In two cases the regulations are suspected of having a differential impact largely because smaller businesses were more likely to be engaging in the regulated activity. The mattress flammability standard studied by Linneman apparently forced smaller producers to upgrade the quality of their mattresses, whereas larger producers were already in compliance.[40] The evidence that smaller producers were adversely affected by the standard is somewhat shaky. The mining safety requirements studied by Neumann and Nelson allegedly had a more serious impact on smaller mines because these mines were unable to afford the safety equipment and procedures required by the regulations.[41] But these smaller mines were demonstrably more accident prone than larger mines. Scale economies in compliance are not a big part of the story told by these two studies. The three other studies use survey data to determine directly whether there are scale economies in compliance. Arthur Andersen's study of ERISA costs, the Federal Home Loan Bank Board's study of savings and loan reporting requirements, and Phillips and Knight's study of the Davis Bacon Act all find that average compliance costs decrease dramatically with firm size.[42] These studies provide the best evidence of fixed compliance costs.

LINNEMAN MATTRESS INDUSTRY STUDY

Linneman examines the impact of the Consumer Product Safety Commission (CPSC) mattress flammability standard on the size distribution of sales and profits in the mattress industry. At the time of his study, this industry had about one hundred firms. A quarter of industry sales were made by the four largest producers, and a half of industry sales were made by the fifty largest producers. The mattress flammability standard, which was adopted in 1973 after a year of debate, required that "mattresses not burn when exposed to cigarettes" and established "recordkeeping and testing procedures for manufacturers." Eighty percent of mattresses produced by this industry satisfied the flammability standard before its adoption.

Linneman notes that most large producers already complied with the standard, whereas most small producers did not. Small producers therefore had to upgrade their production standards. Since large producers met the standard as a result of unconstrained profit maximization, whereas small producers did not, he conjectured that the standard conferred a comparative advantage on large producers. He also noted that a "large portion of the compliance costs are relatively fixed, such as learning and implementing the testing and recordkeeping requirements of the standard." This observation is questionable. The technology for producing up to standard was apparently well known, and the cost of complying with recordkeeping requirements is uncertain.

Linneman provides two types of evidence to support his hypothesis that the mattress flammability standard had a disparate impact on smaller producers. He cites a survey of compliance conducted by the CPSC in 1973 and 1974. These surveys found that 20 percent of surveyed manufacturers were not in compliance with the standard or its administrative requirements, with most violations being for the latter. Of these violations, 43 percent were for firms with annual sales of less than $100,000, 81 percent were for firms with annual sales of less than $500,000, and only 5 percent were for firms with sales of over $3.5 million. The ratio of the share of violations to the share of wholesale sales was six to one for producers with annual sales of under $500,000 and one to three for producers with sales of over $3.5 million. It is hard to know what to make of this evidence. First, the data presented by Linneman do not necessarily show that small firms are less likely to comply than large firms. These data show only that small firms have a greater share of the violations, and more violations per dollar of sales. These results are not surprising, given that 95 percent of the mattress producers account for less than 50 percent of industry sales. They provide little information about the relationship between the probability of compliance and firm size. Second, to the extent that small firms are less likely to comply with the regulations than large firms are, the differential impact on small firms is reduced. Perhaps the CPSC compliance surveys and penalties imposed for noncompliance (if any—Linneman does not say) encouraged small firms to comply in later years. We simply do not know.

Linneman also examined the impact of the mattress flammability standard on the size distribution of industry sales and pretax income. He used data for the years 1959–1976 from annual industry surveys conducted by the National Association of Bedding Manufacturers (NABM). The survey is sent to all NABM members, of whom approximately 10 percent respond. This response rate is poor. He regressed the share of industry sales, average sales, share of pretax income, and average pretax income against a dummy variable equal to one for the poststandard years and zero otherwise and against several control variables, including the annual national production index, a time trend, and the level of advertising expenditures for four size categories of firms. Table 5.16 reports his results. The share of sales decreased for the three smallest size categories and increased for the largest size category. It is not possible to reject the hypothesis that the estimated coefficients are equal to zero for all four size categories. Thus, it is not possible to reject the hypothesis that the mattress standard had no impact on the size distribution of sales in the mattress industry. The results for average industry sales by each size category are somewhat harder to interpret. The average sales of the smallest producers decreased (but the decrease was not statistically significant), whereas the average sales of the largest producer increased (the increase was statistically significant for the two largest size categories but not for the third). This result together with the result for the share of sales suggests that (1) the number of the smallest producers increased (since they experienced a negligible reduction in their share but a decrease in their average size), (2) the number of the next-to-smallest producers ($580,000–$2,300,000) decreased (since they experienced a reduction in their share but an increase in their average size), and (3) the number of the largest producers may have increased or decreased (since their share and their average size both rose). The implications of these results are unclear.

Linneman's results for the share and average of pretax net income do

TABLE 5.16

Estimated Impact of the 1973 Mattress Flammability Standard on Different Business Sizes

	Size Categories in Terms of Annual Sales			
	$0–548,000	*$548,000–$1,000,000*	*$1,000,000–$2,300,000*	*Over $2,300,000*
Share of sample sales	−.001 (0.15)	−.048 (1.92)	−.015	.064 (1.30)
Average category sales	−42,000 (0.89)	40,000 (1.20)	120,000 (2.41)	1,900,000 (2.63)
Share of pretax net income	−.013 (0.51)	−.138 (2.79)	.032	.119 (0.86)
Average category pretax net income	−5,000 (0.82)	−18,000 (2.80)	3,000 (0.15)	18,000 (1.82)

SOURCE: Peter Linneman, "The Effects of Consumer Safety Standards: The 1973 Mattress Flammability Standard," *Journal of Law and Economics* (October 1980): 461–479, table 4.

NOTE: Absolute t-values are in parentheses.

not help clarify matters. Tiny producers experienced a statistically insignificant decrease in the share and average of pretax net income. Producers in the next-to-smallest size category experienced a statistically significant decrease in the share and average of pretax net income. It appears that the next-to-smallest producers, those with sales between $548,000 and $1 million, fared the worst in the poststandard period. Their numbers apparently decreased and their profitability declined. The mattress flammability standard had little discernible impact on either very small producers (those with annual sales of below $548,000) or larger producers (those with annual sales of more than $1 million). Perhaps the smallest producers could evade the regulation with greater impunity than the larger producers, so that the impact was felt primarily by the producers in the next-to-smallest size category. Or perhaps substandard producers were concentrated in the next-to-smallest size category. Or finally, perhaps these results are spurious: given the low response rate for the survey data used and the general lack of precision of the estimates obtained, it would be unwise to place much credence in Linneman's regression results.

NEUMANN AND NELSON COAL MINE HEALTH AND SAFETY ACT STUDY

Neumann and Nelson examine the impact of the Coal Mine Health and Safety Act on labor productivity and accident rates in bituminous coal mining. This act mandated quarterly inspection of mines and established detailed safety requirements. Anecdotal evidence suggests that the act forced some small mines out of existence. *Business Week* reported, "One third of the 400-odd small coal producers—those with fifteen or fewer employees—shut down in the past two years rather than spend to meet the standards of the 1969 Coal Mine and Safety Act." Neumann and Nelson conjecture that the impact of the act has been felt at least partly by the closure of small, unsafe mines.

Neumann and Nelson regress the average productivity of labor and the accident rate against a dummy variable indicating the pre- or postact period, the share of small mine output, the wage rate, and indices of the costs of accidents. They find that the act reduced labor productivity by 12.6 percent holding industry composition constant. They observe that the share of output produced by small mines declined from 1.16 percent in 1970 to 1.01 percent in 1976. They attribute all of this decline to the act. This assumption is not well supported. They note that the share of output was declining in the 1960s but that there was a slowing of this decline around 1970. Using a regression (which they do not report) of the share against a linear time trend and an indicator for the regulatory period, they predict that the act caused a decline slightly larger than that observed. This regression ignores changes in industry demand and factor prices, which presumably affect the share of small mine output. Without further information on the goodness of fit of the regression equation for predicting the share, there is little basis for accepting this critical assumption. In any case, under the assumption that the full decline in small firm output was due to the act, the change in industry composition increased average labor productivity by 1.4 percent. Thus the net decrease in labor productivity was 11.2 percent.

They also find that the act increased the accident rate. They attribute this finding to a shift from fatal accidents to nonfatal accidents. They find that the act decreased fatal accidents both directly and indirectly by reducing the number of unsafe small mines. Their regressions indicate a large but statistically insignificant reduction of 9 percent in the fatality rate subsequent to the enactment of the act. Their regressions also indicate that a 10 percent increase in the shares of small mines leads to a 1.7 percent increase in the fatality rate. Making the assumption that the entire decline in the share of small mine output between 1970 and 1976 was due to the act, they estimate that the reduction of small mines caused four fewer deaths per year. They note that this number is not overly large and must be weighed against the potential loss of competition. They also note that the manner in which the act was enforced—restrictions on allowable equipment and procedures—may impose unnecessary costs on small mines. The difficulty with these conclusions is that they are based on no hard evidence concerning the impact of the act on the exit rate or market shares of small mines.

SAVINGS AND LOAN INSTITUTION REPORTING COSTS

The Federal Home Loan Bank Board (FHLBB) commissioned Peat, Marwick, and Mitchell (PM&M) to survey the costs to savings and loan institutions (S&Ls) of meeting government reporting requirements. More than four thousand S&Ls must submit periodic reports to the FHLBB and twelve federal home loan district banks.

PM&M sent questionnaires concerning compliance costs to 1,665 institutions stratified into five asset size classes. They received usable responses from 820 institutions. They found that the average annual reporting cost was $2,140 per S&L, or $10.3 million when projected up to the industry level. The costs varied dramatically by asset size class, as shown in Table 5.17. The average cost for the smallest institutions was almost twenty times the average cost for the largest institutions. The smaller institutions experienced higher average costs partly because they were more likely to use manual (rather than automated) data processing than were larger institutions. PM&M do not report standard deviations for the costs reported in Table 5.17. Therefore, it is not possible to determine whether the differences between size classes are statistically significant.

TABLE 5.17

Annual Reporting Cost Burden per Million Dollar Assets, by Association Asset Size, for Savings and Loan Institutions

Association Asset Size (millions of dollars)	*Annual Cost per Million Dollar Assets*
0–9.9	275
10–24.9	120
25–99.9	56
100–199.9	20
200 +	15

SOURCE: Frank J. Crowne, "Industry Reporting Requirements—Benefit or Burden?" *Federal Home Loan Bank Board Journal* (March 1977): 7–12, chart 5.

Several factors, however, suggest that these differences are not spurious. First, average cost declines consistently and dramatically across asset size categories. Second, PM&M report that costs are fairly constant across the districts surveyed within each size category. Therefore, the PM&M findings suggest that there are rather pronounced scale economies in complying with government reporting requirements for S&Ls.

PHILLIPS AND KNIGHT DAVIS-BACON ACT STUDY

The Davis-Bacon Act requires construction firms with federally financed contracts to pay their employees at least the "prevailing wage" as determined for each locality by the U.S. Department of Labor. Phillips and Knight examine whether the excess labor and administrative costs caused by the act are disproportionately higher for smaller firms. In order to address this question, they analyzed the responses of 603 construction firms to a national survey of 16,000 construction companies conducted by the Associated Builders and Contractors (ABC).[43] The response rate of 3.7 percent is extremely poor and raises the specter of selectivity bias. Although the respondents appear representative of the major types of construction firms (general, heavy, and special construction), the respondents overrepresent moderate-size construction firms (5–99 employees) and underrepresent tiny construction firms (0–4 employees) and large construction firms (100 or more employees).[44]

Phillips and Knight regressed alternatively the monthly percent increase in labor costs and the monthly percent increase in administrative costs attributed by the respondents to the Davis-Bacon Act against firm size (measured alternatively by employment and sales), the percent of federal contract construction performed by the firm, and a dummy variable equal to one for firms located in SMSAs and zero otherwise). Their regression results for labor costs are reported in Table 5.18. The low R^2's are not that unusual given that the underlying data are disaggregate and based on subjective estimates of costs. The fact that the coefficients of both employment and sales are negative and statistically significantly different from zero is consistent with the hypothesis that the Davis-Bacon Act imposes disproportionately higher labor costs on small firms. Phillips and Knight performed a similar set of regressions for administrative costs but found no evidence that administrative costs are disproportionately higher for smaller firms.[45]

The mechanism by which the Davis-Bacon Act imposes a disproportionate regulatory burden on smaller businesses is similar to the coal mine safety and mattress flammability regulations discussed above. The purpose of the Davis-Bacon Act is to limit "excessive" wage competition in the construction industry in general and to hamper union busting in particular.[46] Smaller firms incur proportionately higher labor costs apparently because they often rely on cheaper labor than do larger firms, presumably because they are less likely to be unionized than are larger firms. Since the purpose of this regulation is to discourage exactly this kind of competi-

TABLE 5.18

The Relationship Between the Percentage Increase in Labor Cost Due to the Davis-Bacon Act and Company Size

Constant[a]	*Employment*[a]	*Sales*[a]	*Urban Dummy*[a]	*F*	R^2
		All Observations			
31.68	—	−0.0007	2.27	4.93[b]	.020
(9.48)	—	(−3.07)	(0.63)		
31.54	−0.056	—	2.55	3.28[c]	.014
(9.38)	(−2.51)	—	(0.71)		
		Urban Observations Only			
34.16	−0.057	—	—	5.81[c]	.014
(19.26)	(−2.41)	—	—		
33.94	—	−0.0007	—	8.06[b]	.020
(20.41)	—	(−2.84)	—		

SOURCE: Bruce D. Phillips and William Knight, "The Davis-Bacon Act Reconsidered: A 'New' Small Business Tax," in *Proceedings* (1982 Small Business Research Conference, Bentley College, Waltham, Mass., March 1982), pp. 330–352, table 5.

[a] Figures given are regression coefficients. T-statistics are in parentheses.

[b] Statistically significant at the .95 level.

[c] Not statistically significant at the .95 level.

tion, it is not surprising that the act imposes a competitive disadvantage on smaller firms.

ARTHUR ANDERSEN'S ERISA STUDY

Arthur Andersen & Co. calculated the additional cost companies incurred in 1977 for complying with the provisions of the 1974 Employment Retirement Income Security Act (ERISA). The forty-eight large companies that supplied data incurred $61 million of additional costs in 1977, of which $44 million was for providing the enhanced benefits and insurance required by ERISA and $17 million was for recordkeeping, preparation and filing of required forms, and other added administrative chores.

Arthur Andersen found dramatic scale economies in meeting ERISA's administrative requirements:

> The incremental administrative costs of ERISA were disproportionately greater for smaller employers than for larger ones. For example, the ten smallest employers in the study incurred average incremental administrative costs per employee in 1977 nearly seven times those of the ten largest. ERISA's reporting requirements were essentially the same for smaller employers as they were for larger employers. As a result, companies with fewer employees incurred higher incremental costs per employee.[47]

Although all of the firms included in the Arthur Andersen study are large, the fact that there are scale economies among these firms suggests that there are scale economies across smaller firms as well. Some of the executives interviewed by Arthur Andersen observed that ERISA's regulatory burden discourages small employers from developing plans. The fact that the ratio of new plans to terminated plans declined from 14.4 in 1973 (the year before ERISA was enacted) to 3.7 in 1975 (the first full year after ERISA's enactment) and to 2.2 in 1977 may reflect the substantial administrative costs of complying with ERISA.

Summary and Conclusions

No empirical study is perfect. Data are seldom as plentiful or as reliable as researchers would like. Statistical techniques often rely upon assumptions that, at best, hold only as crude approximations. Empirical relationships are frequently confounded by factors that the researcher is either unaware of or cannot control for.

In determining whether we should give credence to an empirical study, we must ask not whether it has any flaws—for all empirical studies do—but whether the flaws are serious enough to cast suspicion on the results obtained by the study. Unfortunately, most of the studies reviewed above are so flawed that we must view their findings with skepticism. Each study has one or more of the following deficiencies.

First, the Booz-Allen and Hamilton, Neumann and Nelson, and Pashigian studies examine the impact of increases in regulatory compliance costs during the 1970s on business formations, dissolutions, and growth. But they fail to control for changes in economic conditions, besides increasing regulation, that affect business behavior. For example, they fail to control for changes in industry demand and therefore erroneously ascribe observed decreases in the small business share entirely to increases in regulatory costs.[48] Booz-Allen and Hamilton and Pashigian compare changes in the small business share in heavily and lightly regulated industries during the 1970s. Over this period, demand increased more rapidly in heavily than in lightly regulated industries. Businesses expand when industry demand increases and therefore migrate into larger size categories. The small business share therefore decreases relatively more in more rapidly growing industries. The differential growth in demand rather than the differential impact of regulations may have caused the relative decrease in the small business share in more heavily regulated industries.

Second, almost all the studies either fail to test whether an observed correlation between increases in regulatory costs and changes in the size distribution of businesses is statistically significant or find that the observed correlation is not statistically significant. Arthur Andersen, Booz-Allen and Hamilton, and the Federal Home Loan Bank Board do not test whether their findings are due to chance.[49] Linneman finds that the impact of the mattress flammability standard on the small business share of sales and profits is statistically insignificant. Using Pashigian's data, it is impossible to reject the hypothesis that the small business share changed to the same extent in heavily as in lightly regulated industries during the 1970s.[50]

Third, Booz-Allen and Hamilton and Pashigian examine the impact of increasing regulatory costs on establishments rather than enterprises. Many small establishments are owned by large enterprises. Consequently, it is impossible to determine from these studies whether regulations have had a differential impact across firm sizes. It may be that fixed regulatory costs are incurred at the firm level and that large firms can average these costs across the many establishments they own. Small enterprises might lack this ability and be placed at a competitive disadvantage. Examining establishment data rather than enterprise data could mask this relationship. Alternatively, it could be that regulators wink at small establishments owned by small firms but not at small establishments owned by large firms. Examining establishment data rather than enterprise data could mask this relationship as well. Since the ultimate interest of policy makers is in the differential impact of regulations across businesses rather than across the establishments owned by these businesses, results based on establishment data leave too many questions unanswered.

Fourth, the low response rates for the survey data analyzed by Cole and Sommers, Linneman, and Knight and Phillips raise the possibility of selectivity bias.[51] Firms that are particularly hostile to regulation—either because they have unusually large regulatory costs or because they have a political ax to grind—are probably more likely to respond to these surveys than are other firms. Consequently, regulatory costs reported by responding firms may not accurately represent regulatory costs for the typical firm in the population.[52] The self-selection of firms into the samples analyzed by these authors makes the findings reached by them concerning the magnitude of regulatory costs and the distribution of regulatory costs across firm size suspect.[53]

Despite these serious flaws in the design and execution of existing studies of the impact of regulatory costs across firm sizes, it is possible to draw some tentative conclusions that deserve both further study and the attention of policy makers faced with the design of policy toward small businesses. Table 5.19 summarizes the studies.

First, there is reliable evidence that paperwork-intensive regulations lead to substantial scale economies in regulatory compliance. The studies of ERISA and FHLBB regulations—two regulations whose major burden involves the completion of forms—found that average cost of regulatory compliance differed by an order of magnitude between the smallest and the largest firm in the sample.

Second, several regulations apparently have a disparate impact on smaller businesses because these businesses were more likely to engage in the behavior proscribed by the regulation. The mattress flammability standard, coal mine safety regulation, and Davis-Bacon Act have had a disparate impact on smaller businesses because these businesses were more likely to be engaging in the behavior policy makers wished to discourage. Small mattress producers were producing more flammable mattresses, small coal mines had higher accident rates, and small construction companies relied more heavily on cheap, nonunion labor than did larger businesses in the respective industries. In these cases, the regulation itself rather than scale economies in regulatory compliance had a disparate impact on small businesses.

Third, there is no credible evidence that environmental or health and safety regulations have had a widespread disparate impact on smaller manufacturing plants. The statistical results reported by Booz-Allen and Hamilton and Pashigian do not enable us to reject the hypothesis that regulations have had a neutral impact across plant sizes and that there are no scale economies in regulatory compliance. Preliminary results from our own study, reported in the next chapter, are consistent with this conclusion. Given the extent of tiering that exempts small businesses from certain requirements and the strong incentives that regulators have to skew enforcement efforts toward larger businesses, this finding is not

TABLE 5.19

The Impact of Regulations Across Business Sizes: Summary of the Evidence

SIC Code	*Industry*	*Regulations Examined*	*Period Examined*	*Study*	*Major Finding*	*Statistical Significance*
10–89	All	All	1979	Cole and Sommers	Average regulatory costs higher and more variable for smaller firms	No or indeterminate
20–39	Manufacturing	EPA	1970–1980	Booz-Allen and Hamilton	Greater decrease in small business market share in more heavily regulated industries and greater dissolution rate of businessess in more heavily regulated industries	No or indeterminate
20–39	Manufacturing	EPA and OSHA	1963–1977	Pashigian	Regulations decreased average firm size and decreased small business market share	Yes for average firm size; no for small business market share
All	All	ERISA	1977	Arthur Andersen	Average cost of complying with ERISA administrative requirements 10 times higher for larger than for smaller firms in sample	Indeterminate
28	Chemical industry	EPA and OSHA	1977	Arthur Andersen	Average cost of regulatory compliance constant across firm size for larger firms	Not applicable

TABLE 5.19 (Cont'd)

The Impact of Regulations Across Business Sizes: Summary of Evidence

SIC Code	*Industry*	*Regulations Examined*	*Period Examined*	*Study*	*Major Finding*	*Statistical Significance*
48	Communications	EEO	1977	Arthur Andersen	Average cost of regulatory compliance constant across firm size for larger firms	Not applicable
36	Electrical	EPA and OSHA	1977	Arthur Andersen	Average cost of regulatory compliance constant across firm size for larger firms	Not applicable
60	Banking	FHLBB	1977	FHLBB	Average cost of regulatory compliance 13 times higher for smallest banks than for largest banks in sample	Indeterminate
2515	Mattress	Mattress Flammability Standard	1975	Linneman	Regulation decreased small business market share and small business share of profits	No
12	Mining	Mine Safety	1950–1976	Neuman and Nelson	Regulation decreased small business market share	Indeterminate
15–17	Construction	Davis-Bacon Act	1981	Phillips and Knight	Average increased labor cost due to the regulation higher for smaller firms but average increased administrative cost due to the act not higher for smaller firms	Yes

terribly surprising. Of course, the fact that environmental and health and safety regulations do not appear to have a disparate impact on smaller businesses does not imply that tiering and the provisions of the Regulatory Flexibility Act are unjustified. Rather, it attests to the success of tiering—both tacit and explicit—in attenuating the impact of regulations on smaller businesses.

6

EMPIRICAL ANALYSIS OF BUSINESS FORMATION, DISSOLUTION, AND GROWTH

This chapter shows how the models described in Chapter 3 can be used to guide empirical research on the formation, dissolution, and growth of small businesses. It reports preliminary results from three studies we are currently performing.[1] The first study uses data from a sample of firms drawn from the Small Business Data Base to test some of the implications of Boyan Jovanovic's theory of firm growth and industry evolution.[2] The second study uses data from the 1980 Public Use Sample of the Bureau of the Census to investigate the relationship between demographic characteristics, the decision to become self-employed, and self-employment earnings.[3] The third study uses industry data drawn from a variety of sources to examine the impact of environmental and safety regulations on the size distribution of manufacturing establishments.[4]

Firm Growth, Size, and Age
A Test of Jovanovic's Model

THE EMPIRICAL IMPLICATIONS OF JOVANOVIC'S MODEL

As discussed in Chapter 3, Jovanovic considers an industry that is small relative to the economy as a whole so that firms take factor prices as given, produce a homogeneous product, and face a known and deterministic path of demand over time.[5] Random costs for each firm at time t are given by $c(q_t,x_t) = c(q_t)x_t$, where x is a firm-specific random efficiency factor drawn from the density $x_t = \xi(\eta_t)$ where $\eta_t = \theta + \epsilon_t$. The term θ represents the deterministic but unknown ability level of an individual who manages firm x and the term ϵ represents firm-specific shocks. The distribution of ability across the population of potential managers is normal with mean θ^* and variance γ^2. The distribution of shocks is normal with mean zero and variance σ^2.

At the start of the industry each individual in the population of potential managers estimates that his ability level is average, i.e., $\theta = \theta^*$. An individual who starts a firm observes his costs and revises his estimate of θ accordingly through a Bayesian learning process. New estimates of θ over time are obtained by taking a weighted average of the original estimate of θ and the estimates of θ inferred from observed costs. Let $y_t = \xi^{-1}(x_t)$. Then, given t observations of x_t,

$$\theta_{t+1} = [\theta^* + vy_t]/[1 + vt]$$

where

$$v = \gamma^2/\sigma^2$$

and

$$y_t = [\sum_{i=1}^{t} y_i]/t$$

The estimated θ will converge to the true θ for individuals who remain in business for a long period of time. An individual withdraws from business when the present discounted value of expected future profits, conditional on his most recent estimate of θ, is less than his alternative opportunity cost. Jovanovic shows that a unique perfect foresight equilibrum solution exists for this model under certain technical assumptions concerning the nature of costs and demand.

At this level of abstraction, the main empirical implication of this model concerning firm growth is that younger firms have higher and more variable growth rates than do older firms.[6] It is possible to impose two assumptions on Jovanovic's model under which several other interesting empirical implications hold. First, firm growth is independent of firm size for mature firms (i.e., firms whose estimated θ has converged to its true value) if and only if costs are Cobb-Douglas, $c(q) = Aq^b$. Second, firm growth and its variance are independent of firm size for firms of the same age if x_t is lognormally distributed.[7] The validity of these assumptions is important because Jovanovic's model provides an empirically tractable structural equation for analyzing business growth when these assumptions are imposed.[8]

EMPIRICAL FRAMEWORK

The relationship between firm growth and firm size can be represented by the following general equation

$$s_{t+1} = [g(a_t, s_t)][s_t]e_t \qquad (6.1)$$

where t denotes time, s denotes size, a denotes age, and e is a lognormally distributed error term with a mean log value of 0 and a variance that may vary across firms.[9] Taking logs of both sides of equation (6.1), subtracting $\ln s_t$ from both sides, and taking a second-order expansion of $\ln g(a,s)$ yields the following estimable equation[10]

$$\begin{aligned} \ln s_{t+1} - \ln s_t = b_0 &+ b_1 \ln s_t + b_2[\ln s_t]^2 \\ &+ b_3 \ln a_t + b_4[\ln a_t]^2 \\ &+ b_5 \ln a_t \ln s_t \\ &+ u_t \end{aligned} \qquad (6.2)$$

where u_t has mean zero and variance that may vary across firms. The estimation also includes as regressors a vector of dichotomous variables that adjust for differences in mean growth rates across regions of the country, across multiestablishment and single-establishment firms, and across industries.

SUMMARY OF DATA

The sample for estimation was drawn from the Small Business Data Base, which was constructed by the Office of Advocacy of the U.S. Small Business Administration from information originally collected by Dun and Bradstreet.[11] Data are available on firm age, number of employees, sales, and various aspects of corporate structure for 1976, 1978, 1980, and 1982. Employment data are available for more firms and are more reliable than are sales data.[12] Asset data are not available. Consequently the study uses employment as a measure of firm size.[13] The data set includes most manufacturing firms with employees.[14]

The fact that a firm has data on a file for a particular year does not necessarily mean that the data apply to that year. Because of reporting and collecting delays, the data for some firms are older than the data for other firms. In order to ensure that the growth rates apply to roughly the same time period, firms were included in the analysis only if their data were less than two years old in both 1976 and 1982. Roughly a third of all firms were excluded for this reason.[15] The growth rates used in the study are average annual growth rates between the date at which data on the 1976 file applied and the date at which the data on the 1982 file applied.[16] The dependent variable is therefore defined as

$$100[\ln s_{t+t'} - \ln s_t]/12t' \quad (6.3)$$

where t is measured in months and t′ is the number of months between observations.

Age is reported by year for firms under seven years of age and by six age intervals for firms seven years of age or older. We assumed that age was distributed lognormally in the population of firms and estimated the average age of firms for each age interval.[17] In the regression analysis, we used age as a continuous variable (using estimated age for firms for which interval data are reported) and included dummy variables for the age intervals in order to attenuate biases caused by this substitution.

A sample of 27,046 firms stratified by firm size was obtained from the data set. Larger firms were oversampled. Of 22,266 surviving firms, data less than two years old were available for 16,570.[18] Table 6.1 reports the number of firms in each age-size class. Table 6.2 reports the average growth rate of employment size between 1976 and 1982 for each age-size category.[19] Table 6.3 reports the exit rates between 1976 and 1982 for each age-size category.[20] Exit rates generally decline with the age and size of firm. Table 6.4 reports the mean and standard deviations of the variables used in the statistical analysis.

ESTIMATION METHODS AND RESULTS

In order to obtain consistent estimates of the coefficients, standard errors, and related test statistics for equation (6.2), it is necessary to address two statistical issues. The first issue concerns heteroskedasticity. There are strong a priori grounds for expecting the variance of the disturbance terms in these equations to differ across firms.[21] Indeed, using a test proposed by

TABLE 6.1
Number of Surviving Firms, by Size and Age

	Number of Employees							
Age	*1–19*	*20–49*	*50–99*	*100–249*	*250–499*	*500–1,000*	*1,000+*	*Total*
1–7	2,795	450	381	284	96	26	5	4,037
8–20	2,757	1,021	983	710	259	64	34	5,828
21–45	1,607	901	1,054	986	448	160	51	5,207
46–95	169	152	202	356	256	125	140	1,400
96+	6	5	11	17	17	19	23	98
Total	7,334	2,529	2,631	2,353	1,076	394	253	16,570

TABLE 6.2

Average Growth Rate of Surviving Firms, by Size and Age

Age in 1976	*1–19*	*20–49*	*50–99*	*100–249*	*250–499*	*500–1,000*	*1000+*	*Mean*
	Number of Employees in 1976							
1–7	9.1	2.3	−2.4	−4.2	−7.6	−6.5	−13.8	5.1
8–20	3.6	0.0	−1.1	−3.5	−5.9	−10.4	−18.8	0.6
21–45	−2.3	−0.7	−1.6	−3.3	−6.4	−7.2	−11.1	−1.2
46–95	6.6	0.1	−1.0	−3.2	−4.8	−5.3	−7.6	−2.5
96+	2.8	6.8	6.7	−6.9	−3.3	−8.2	−5.1	−3.3
Mean	5.0	0.4	−1.4	−3.5	−6.0	−7.1	−9.9	0.9

NOTE: Entries equal average annual logarithmic growth rate of employment for firms in the age-size category between 1976 and 1982 times 100.

TABLE 6.3

Average Dissolution Rate, by Size and Age

Age	*1–19*	*20–49*	*50–99*	*100–249*	*250–499*	*500–1,000*	*1000+*	*Mean*
	Number of Employees 1976							
1–7	40.4	32.3	29.8	24.9	29.4	21.2	0.0	37.4
8–20	22.6	14.3	13.0	12.0	12.2	9.9	12.8	17.8
21–45	20.2	10.9	10.2	11.0	7.1	5.9	8.9	13.4
46–95	18.0	11.6	14.0	6.6	6.9	4.6	2.1	9.3
96+	0.0	16.7	15.4	10.5	5.6	5.0	8.0	8.4
Mean	30.0	16.9	14.9	12.6	10.7	10.8	5.6	21.0

NOTE: Entries equal the percentage of firms in age-size category that failed between 1976 and 1982.

White it is possible to reject the null hypothesis of homoskedasticity for equation (6.2) at the 0.0001 level of statistical significance.[22]

Two alternative schemes for purging the heteroskedasticity were considered. The first scheme assumed that the variance of the disturbance is inversely proportional to firm age.[23] The second scheme assumed that the variance of the disturbance is inversely proportional to firm size. With both schemes, it was not possible to reject the hypothesis that the residuals obtained from generalized least squares estimation were homoskedastic at the .01 level of statistical significance.[24] The size weighting scheme was used for subsequent regressions since the size variable is subject to less measurement error than the age variable.[25]

The second question concerns selectivity bias. The theory that gives rise to equation (6.2) applies to firms that fail as well as to firms that survive over the time period under consideration. But the sample upon which equation (6.2) is estimated excludes firms that fail. To the extent that the probability of survival is correlated with the disturbance term in equation (6.2), ordinary least squares estimates of the coefficients of this equation will be biased.

In order to correct for this potential bias, the generalized least squares method proposed by Heckman was used.[26] The method involves estimating a probit equation for survival, including the Mill's ratio obtained from this equation as a regressor in equation (6.2), using estimated parameters from equation (6.2) to form weights, and performing a generalized least squares regression using these weights.[27] The estimates are reported in Table 6.5. It is not possible to reject the null hypothesis of no selection bias. Moreover, the correction for selection bias has little effect on the estimated parameters.[28]

The growth equation estimates reported in Table 6.5 imply the following relationships between growth, size, and age. First, the first derivative of lng(a,s) with respect to lng implies that firm growth decreases with firm size for firms younger than thirteen years, increases with firm size for firms older than thirteen years but smaller than a critical size level $\ln s_c$ given by

$$\ln s_c = [-2.55 + 0.98 \ln a]/.70$$

that varies with firm age; and decreases with firm size for firms older than thirteen years but larger than the critical size level given above. Second, the first derivative of lng(a,s) with respect to lna implies that firm growth decreases with firm age for firms with fewer than twenty-three employees and increases with firm age for firms with more than twenty-three employees. These results are not consistent with the general version of Jovanovic's model, which predicts that firm growth will decrease monotonically with age. This prediction is confirmed for smaller firms but not for larger firms.[29]

Two other key implications of Jovanovic's model are confirmed. The

TABLE 6.4

Summary Statistics for Variables Used in Regression Analysis

Variable	*Mean*	*Standard Deviation*
Ln[Size]	3.08	1.68
$Ln[Size]^2$	12.35	11.67
Ln[Age]	2.49	0.98
Ln[Age]Ln[Size]	8.41	6.43

TABLE 6.5
Estimated Growth and Survival Equations with Sample Selection Correction (All Firms)

Growth (Generalized Least Squares Estimates)			*Survival (Probit Estimates)*	
Variable[a]	*Coefficient*	*Standard Error*	*Coefficient*	*Standard Error*
Constant	10.8670*	(3.7630)	14.9247*	2.6582
Size	−2.2490*	(0.4386)	0.1142*	0.0189
$Size^2$	−0.3491*	(0.0594)	−0.0005*	0.0001
Age	−3.0223*	(1.0570)	4.8259*	0.2299
Age^2	—	—	−0.0483*	0.0034
Age* Size	0.9778*	(0.1532)	−0.0272	0.0439
Lambda	6.8500	(4.2190)	—	—
Summary Statistics:				
Observations	8264		10638	
Exogenous variables	38		6	
R^2	0.1533		—	
Log-likelihood function	—		−5249.6	
Standard error	15.06		—	

NOTE: Asterisk indicates statistically significantly different from zero at .01 level of significance.

[a] In addition to the variables listed below, dummy variables for twenty two-digit SIC industry codes, nine census regions were included, and four age categories were included in the dissolution equation. Estimates of the coefficients of these dummies are available from the author upon request. Continuous variables entered in levels for dissolution equation and in natural logs for growth equation {i.e., $Age^2 = (Ln[Age])^2$ for growth equation}.

survival equation estimates reported in Table 6.5 indicate that the probability of firm survival increases at a diminishing rate with firm age and firm size. These results are consistent with Jovanovic's model. We have also obtained estimates of the relationship between the variability of firm growth, firm age, and firm size.[30] These estimates indicate that the variability of firm growth decreases at a diminishing rate with firm age and firm size. These results, too, are consistent with Jovanovic's model.[31]

The results reported above indicate that three key implications of Jovanovic's model are confirmed for smaller firms—firm growth, the probability of firm dissolution, and the variability of firm growth all decrease with firm age. As a theory of the formation, growth, and dissolution of small firms, Jovanovic's model is consistent with observed patterns of industry evolution. A key implication of Jovanovic's model, however, is not confirmed for larger firms—firm growth increases with firm age for large firms—although the two other implications are confirmed for larger firms as well as for smaller firms. Further work is needed to develop models of business formation, growth, and dissolution that apply across the full size distribution of firms. Jovanovic's model will clearly provide a useful starting point for future work in this area.

Entrepreneurial Choice and Success

Approximately nine million men and women in this country work primarily for themselves.[32] They constitute almost 9 percent of the work force and operate the vast majority of businesses.[33] Yet little is known about the factors that influence an individual's decision to work for himself or the factors that determine his earnings from self-employment.

This empirical lacuna is partly due to a theoretical one. Individuals who work for themselves are entrepreneurs according to the definition of the entrepreneur given by Frank Knight and accepted by many economists.[34] But economists have largely suppressed the role of the entrepreneur in modern theory by relying on abstract product functions to describe the firm and by ignoring the process by which the economy evolves over time. Empirical work has shared this bias: there have been countless empirical studies of production functions but few of entrepreneurs. Economists have left the study of entrepreneurs to sociologists and psychologists.[35] Given the importance of the entrepreneur to firm formation, innovation, and other dynamic aspects of economic growth, this abdication is not desirable.

Several economists have recently proposed theories of entrepreneurial choice.[36] Lucas has developed a model in which people who have relatively more "entrepreneurial ability" become entrepreneurs and those who have relatively less become workers.[37] Kihlstrom and Laffont and Kanbur have developed models in which people who are relatively less averse toward risk become entrepreneurs and those who are relatively more risk averse become workers.[38] These theories provide a useful starting point for an empirical investigation of the determinants of entrepreneurial choice.[39]

The study reported in this section makes several contributions. First, it develops an empirical framework within which key assumptions and implications of existing economic, psychological, and sociological theories of the entrepreneur can be tested. The empirical framework consists of a structural equation for entrepreneurial choice derived from expected utility maximization and the reduced-form equation implied by this structural equation. Second, it reports estimates of a reduced-form equation for entrepreneurial choice and investigates the impact of various demographic and human capital characteristics on the probability that an individual will choose to become an entrepreneur. Third, it uses the estimated reduced-form equation to obtain consistent estimates of an earnings equation for entrepreneurs in the face of self-selection into the sample of entrepreneurs. It then investigates the impact of various demographic and human capital characteristics on entrepreneurial earnings. Further research will estimate a structural equation for entrepreneurial choice, test alternative specifications of the underlying utility function, and test whether the estimated structural coefficients are consistent with various theories of entrepreneurial choice. The estimates reported in this chapter are based on a sample of male self-employed and wage and salary workers drawn from the Public Use Sample of the 1980 Decennial Census.

Several words of caution are in order. Many of the interesting questions about entrepreneurial choice and success concern dynamics. Sufficient data necessary for addressing such questions are not available at present. Consequently, we develop a static model of entrepreneurial choice and success in order to explain which people select themselves into self-employment at any point in time. We estimate this model with census data that contain information on many but by no means all demographic and human capital attributes that might affect entrepreneurial choice and success. Although this approach is not entirely satisfactory, we hope it will provide a useful starting point for the development of dynamic theories of entrepreneurship and will stimulate the development of longitudinal data bases necessary to test such theories. The empirical results reported below are highly preliminary and may change when better data become available.

AN ESTIMABLE MODEL OF ENTREPRENEURIAL CHOICE

Most neoclassical economists view an entrepreneur as anyone who has control over the direction and operation of a business and bears risk as the residual claimant of business profits. Austrian economists have criticized this definition for not capturing the essential features of the entrepreneur. They view the entrepreneur as a spotter of opportunities. Since the entrepreneur can shift risks onto the capitalist, risk bearing is not essential to entrepreneurship, although capital market imperfections may link risk bearing and spotting.[40]

The Austrian view is useful for thinking about innovation and economic growth. But it is less useful for empirical investigations of entrepreneurial choice and success because it is generally not possible to distinguish a "spotter" from a "risk bearer." Consequently, this study adopts the neoclassical definition of the entrepreneur.

Much of what we know about the characteristics of entrepreneurs comes from sociological and psychological studies of select groups of small businessmen.[41] Studies by David McClelland and David Winter, D. F. Collins, D. G. Moore, D. B. Unvala, and Albert Shapero reviewed in Chapter 3 find that entrepreneurs have several common characteristics. Entrepreneurs are more likely than the average individual to be immigrants or the sons of immigrants; to be orphans or half orphans or to have had fathers who were away for long periods of time; to have had fathers who were company owners, professionals, or otherwise self-employed; to be college educated; and to be displaced persons whose niche in life has been upset through job loss, divorce, or military discharge. They also have common psychological characteristics. They are unwilling to submit to authority. They push themselves more. They feel that they have a great deal of influence over the course of events. Finally, they receive much different scores from nonentrepreneurs on psychological tests. Unfortunately, these studies rely on small and often noncomparable samples. Whether their results hold true for entrepreneurs generally is not known.

In the last several years, some economists have developed theories of entrepreneurial choice. These theories assume that each individual has some characteristic that is associated with the propensity for entrepreneurship. Individuals who have more of this characteristic are more likely to become entrepreneurs than individuals who have less of this characteristic. Lucas assumes that this characteristic is "entrepreneurial" ability. People with great entrpreneurial ability can earn more money by running their own businesses than by working for someone else. Kihlstrom and Laffont and Kanbur assume that this characteristic is a "taste for risk." Running a business is more risky than working for someone else. People who have a stronger taste for risk are more likely to operate their own businesses.

The economic, psychological, and sociological literature reviewed above suggests that the probability that an individual chooses to become an entrepreneur depends on the following attributes of that individual. First, certain observable personal attributes such as whether the person has suffered a trauma such as divorce or military service and whether the individual is an immigrant.[42] Second, entrepreneurial ability. People who can earn more working for themselves than working for someone else tend to become entrepreneurs. Entrepreneurial ability may depend on observable characteristics such as work experience and education and on unobservable characteristics such as "drive."[43] Third, the "taste for entrepreneurship." People who have a stronger taste for risk or a stronger taste for being their own boss tend to become entrepreneurs.[44] This section develops an empirical framework that incorporates these various determinants of entrepreneurship.

Following Kihlstrom and Laffont, individuals maximize expected utility. Utility is given by

$$U(I(x|s),z,a|\rho,s) \tag{6.4}$$

where I is wage (s = 0) or entrepreneurial (s = 1) earnings, x, z, and a are characteristic vectors that vary across individuals, and ρ is a vector of parameters that measure risk aversion. The vector x measures observable characteristics of individuals that affect their expected income from working or entrepreneuring. These characteristics include the usual demographic and human capital indicators. The vectors z and a summarize, respectively, observable and unobservable characteristics of individuals that affect the utility they derive from income.[45] Observable characteristics include the individual's family status, such as whether a person has been divorced, and other demographic attributes, such as a person's race. Unobservable characteristics include psychological differences across individuals that affect their relative enjoyment of entrepreneurship (following McClelland and Winter, who find that entrepreneurs like to be in charge).

In order to obtain an estimable model it is necessary to place more structure on the utility function given by (6.4). First, it is useful to assume that utility is separable in income, observable taste characteristics, and unobservable taste characteristics:

$$U(I(x|s),z,a|\rho,s) = U(I(x|s),\rho)v(z|s)u(a|s) \tag{6.5}$$

Second, it is useful to assume that the income component of utility is given by the following approximation:

$$U(I(x|s),\rho) = \exp[\gamma \ln I(x) + \tfrac{1}{2}\beta(\ln I(x))^2] \tag{6.6}$$

where ρ = (γ, β). This approximation allows the degree of risk aversion to vary across income levels and includes constant relative risk aversion as a special case. The properties of this utility function are explored below.

Entrepreneurial and wage earnings are given by

$$\ln I(x|s = 1) = \ln e(x) + \epsilon_e \tag{6.7}$$

$$\ln I(x|s = 0) = \ln w(x) + \epsilon_w \tag{6.8}$$

where ϵ_e is normally distributed with mean zero and variance σ_{ee} and ϵ_w is normally distributed with mean zero and variance σ_{ww}. Thus entrepreneurial earnings and wage earnings are both uncertain from the standpoint of the individual choosing between these alternative pursuits.[46] The degree of uncertainty is proportional to expected earnings.[47]

An individual chooses to entrepreneur (s = 1) if the expected utility from entrepreneurship exceeds the expected utility from working:

(6.9) $$E\{U(I(x|s = 1),z,a|\rho,s = 1)\} > E\{U(I(x|s = 0),z,a|\rho,s = 0)\}$$

and chooses to work (s = 0) if ">" in (6.9) is replaced by "<". Substituting from (6.5) into (6.9) yields

(6.10) $$\begin{aligned} &E\{U(I(x|s = 1),\rho)v(z|s = 1)u(a|s = 1)\} \Longrightarrow \\ &\quad >E\{U(I(x|s = 0),\rho)v(z|s = 0)u(a|s = 0) \\ &v(z|s = 1)u(a|s = 1)E\{U(I(x|s = 1),\rho)\} \\ &\quad >v(z|s = 0)u(a|s = 1)E\{U(I(x|s = 0),\rho)\} \end{aligned}$$

It is straightforward to show that

$$\begin{aligned} &E\{U(I(x/s = 1)\} \\ &= \{\exp[\gamma \ln I(x/s = 1) + \tfrac{1}{2}\beta(\ln I(x/s = 1))^2]\} \\ &= E\{\exp[\gamma \ln e(x) + \epsilon_e)) + \tfrac{1}{2}\beta(\ln e(x) + \epsilon_e))^2]]\} \end{aligned}$$

(6.11) $$= \exp\{c_{e0} + c_{e1}\ln e(x) + c_{e2}[\ln e(x)]^2\}$$

where

(6.12) $$c_{e1} = \gamma + \{\gamma\beta/[(1/\sigma_{ee}) - \beta\sigma_{ee}\}$$

(6.13) $$c_{e2} = \tfrac{1}{2}\beta + \{\beta^2/2[(1/\sigma_{ee}) - \beta\sigma_{ee}]$$

and c_{e0} is a function of γ, β, and σ_{ee}. Similarly

(6.14) $$E\{U(Ix|s = 0)\} = \exp\{c_{wo} + c_{wl}\ln w(x) + c_{w2}[\ln w(x)]^2\}$$

where

(6.15) $$c_{wl} = \gamma + \{\gamma\beta/[(1/\sigma_{ww}) - \beta\sigma_{ww}]\}$$

(6.16) $$c_{w2} = \tfrac{1}{2}\beta + \{\beta^2/2[1/\sigma_{ww}) - \beta\sigma_{ww}]\}$$

and c_{wo} is a function of γ, β, and σ_{ww}.

The event s = 1 implies (6.9), which implies that

$$\ln E\{U(I(x|s = 1),z,a|\rho,s = 1)\} > \ln E\{U(I(x|s = 0),z,a|\rho,s = 0)\}$$

$$\Longrightarrow$$

(6.17) $$\begin{aligned} &\ln v(z|s = 1) + \ln u(a|s = 1) + \ln E\{U(I(x|s = 1),\rho)\} \\ &\quad > \ln v(z|s = 0) + \ln u(a|s = 1) + \ln E\{U(I(x|s = 0),\rho)\} \end{aligned}$$

Substitution of (6.11) and (6.14) into (6.17) yields

$$(6.18)\quad \begin{aligned} &[c_{e0} - c_{w0}] \\ &+ [c_{e1}\ln e(x) - c_{w1}\ln w(x)] \\ &+ [c_{e2}[\ln e(x)]^2 - c_{w2}[\ln w(x)]^2] \\ &+ [\ln v(z|s = 1) - \ln v(z|s = 0)] \\ &> -[\ln u(a|s = 1) - \ln u(a|s = 0)] \end{aligned}$$

Denote the left-hand side of (6.18) by

$$(6.19)\quad \begin{aligned} V = &[c_{e0} - c_{w0}] \\ &+ [c_{e1}\ln e(x) - c_{w1}\ln w(x)] \\ &+ [c_{e2}[\ln e(x)]^2 - c_{w2}[\ln w(x)]^2] \\ &+ [\ln v(z|s = 1) - \ln v(z|s = 0)] \end{aligned}$$

Assume that the unobservable quantity

$$(6.20)\quad \nu_p = [\ln u(a|s = 1) - \ln u(a|s = 0)]$$

is distributed normally with mean 0 and variance σ_{pp} where σ_{pp} is assumed to be constant across individuals.[48]

The probability that an individual with characteristics x and z will choose entrepreneurship is therefore given by

$$(6.21)\quad P(s = 1|x,z,\rho) = P(\nu_p > - V/\sigma_{pp}) = F(V/\sigma_{pp})$$

where P denotes the probability of an event and F is the cumulative normal distribution with mean 0 and variance σ_{pp}.

The estimation framework is completed by postulating explicit forms for ln e(x), ln w(x), and [ln v(z|s = 1) − ln v(z|s = 0)]

$$(6.22)\quad [\ln v(z|s = 1) - \ln v(z|s = 0)] = \tau' z$$

$$(6.23)\quad \ln e(x) = b'_e x$$

$$(6.24)\quad \ln w(x) = b'_w x$$

where z is a vector of variables. Note that with an appropriate specification of the random disturbance as seen by the analyst and using one of the available methods for correcting selection biases it may be possible to obtain consistent estimates of ln e(x) and ln w(x).[49] Substitution of (6.22) – (6.24) into (6.19) yields

(6.25)
$$V = [c_{e0} - c_{w0}] + [c_{e1}b'_{e}x - c_{w1}b'_{w}x] + [c_{e2}[b'_{e}x]^2 - c_{w2}[b'_{w}x]^2] + \tau'Z$$

It is clear from inspection of (6.25) that the reduced-form of V in the x's and z's is given by

(6.26)
$$V = d_0 + d_1'x + d_2'z^* + d_3'y$$

Where z^* consists of the elements of z not contained in x, y consists of the squares and cross-products of the x's, and the d's are functions of the structural parameters of the model. This reduced-form equation will prove useful for performing specification tests and for obtaining consistent estimates of lne(x) and lnw(x) in the face of self-selection into the alternative occupations.[50]

It is now useful to explore the properties of the utility function given by (6.6). Marginal utility is given by

(6.27)
$$U_I = [\gamma + \beta \ln I](U/I)$$

which is positive when

(6.28)
$$\frac{\beta}{\gamma} > -\frac{1}{\ln I}, \gamma \neq 0$$
$$\beta > 0, \gamma = 0$$

U_{II} is given by

(6.29)
$$U_{II} = [(\gamma + \beta \ln I)^2 - (\gamma + \beta \ln I) + \beta][U/I^2]$$

Expanding (6.29), collecting terms in lnI and $(\ln I)^2$, and solving for the roots yields

(6.30)
$$r_1, r_u = \{(1 - \gamma) \pm \beta(1 - 4\beta)^{1/2}\}/2\beta$$

which implies

(6.31)
$$U_{II} < 0 \text{ for } r_1 < \ln I < r_u$$
$$U_{II} > 0 \text{ for } \ln I < r_1, \ln I > r_u$$

Thus, depending upon the values of γ and β, individuals may be risk preferrers at low and high values of income. The Arrow-Pratt measure of risk aversion $R = -U_{II}/U_I$ also varies across income levels.

The utility function (6.6) allows risk behavior to vary in a complicated way across income levels. It includes several simpler utility functions as special cases. When $\beta = 0$ we have the case of constant relative risk aversion

$$R = -(\gamma - 1)/I$$

With $0 < \gamma < 1$ for risk aversion, $\gamma = 1$ for risk neutrality, and $1 < \gamma$ for risk preferring. When $\gamma = 1$ and $\beta \neq 0$ we have

$$\beta > -1/\ln I, \text{ for } U_I > 0 \text{ and}$$

$$\frac{-\sqrt{1-4\beta}}{2\beta} < \ln I < \frac{\sqrt{1-4\beta}}{2\beta}, \text{ for } U_{II} < 0.$$ We have constant relative risk neutrality when $\beta = 0$ and $\gamma = 1$.

Several aspects of this estimation framework are noteworthy. First, it is possible to obtain consistent estimates of expected log earnings $\ln e(x)$ and $\ln w(x)$ from log-earnings regressions for self-employed and wage and salary workers, respectively, using the reduced-form equation (6.26) to correct for selection bias. Second, the structural equation given by (6.25) is nonlinear in the risk-aversion parameters γ and β and the earnings variances σ_{ee} and σ_{ww}. Securing estimates of such a nonlinear system is generally a difficult task. Moreover, the structural parameters are not necessarily identified without further restrictions of these parameters or on the error process generating the disturbances.[51]

DATA

The data used for this study were obtained from the 1980 Public Use Samples (PUS) prepared by the U.S. Bureau of the Census as part of its decennial survey of the population. All self-employed workers and 8 percent of wage and salary workers were drawn from the 1980 PUS. The purpose of this sample design was to obtain the most statistically reliable estimates of the determinants of the probability of self-employment given an overall limitation on the number of individuals we could include in our sample. There is some limited evidence that the best sample for this purpose contains roughly equal proportions of the two categories being considered (in our case self-employed workers and wage and salary workers).[52] Thus, the objective of our sample design was to obtain roughly equal size samples of self-employed and wage workers.

Only men who worked full time in the preceding year were included in the sample.[53] Part-time self-employed workers are probably substantially different from full-time self-employed workers. Part-time self-employed workers probably include individuals engaging in self-employment in order to tide them over between wage jobs. Part-time workers probably also include retired individuals who are supplementing their pensions with self-employment.[54] Although the determinants of part-time self-employment may be interesting in their own right, they are likely to differ from the determinants of full-time self-employment. Professionals (doctors, lawyers, dentists, and veterinarians) were excluded from the sample because individuals in these occupations are predominantly self-employed and because the determinants of self-employment choice and success for these groups are probably substantially different from the determinants for occupations where there is less need for substantial investment in human capital. Farmers were also excluded for a similar set of reasons. Finally, only individuals between the ages of eighteen and sixty-five were considered. Older workers were excluded because the determinants of self-employment are likely to change upon retirement.[55]

It is useful to compare the characteristics of self-employed and wage and salary workers. Table 6.6 reports some characteristics of male self-employed and wage workers. Self-employed workers are slightly older and much less likely to be black than are wage and salary workers. The self-employed are just about as likely as other workers to be veterans, immigrants, urban dwellers, or college educated. Table 6.7 defines the variables used in the statistical analysis.

TABLE 6.6
Characteristics of Self-Employed and Wage and Salary Workers, Males 1980

	(percentage)	
Characteristic	*Self-Employed Workers*	*Wage and Salary Workers*
Age*	43.6	39.6
College-educated	23.8	22.6
Veteran	52.6	52.5
Black	2.6	8.1
Urban	78.5	82.5
Immigrant	6.9	7.2
Professional	9.0	14.3
Sales	23.2	8.4
Clerical	1.2	7.0
Service	4.5	7.6
Management	24.6	16.9
Craft	28.7	23.5
Operator	8.8	22.4

*Arithmetic average age. Other variables are percentages of population with given characteristic.

TABLE 6.7

Definition of Variables Used for Entrepreneurial Choice and Success Analysis

Variable	*Definition*
Dichotomous Variables[a]	
SELFEMP	Individual is self-employed
URBAN	Individual resides in an urban area
LITKID	Household has child under 6
OLDKID	Household has child between 6 and 17 but no child under 6
NOKID[b]	Household has no children
MARHLD	Married couple household
BLACK	Individual is black
ASIAN	Individual is of Asian descent
WHITE[b]	Individual is not black or Asian
IMMIG	Individual not born in U.S. or abroad of U.S. parents
BADENG	Individual has no or little command of English language
ELEM	Individual has less than high school education
HSDROP	Individual dropped out of high school
HSGRAD[b]	Individual graduated from high school
COLDROP	Individual dropped out of college
COLGRAD	Individual graduated from college
POSTGRAD	Individual has postgraduate education
HANDICAP	Individual has some physical handicap
MARO	Individual never married
MAR1[b]	Individual married only once for 1980
MAR2	Individual married more than once for 1980
NEWVET	Individual veteran of post-Vietnam era
VIETVET	Individual veteran of Vietnam area
PREVIET	Individual veteran of era between Korean and Vietnam eras
KORVET	Individual veteran of Korean era
WWIIVET	Individual veteran of World War II
OTHVET	Individual veteran of other era (includes pre-1940 and 1947–1950 veterans for 1980
NONVET[b]	Individual not a veteran
MANAGE	Management occupation
PROF	Professional occupation
SALES	Sales occupation
CLERIC	Clerical occupation
SERVICE	Service occupation
CRAFT	Craft occupation
OPERATOR[b]	Machine operator occupation
Continous Variables	
IMGYRS	Number of years individual has been in this country
YRSIMG	IMMIG*IMGYRS
AGE	Individual's age in years divided by 10
AGESQ	AGE*AGE
EDUC	Number of years of education
VETAGE	VET*AGE

TABLE 6.7 (Cont'd)
Definition of Variables Used for Entrepreneurial Choice and Success Analysis

Variable	*Definition*
EDVET	VET*EDUC
LINC	Lograrithmic value of sum of all income received by individual
SPSEINC	Difference between family income and individual income divided by 1,000,000

[a] Variable equals 1 if individual possesses characteristic and 0 otherwise.

[b] Base category for regression analysis.

ESTIMATION RESULTS

Entrepreneurial Choice

We first consider the determinants of the probability that an individual will become self-employed rather than become a wage earner. We approach this problem in two steps.

In the first step we examine the influence of a large set of potential explanatory variables on the probability of self-employment using the linear probability model.[56] The linear probability model is convenient because it can be estimated with simple regression techniques. It provides a relatively inexpensive method for estimating and testing alternative models. Unfortunately, the linear probability model is not appropriate with a choice-based sample. We therefore estimated this model with a random sample.[57]

In the second step we estimate the reduced-form estimates of the probit model of self-employment choice given by (6.26). Aside from the fact that the theory presented above suggests its use, the probit model has two practical advantages. First, estimates from the probit model enable us to test for selectivity bias in the earnings equations (6.23) and (6.24). We discuss this issue in more detail below. Second, the probit model, unlike the linear probability model, enables us to obtain valid estimates with a choice-based sample. The probit estimates reported below are based on the WESML estimator proposed by Manski and Lerman.[58]

We begin with the tests based on the linear probability model. The first set of variables we examine concern the marital and family status of the household. The marital status of the household may affect the taste for entrepreneurship. Men with small children may be less willing to take on the risks associated with entrepreneurship. On the other hand, men with older children may have a greater propensity to operate their own business because their children provide a cheap and reliable source of labor. Finally, according to Shapero's theory of the entrepreneur as a displaced person, people who have been divorced are more likely to be entrepreneurs.[59]

In order to test these hypotheses we estimated the coefficients of variables that indicate the number of times the individual has been married, whether the individual is currently married, whether the individual has children age six or younger living at home, and whether the individual has children older than six living at home. The estimated coefficients of these variables are relatively small and imprecise. They are not statistically significantly different from zero taken singly or jointly. These findings indicate that marital and family status have little influence on the probability of self-employment. Another variable of interest is the amount of income earned by a man's wife. We tested and rejected the hypothesis that the probability of self-employment increases with the spousal income.

The second set of variables considered concern education. Education may affect the probability of self-employment in two ways. First, the difference between self-employment and wage earnings may vary with educational level. People with relatively little education may find it difficult to satisfy the hiring criteria for many employers and may therefore find that self-employment is their best available alternative. Second, the taste for self-employment may vary systematically with educational level.

We tested these hypotheses by including several variables that indicate the individual's education attainment. We included dummy variables that indicate whether an individual has only an elementary school education, is a high school dropout, a high school graduate, a college dropout, a college graduate, or has done some postgraduate work. We also included the product of age and the number of years of education—this variable allows the impact of education to vary with age—and the product of veterans status and the number of years of education. These coefficients on these variables were not statistically significantly different from zero when taken either singly or together.

The third set of variables we consider concern whether and when an individual was in the military. We include dummy variables indicating whether the individual saw military service after the Vietnam War, during the Vietnam War, between the Korean and Vietnam wars, during the Korean War, during World War II, or during some other time. We found that men who saw military service during or after the Vietnam War are statistically significantly less likely than nonveterans or veterans of other eras to become self-employed.

The fourth set of variables we consider concern the age of the individual. We find that the probability of self-employment increases at a diminishing rate with age. This relationship is statistically significant.

Finally, we consider three demographic characteristics. We find that black men are statistically significantly less likely than white men to become self-employed. We find that urban dwellers are statistically significantly less likely than nonurban dwellers to become self-employed. We find that immigrants are no more or less likely than nonimmigrants to choose self-employment.

Variables or sets of variables that were statistically significantly different from zero at the 10 percent level or greater were included in probit estimation. Table 6.8 reports the probit estimates. Table 6.9 reports the estimated impact of each variable at the mean value for the sample.

Entrepreneurial Success

In order to obtain valid estimates of the influence of personal attributes on the entrepreneurial earnings that a typical individual might expect, it is necessary to address a statistical issue known as sample-selection bias. Entrepreneurial earnings are determined by observable characteristics such as age and education and unobservable characteristics such as entrepreneurial ability. In estimating the impact of observable characteristics on entrepreneurial earnings we assume that unobservable characteristics can be summarized by a random variable that has an average value of zero across the population and is uncorrelated with the observable characteristics.[60] If we could observe entrepreneurial earnings for each individual in the population, we could with no problem estimate the impact of observable characteristics on entrepreneurial earnings. But we only observe entrepreneurial earnings for individuals who have chosen to become entrepreneurs. In the language of statistics, we only observe entrepreneurial earnings for individuals who have "self-selected" themselves into our sample.

People who have decided to become entrepreneurs will generally have different unobservable characteristics than people who have decided to become workers. Such self-selection creates two problems. First, if the average value of the unobservable characteristics is zero for the population, there is no reason to believe that the average value will remain zero for the sample of individuals who have self-selected themselves into entrepreneurship. Second, to the extent that the determinants of entrepreneurial choice are correlated with the determinants of entrepreneurial earnings, the random variable that measures the influence of unobservable characteristics for entrepreneurs will be correlated with the observable characteristics of entrepreneurs. It turns out that this correlation biases the coefficient estimates so that our estimated coefficients may bear little relationship to the true coefficients.

Fortunately, there are statistical methods available for eliminating these biases and securing reliable estimates of the true coefficients. The method we use in this study is often called the lambda method.[61] The method involves calculating a variable that reflects the probability that an individual will self-select himself into the sample and including this variable in

TABLE 6.8

Probability of Self-Employment, Reduced-Form Probit Model Estimates, Males 1980

Variable	*Coefficient (Standard Error)*
URBAN	−0.1510**
	(0.0565)
BLACK	0.4275***
	(0.1162)
IMMIG	−0.0148
	(0.0902)
HANDICAP	0.2255**
	(0.0971)
AGE	0.5503***
	(0.0153)
AGESQ	−0.0475**
	(0.0178)
EDVET	−0.0005
	(0.0104)
VETAGE	−0.0159
	(0.0291)
NEWVET	−0.4237*
	(0.0191)
VIETVET	−0.1656
	(0.0869)
SALES	0.9270***
	(0.0680)
CRAFT	0.4728***
	(0.0572)
MANAGE	0.5889***
	(0.0621)
CONSTANT	−2.8167***
	(0.3177)
Summary statistics	
Observations	6,205
Likelihood function	−1939.9
Exogenous variables	14

NOTE: These are weighted maximum likelihood estimates of probit model. Asymptotic standard errors in parentheses.

* Statistically significantly different from 0 at 5 percent level.

** Statistically significantly different from 0 at 1 percent level.

*** Statistically significantly different from 0 at 0.1 percent level.

TABLE 6.9
Net Impact of Demographic Characteristics on the Probability of Self-Employment. 1980

Characteristic	*Percentage Impact*
Urban	−21.9[a]
Black	−54.4[a]
Immigrant	−2.5
Post-Vietnam era veteran	−54.9[a]
Vietnam era veteran	−24.9[a]
Age[b]	15.5[a]

NOTE: Percentages are calculated from reduced-form probit model estimates reported in Table 6.8.

[a] There is a less than one out of twenty chance that the true impact is 0.

[b] Percentage change in the probability of self-employment per additional year of age, calculated for a forty-two-year-old man.

the equation. This variable is usually called lambda. The estimated coefficient of lambda can be used to determine whether people who have self-selected themselves into the sample have relatively high or relatively low earnings.[62] If lambda is not significantly different from zero, we may conclude that entrepreneurs have roughly the same unobservable characteristics as workers. If lambda is significantly different from zero, we may conclude that they have different unobservable characteristics and are therefore intrinsically different kinds of people.

Table 6.10 reports the regression estimates for self-employed workers. The estimated coefficient of lambda is negative and significantly different from zero. The estimated wage equation for wage workers is also reported for comparison.

Table 6.11 reports the estimated impact of various demographic characteristics on entrepreneurial earnings. Two kinds of numbers are reported. For continuous variables we report the percentage change in entrepreneurial earnings due to a percentage change in the variable under consideratiion (and under the assumption that all the other variables stay the same). Thus a number like 1.5 for age would imply that a 1 percent change in age leads to a 1.5 percent change in entrepreneurial earnings.[63] For dichotomous variables we report the percentage difference in earnings between people who possess the characteristic measured by the variable and people who do not possess the characteristic but are otherwise comparable. Thus a number like 7.5 for Asians implies that Asians earn 7.5 percent more than non-Asians with the same education, age, and other demographic characteristics.

Several interesting relationships appear:

TABLE 6.10

Self-Employment and Wage Earnings Regression Results, Males 1980

Variable	*Self-Employment Coefficient (Standard Error)*	*Wage Coefficient (Standard Error)*
URBAN	0.3630***	0.0580*
	(0.0432)	(0.0301)
BLACK	0.1799	−0.2614***
	(0.1143)	(0.0508)
ASIAN	0.0542	−0.1309
	(0.1183)	(0.1077)
YRSIMG	0.0170***	−0.0020
	(0.0030)	(0.0028)
IMMIG	−0.3627***	−0.0013
	(0.0902)	(0.0751)
BADENG	−0.1220	−0.3463***
	(0.1440)	(0.0924)
ELEM	0.0845	−0.0474
	(0.0863)	(0.0752)
HSDROP	−0.0807	−0.0802
	(0.0490)	(0.0418)
COLDROP	−0.0032	0.0939**
	(0.0409)	(0.0352)
COLGRAD	0.1259*	0.2305***
	(0.0615)	(0.0539)
POSTGRAD	−0.0652	0.2254**
	(0.0824)	(0.0682)
HANDICAP	−0.4707***	−0.1031*
	(0.0664)	(0.0535)
NEWVET	0.5334**	−0.2499***
	(0.1639)	(0.0761)
VIETVET	0.0968	0.0585
	(0.0725)	(0.0441)
PREVIET	0.0117	−0.0152
	(0.0582)	(0.0441)
KORVET	−0.0273	−0.0499
	(0.0614)	(0.0510)
WWIIVET	−0.0302	−0.1177
	(0.0818)	(0.0733)
OLDVET	−0.1596	0.0595

TABLE 6.10 (Cont'd)

Self-Employment and Wage Earnings Regression Results, Males 1980

Variable	*Self-Employment Coefficient (Standard Error)*	*Wage Coefficient (Standard Error)*
	(0.1773)	(0.1475)
MANAGE	−0.2631***	0.0944*
	(0.0409)	(0.0450)
PROF	0.0026	−0.0257
	(0.0634)	(0.0439)
SALES	−0.7491***	−0.0033
	(0.1892)	(0.0520)
CLERIC	0.1021	−0.0742
	(0.1215)	(0.0489)
SERVICE	−0.1160	−0.1490**
	(0.0725)	(0.0468)
CRAFT	−0.5150***	0.0569
	(0.1076)	(0.0331)
AGE[a]	—	0.5673***
		(0.0902)
AGESQ	−0.0197***	−0.0627***
	(0.0041)	(0.0100)
EDAGE	0.0092***	0.0087***
	(0.0027)	(0.0022)
VETAGE	−0.0278	0.0611**
	(0.0266)	(0.0232)
EDVET	0.0127	−0.0192**
	(0.0079)	(0.0065)
LAMBDA	−1.2993***	−0.0013
	(0.0240)	(0.0017)
CONSTANT	11.9592***	8.0421***
	(0.5344)	(0.1749)
Summary statistics		
Observations	3,751	2,386
R^2	0.1507	0.2486
Standard error	0.7762	0.5398
F-statistic	22.7784	25.9733

[a] Variable could not be included because of high collinearity with EDAGE.

* Statistically significantly different from 0 at 5 percent level.

** Statistically significantly different from 0 at 1 percent level.

*** Statistically significantly different from 0 at 0.1 percent level.

TABLE 6.11

Impact of Demographic Characteristics on Self-Employment Earnings, 1980

Characteristic	*Percent Differences*
Urban	43.73*
Black	19.71
Asian	5.57
Immigrant	−30.42*
Poor English	−11.49
Elementary school education	8.82
High school dropout	−7.75
High school graduate	0.00
College dropout	−0.32
College graduate	13.42*
Postgraduate	−6.31
Handicapped	−37.54*
Post-Vietnam War era veteran	70.47*
Vietnam War era veteran	10.16
Pre-Vietnam War era veteran	1.18
Korean War era veteran	−2.69
World War II era veteran	2.97
Other veteran	−14.75
Nonveteran	0.00
Manager	−23.13*
Professional	0.26
Salesman	−52.72*
Clerical worker	10.75
Service worker	−10.95
Craftsman	−40.25*
Operator	0.00
Percent change in earnings per year of:[a]	
Education	0.71 + 0.09 Age*
Age	9.04 − 0.39 Age*
Residence in this country for immigrant	1.70*

NOTE: Figures calculated from the estimated earnings equations reported in Table 6.9. Entries equal the percentage difference in earnings between people who possess the characteristic and otherwise comparable people who do not possess the characteristic.

[a] The percentage change in earnings due to a change in education or age varies with age level. To find the percentage change at any particular age level insert the relevant value of age (e.g., 42 for the average individual in the sample) for Age in the expression.

* Difference is statistically significant.

First, relative to nonveterans, veterans of the post-Vietnam era earn 70 percent more, veterans of the Vietnam era earn 10 percent more, veterans of the era between Korea and Vietnam earn 1.2 percent more, veterans of the Korean era earn 2.7 percent less, veterans of World War II earn 3 percent less, and veterans of the pre-World War II era earn 14.8 percent less. All of these differences except that for recent veterans could be due to chance.

Second, blacks earn almost 20 percent more than do otherwise comparable nonblacks. Asians earn almost 6 percent more than do otherwise comparable non-Asians. These differences, however, might be due to chance.[64]

Third, an immigrant to this country initially earns almost 44 percent less than an otherwise comparable nonimmigrant. But his earnings increase by 1.7 percent for every year he remains in this country. By the time he has been in this country for twenty-one years, he makes as much as otherwise comparable nonimmigrants. Immigrants who have been in this country for more than twenty-one years earn more than nonimmigrants.

Fourth, entrepreneurial earnings vary systematically with education.[65] Relative to individuals who have a high school education, men with only an elementary school education earn 18.5 percent less, men who dropped out of high school earn 13.4 percent less, men who dropped out of college earn 9 percent more, men who completed college earn 36.1 percent more, and men who went on to graduate work earn 23 percent more. It is notable that men who have done postgraduate work actually earn less than men who stopped at college.[66]

Fifth, entrepreneurial earnings initially increase and then decrease with age. For men with twelve years of education, a forty-two-year-old man makes 17.7 percent more than a sixty-year-old man and 3.5 percent less than a twenty-four-year-old man. Earnings decline with age for men older than twenty-eight who have twelve years of education. For men with sixteen years of education, a forty-two-year-old man makes 10.1 percent more than a sixty-year-old man and 3.1 percent more than a twenty-four-year-old man. Earnings decline with age for men older than thirty-seven who have sixteen years of education.

Finally, collecting some miscellaneous results, handicapped men earn 47.6 percent less than otherwise comparable nonhandicapped men. (This difference is significantly different from zero.) Men who speak English poorly earn 11.5 percent less than otherwise comparable men who speak English well. (This difference could be due to chance.) Men who reside in urban areas earn 43.7 percent more than men who reside in rural areas. (This difference is significantly different from zero.[67]) Relative to men in operator occupations, men in management occupations earn 23.2 percent less, men in sales occupation 62.8 percent less, men in craft occupations 40.2 percent less, men in service occupations 10.5 percent less, men in professional occupations 0.3 percent more, and men in clerical occupations 10.8 percent more. (The differences are significantly different from zero for management, sales, and craft occupations.)

The first result reported above for veterans of the Vietnam War and post-Vietnam War eras could be spurious. It might result from the partial failure of our statistical analysis to control for the relationship between earnings and age. In order to test for this possibility, we estimated the earnings equations for men who came of draft age during or after the Vietnam War era and who therefore belong to the same age cohort.[68] We found that there were no statistically significant differences (the differences were numerically small) between the earnings of otherwise comparable self-employed veterans and nonveterans.

SUGGESTIONS FOR FURTHER RESEARCH

The study reported above develops what we believe to be a promising approach toward the study of self-employed workers, identifies a number of empirical relationships concerning entrepreneurial choice and success, and discards some theories—that immigrants are more likely to become self-employed, for example—that were based on limited evidence. Although the study has addressed some interesting questions concerning the determinants of entrepreneurial choice and success, many other questions remain unanswered because of the limited data available on people who work for themselves.

Two kinds of additional data would prove useful. Data on previous work experience (e.g., in either self-employment or wage work, in related or unrelated occupations, in family-owned and other businesses), type of education (e.g., vocational training or college major), and IQ would help us gain a better understanding of the impact of an individual's "human capital" on entrepreneurial choice and success. Longitudinal data would also help us determine when and why people switch between self-employment and wage work and would help us sort out the influence of human capital accumulated in wage work on subsequent self-employment income and vice versa. Collection of such data should be a major objective of future research on entrepreneurial choice and success.

The study reported above faces several problems which we plan to investigate in further work. First, the inclusion of the occupational dummies in the regressions is questionable. Choice of occupation is probably endogenous. Preliminary work indicates that our general results are not sensitive to the inclusion of these dummies. Second, it is well known in the sample selection literature that distinguishing sample selection from untreated nonlinearities in the behavioral equation (here the wage equation) is a difficult matter. The high correlation between the disturbances in the self-employment selection and wage equations may indicate true sample selection or it may indicate misspecification of the self-employment wage equation. Indeed, the fact that the correlation coefficient implied by the estimates lies outside the unit interval suggests that the model is not correctly specified. The lambda term may be acting as a proxy, perhaps, for untreated nonlinearities in the wage equation. Third, studies such as this face a number of serious specification problems. Of particular concern is heteroskedasticity. If the disturbance term in the self-employment selection equation is heteroskedastic, standard errors *and* coefficient estimates are inconsistent. Moreover, if this disturbance term is heteroskedastic, the traditional methods for correcting sample-selection bias are not valid. We do not have a bivariate normal problem: using bivariate maximum likelihood or Heckman's lambda method will lead to inconsistent estimates of the true model parameters.

The Impact of Environmental and Safety Regulations on the Size Distribution of Establishments

As discussed in the previous chapter, few studies have either documented that average regulatory costs decrease with firm size or shown that regulations have distorted the size distribution of businesses. Arthur Andersen's study of pension regulations and the Federal Home Loan Bank Board's study of savings and loan regulations both found that average compliance costs decrease with firm size.[69] But these studies are for paperwork-intensive regulations. Reliable data on average compliance cost for more capital-intensive regulations such as those administered by EPA or OSHA are not available. This lack is unfortunate because capital-intensive regulations impose the vast bulk of the costs incurred by businesses for complying with federal regulations. Arthur Andersen found that EPA and OSHA regulations accounted for 84.5 percent of the regulatory costs incurred by the forty-eight firms it surveyed.[70]

Several studies have examined whether regulations have altered the size distribution of businesses. Booz-Allen and Hamilton compared the market shares of small businesses and the failure rates of small businesses in heavily and lightly regulated industries. They found that regulations have increased small business failures and decreased the market shares of small businesses.[71] A similar study by Pashigian also found that regulations have decreased the market shares of small businesses.[72] Both studies have difficulties that lead us to place little credence in their findings.

This section examines the differential impact of regulations across firm size from two different angles. First, we report pollution abatement cost per employees for three size categories of plants (0–99, 100–499, and 500+) and two types of plants (establishments operated by single-establishment firms and establishments operated by multiestablishment firms) for eighteen two-digit SIC code manufacturing industries in 1974. These estimates are based on a sample of roughly 20,000 establishments surveyed by the U.S. Bureau of the Census. Second, we report estimates of the impact of changes in environmental and safety regulations on changes in average establishment size and the number of small establishments between 1967 and 1977.

AVERAGE POLLUTION ABATEMENT COSTS PER EMPLOYEE

Since 1973 the Bureau of the Census has sent a questionnaire concerning pollution abatement expenditures to approximately 20,000 manufacturing establishments.[73] Data from the returned questionnaires are then used to estimate total pollution abatement expenditures for each manufacturing industry. At our request the Bureau of the Census has retabulated these data in order to estimate average pollution abatement expenditures per employee for several size categories of establishments.[74] The tabulations were performed separately for establishments operated by single-establishment firms and establishments operated by multiestablishment firms. Small establishments operated by single-establishment firms can be viewed unambiguously as small businesses, whereas small establishments operated by multiestablishment firms obviously cannot.

Because of restrictions on the disclosure of data, the most detailed tabulations are for two-digit SIC code industries.[75] For these industries we have data on the average pollution abatement cost per employee for establishments with 0–99, 100–499, and 500 or more employees and for single-unit establishments and multiunit establishments. In order to determine whether there are scale economies in complying with pollution regulations, we calculate the ratio of average pollution abatement cost per employee for each of the six groups of establishments (three size categories times two types of establishments equals six groups) to average pollution abatement cost per employee for multiunit establishments with 500 or more employees. These ratios provide an index of the cost advantage or disadvantage of each establishment group relative to multiunit establishments with 500 or more employees. A ratio greater than one indicates that average pollution abatement cost per employee is greater for the group under consideration than it is for the largest establishments. Groups that have a ratio greater than one are therefore at a cost disadvantage relative to the largest establishments. Similarly, groups that have a ratio of less than one have a cost advantage relative to the largest establishments.

Table 6.12 reports the estimates for pollution abatement capital expenditures. Table 6.13 reports the estimates for pollution abatement operating costs. It is clear from these tables that small establishments operated by single-establishment businesses have a significant cost *advantage* relative to large establishments operated by multiestablishment businesses. For most industries it is also clear that establishments operated by single-establishment businesses have a cost *advantage* relative to establishments of the same size operated by multiestablishment businesses. For some industries it appears that medium-size establishments (100–499 employees) operated by multiestablishment businesses have a cost *disadvantage* relative to large establishments (500 or more employees) operated by multiestablishment businesses.[76]

TABLE 6.12
Distribution of Pollution Abatement Capital Costs per Employee Across Establishment Size, 1974

	Size Category[a] (Number of Employees)				
	Single-Unit Companies			Multiunit Companies	
SIC Industry	*0–99*	*100–499*	*500+*	*0–99*	*100–499*
20. Food	0.36	0.65	0.48	1.78	1.01
21. Tobacco	—	—		—	3.74
22. Textiles	0.07	0.59	2.53	0.36	0.73
24. Lumber	0.19	0.59	—	0.57	0.46
25. Furniture	0.02	0.94	1.76	0.63	0.99
26. Paper	0.03	0.06	—	0.17	0.34
27. Printing	0.15	1.08	3.69	10.38	2.38
28. Chemicals	0.11	0.31	—	0.60	1.31
29. Petroleum	0.32	—	—	0.32	0.84
30. Rubber	0.08	0.11	—	0.23	0.53
31. Leather	1.33	3.33	—	2.00	2.50
32. Stone, clay	0.53	0.44	—	1.82	2.90
33. Primary metal	0.38	0.51	0.35	0.53	1.22
34. Fabricated metal	0.42	0.23	0.08	0.77	0.54
35. Machinery	0.27	0.54	0.63	0.42	0.52
36. Electrical equipment	0.05	0.18	0.53	0.66	0.82
37. Transportation equipment	0.25	0.10	0.13	0.17	0.64
38. Instruments	0.11	0.06	—	0.34	0.30
39. Miscellaneous	0.04	0.27	0.16	0.17	0.63
Number of industries with cost disadvantage[b]	1	2	3	4	7
Number of industries with cost advantage	17	15	7	14	12

NOTE: Each entry equals the ratio of pollution abatement capital costs per employee for the indicated size category to pollution abatement capital costs per employee for multiunit establishments with 500 or more employees. A dash indicates insufficient data.

[a] A single-unit establishment is associated with a firm that has only one establishment. A multiunit establishment is associated with a firm that has more than one establishment.

[b] A cost disadvantage exists when the ratio is greater than 1.00. A cost advantage exists when the ratio is less than 1.00.

These results do not support the hypothesis that environmental regulations place smaller businesses at a competitive disadvantage by conferring artificial scale economies upon larger businesses.[77]

TABLE 6.13

Distribution of Pollution Abatement Operating Costs per Employee Across Establishment Size, 1974

	Size Category[a] (Number of Employees)				
	Single-Unit Companies			*Multiunit Companies*	
SIC Industry	*0–99*	*100–499*	*500+*	*0–99*	*100–499*
20. Food	0.27	0.50	0.40	0.98	0.85
21. Tobacco	—	—		—	2.86
22. Textiles	0.64	0.48	0.91	1.86	1.25
24. Lumber	0.10	0.58	—	0.51	0.64
25. Furniture	0.62	0.73	1.58	0.91	1.00
26. Paper	0.09	0.33	—	0.53	0.46
27. Printing	0.15	0.63	0.22	0.78	1.22
28. Chemicals	0.07	0.34	—	0.71	1.14
29. Petroleum	0.14	—	0.12	0.38	0.54
30. Rubber	0.26	0.29	—	0.41	0.72
31. Leather	0.92	2.00	—	2.00	2.62
32. Stone, Clay	0.36	0.41	—	1.87	2.17
33. Primary metal	0.16	0.29	0.55	0.31	0.64
34. Fabricated metal	0.26	0.40	0.25	1.36	0.89
35. Machinery	0.10	0.36	0.36	0.32	0.53
36. Electrical equipment	0.21	0.40	0.56	0.52	0.63
37. Transportation equipment	0.07	0.28	0.74	0.25	0.42
38. Instruments	0.07	0.84	—	0.70	0.38
39. Miscellaneous	0.18	0.43	—	0.24	0.91
Number of industries with cost disadvantage[b]	0	1	1	4	6
Number of industries with cost advantage	18	17	10	14	13

NOTE: Each entry equals the ratio of pollution abatement capital costs per employee for the indicated size category to pollution abatement capital costs per employee for multiunit establishments with 500 or more employees. A dash indicates insufficient data.

[a] A single-unit establishment is associated with a firm that has only one establishment. A multiunit establishment is associated with a firm that has more than one establishment.

[b] A cost disadvantage exists when the ratio is greater than 1.00. A cost advantage exists when the ratio is less than 1.00.

THE IMPACT OF EPA AND OSHA REGULATIONS ON AVERAGE FIRM SIZE AND THE NUMBER OF SMALL ESTABLISHMENTS

Even without scale economies in regulatory compliance, it is possible that federal regulations have altered the size distribution of businesses. An increase in the cost of doing business that is neutral across business sizes will induce some marginal firms to close down and remaining firms to expand in order to pick up the slack in supply. An increase in the capital requirements for starting a business might deter entry by some smaller businesses if these businesses incur higher capital costs than larger businesses. Finally, although existing firms may not have scale economies in regulatory compliance, potential entrants very well may.

In order to investigate the impact of regulations on the size distribution of establishments, we have collected detailed data on 450 four-digit SIC code industries for the period 1958–1981.[78] We have used these data to examine the impact of changes in the regulatory burden on changes in average establishment size, the number of establishments, and the number of small establishments between 1967 and 1977. We chose 1967 as the base year for the analysis because many of the state and federal regulations were imposed after this year and because reliable data are available from the quinquenenial *Census of Manufactures* for 1967. We chose 1977 as the end year for the analysis because there was little change in the regulatory burden after this year and because 1977 was the last year for which *Census of Manufactures* data were available.

The Lucas model discussed in Chapter 3 provides a useful framework for examining the determinants of changes in the size distribution of establishments over time. Let the cost function for manager x be given by[79]

$$c = c(q;r,w,m,F,t)x \tag{6.32}$$

where q denotes quantity of output, r, w, and m denote the prices of capital, labor, and material, respectively, F denotes fixed regulatory costs, and t denotes variable regulatory costs. Denote product price by p. Then it is straightforward to show that the supply of each manager is given by

$$q = q(p,r,w,m,F,t,x) \tag{6.33}$$

and the marginal manager's efficiency is given by

$$x_m = x_m(p;r,w,m,F,t) \tag{6.34}$$

Total output is given by

$$Q = \int_{x_m}^{\infty} q\,(p,r,w,m,F,t,x)dG(x) \tag{6.35}$$

The total number of establishments is given by

$$(6.36) \qquad N = \int_{x_m}^{\infty} d\, G(x)$$

Let demand be given by

$$(6.37) \qquad p = D(Q,I)$$

where I denotes a vector of factors other than price that influence the demand for the industries product. Solving (6.36)–(6.37) simultaneously for Q, N, and p yields

$$(6.38) \qquad Q = Q(r,w,m,t,F,I)$$

$$(6.39) \qquad N = N(r,w,m,t,F,I)$$

which implies

$$(6.40) \qquad A = Q/N = A(r,w,m,t,F,I)$$

where A denotes average establishment size. The number of small establishments (defined relative to a given size level) is given by

$$(6.41) \qquad S = S(r,w,m,t,F,I)$$

This framework is extremely crude, but we believe that it is likely that more sophisticated frameworks would yield similar relationships.[80] It therefore provides a useful starting point for investigating the impact of regulatory costs on average establishment size, the number of establishments, and the number of small establishments.

In order to obtain an estimable model from equations (6.38)–(6.41), it is necessary to make some assumptions concerning the form of the functions on the righthand side of these equations. We assume that these functions are given by the following double-log approximations.[81]

$$(6.42) \qquad \ln A_t = a_0 + a_1 \ln r_t + a_2 \ln w_t + a_3 \ln m_t + a_4 \ln t_t + a_5 \ln F_t + a_6 \ln I_t$$

$$(6.43) \qquad \ln N_t = b_0 + b_1 \ln r_t + b_2 \ln w_t + b_3 \ln m_t + b_4 \ln t_t + b_5 \ln F_t + b_6 \ln I_t$$

$$(6.44) \qquad \ln S_t = c_0 + c_1 \ln r_t + c_2 \ln w_t + c_3 \ln m_t + c_4 \ln t_t + c_5 \ln F_t + c_6 \ln I_t$$

Taking first differences in the logs between time t = 1977 and time t − 1 = 1967 we obtain

(6.45)
$$\ln A_t - \ln A_{t-1} = a_0 + a_1[\ln r_t - \ln r_{t-1}] + a_2[\ln w_t - \ln w_{t-1}] + a_3[\ln m_t - \ln m_{t-1}] + a_4[\ln t_t - \ln t_{t-1}] + a_5[\ln F_t - \ln F_{t-1}] + a_6[\ln I_t - \ln I_{t-1}]$$

(6.46)
$$\ln N_t - \ln N_{t-1} = b_0 + b_1[\ln r_t - \ln r_{t-1}] + b_2[\ln w_t - \ln w_{t-1}] + b_3[\ln m_t - \ln m_{t-1}] + b_4[\ln t_t - \ln t_{t-1}] + b_5[\ln F_t - \ln F_{t-1}] + b_6[\ln I_t - \ln I_{t-1}]$$

(6.47)
$$\ln S_t - \ln S_{t-1} = c_0 + c_1[\ln r_t - \ln r_{t-1}] + c_2[\ln w_t - \ln w_{t-1}] + c_3[\ln m_t - \ln m_{t-1}] + c_4[\ln t_t - \ln t_{t-1}] + c_5[\ln F_t - \ln F_{t-1}] + c_6[\ln I_t - \ln I_{t-1}]$$

In order to complete the empirical framework we add mean zero error terms ϵ_A, ϵ_M, and ϵ_S to (6.45), (6.46), and (6.47), respectively. These error terms reflect omitted variables, measurement errors, and other stochastic elements not included in the framework.

The coefficients of (6.45)–(6.47) were estimated from data on roughly 300 four-digit SIC code industries.[82] Table 6.14 defines the variables.

TABLE 6.14

Definition of Variables and Summary Statistics for Establishment Analysis[a]

Variable	*Definition* *Change in log value between 1967 and 1977 of*
Capital Price	Price deflator for new capital equipment
Labor Price	Price deflator for labor
Materials Price	Price deflator for materials
Industry Growth[b]	Quantity of shipments
Pollution Capital	Ratio of real pollution abatement capital costs to real capital stock
Pollution Operating	Ratio of pollution abatement operating costs to value added
EPA Inspections	Fraction of establishments inspected by EPA
OSHA Inspections	Fraction of establishments inspected by OSHA

[a] See Wayne Gray, "The Impact of OSHA and EPA Regulations on Productivity Growth," NBER Working Paper 8405 (Cambridge: National Bureau of Economic Research, July 1984) for further discussion of the data. All variables are for 4-digit SIC code industries.
[b] Change between 1963 and 1967.

Average establishment size is measured by value added per establishments. The number of small establishments was defined as those with fewer than 100 employees. The number of large establishments was defined as the those with more than 100 employees. The prices of capital, labor, and materials are given by price deflators.

Variable pollution regulatory costs are measured by the ratio of pollution abatement operating costs to value added in 1977. Fixed pollution regulatory costs are measured by the ratio of the sum of real pollution abatement capital expenditures between 1973 and 1977 to the real capital stock in 1977. This distinction between variable and fixed regulatory costs involves the time period during which costs change. Pollution abatement operating costs may exhibit economies of scale, and pollution abatement capital costs may exhibit diseconomies of scale across establishment sizes for some industries. We assume that both variable pollution regulatory costs and fixed pollution regulatory costs were zero in 1967. This assumption is at best an approximation. The real pollution abatement capital stock, for example, was $3.36 billion in 1960, $5.39 billion in 1967, $11.46 billion in 1970, and $24.25 billion in 1975.

In addition to these measures of the costs of complying with pollution regulations, we included two measures of the enforcement effort by EPA and OSHA. The first measure is the fraction of establishments inspected in each industry by EPA. The second measure is the fraction of establishments inspected in each industry by OSHA. Since we have no measure of the cost of complying with OSHA regulations, the OSHA inspection measure may also be viewed as a proxy for the regulatory burden imposed by OSHA.

It is difficult to construct a proxy for I. The variables in the vector I are supposed to reflect non-price determinants of the level of demand for an industry's product. Ideally, these variables should reflect all the factors that determine the derived demand for an industry's product. For example, for the steel industry these variables should include measures of the demand for automobiles and other products that use steel as an input. Constructing such a list of variables would be an extremely time-consuming and difficult project.

There are two possible solutions. One solution is to include the size of the industry under consideration (measured by output, employment, or value added for example) as a measure of the level of demand. The problem with this solution is that changes in industry size may be correlated with the disturbance terms in (6.45)–(6.47). If so, the inclusion of industry output as a regressor will lead to simultaneous equations bias.

The second solution and the one we have adopted is to assume that the industry growth rate between 1967 and 1977 is a function of the other variables in the model plus the industry growth rate between 1963 and 1967 and its squared valued. The coefficients of the variables other than lagged growth reflect two effects. First, the coefficient of an independent variable reflects the direct effect of this variable on the dependent variable. Second, the coefficient of an independent variable reflects the indirect effect of this variable on the dependent variable through this variable's effect on industry growth. For example, pollution abatement costs change minimum efficient firm size (the direct effect) and change industry growth (the indirect effect through the effect of pollution abatement costs on equilibrium industry price).

Table 6.15 reports the regression estimates. Considering the fact that we are examining changes over a long period of time in a rather crude fashion, the R^2's are respectable although not inspiring. Table 6.16 reports some tests of the statistical significance of the various regulatory variables. Although many of the regulatory variables taken singly are not statistically significantly different from zero, these variables are always jointly significant at the 5 percent level of significance or better. We find a positive association between inspections by EPA and OSHA and average establishment size and a negative association between inspections by EPA and OSHA and the number of both small and large establishments. We find a positive association between relative pollution abatement capital costs and average establishment size and a negative association between pollution abatement capital costs and the number of small but not large establishments. We find a negligible and statistically insignificant relationship between pollution abatement operating costs and average establishment size and the number of small establishments.

These results have two major implications. First, industries that have relatively high inspection rates for EPA and OSHA have experienced relatively large increases in average establishment size and relatively large decreases in the number of establishments of all sizes. The EPA and OSHA inspection variables may simply be acting as proxies for levels of regulatory costs. We would expect EPA and OSHA to inspect establishments more frequently in industries that have stiffer regulations. Second, industries that have experienced relatively large increases in capital costs as a result of environmental regulations have experienced relatively large increases in average establishment size. This result is statistically significant. Increases in relative capital costs have decreased the growth rate of the number of small but not large establishments.

It would be hasty to conclude from these findings that small businesses have borne the brunt of government regulations. First, we must be especially clear about what we mean by a small business. If our definition of a small business is based on an absolute size standard that is independent of the industry in which the business operates, then small businesses have probably not borne the brunt of government regulations. The industries in which regulatory costs are largest are generally those in which small businesses are least prevalent. Therefore, to the extent regulations have decreased average establishment size or decreased the number of establishments they may have done so in industries in which small businesses are relatively unimportant.

TABLE 6.15
Changes in Average Establishment Size and Number of Establishments Regression Results, 1967–1977

Variable	*Average Establishment Size*	*Number of Small Establishments*	*Number of Large Establishments*
Capital price	0.2632	−0.9950	−1.3698*
	(0.8160)	(0.8440)	(0.6923)
Labor price	0.3010	−0.0421	0.1582
	(0.1542)	(0.1583)	(0.1311)
Materials price	−0.6266	0.5465	0.4684*
	(0.8160)	(0.2890)	(0.2329)
Industry growth	0.6869*	0.6855*	0.7440*
	(0.2651)	(0.2739)	(0.2265)
Industry growth squared	−1.0892*	−0.4126	−0.7537*
	(0.4130)	(0.4264)	(0.3514)
EPA inspections	0.0591	−0.4256	−0.0979
	(0.1968)	(0.2202)	(0.1672)
OSHA inspections	0.2029	−0.2250	−0.2611*
	(0.1157)	(0.1454)	(0.0982)
Pollution capital	0.0832*	−0.0566	0.0479
	(0.0405)	(0.0417)	(0.0344)
Pollution operating	−096	0.0376	0.0117
	(0.0248)	(0.0255)	(0.0210)
Constant	1.0143	0.2696	0.9445
	(0.6078)	(0.6242)	(0.5157)
Summary statistics:			
Observations	293	290	292
R^2	0.0841	0.1291	0.1089
F-Statistic	2.5918*	4.13645*	3.4349*
Mean square error	0.2362	0.2566	0.1752

* Statistically significant at five percent level

Second, the results reported above apply to establishments but not necessarily to firms. Given the evidence from the PACE data that pollution abatement costs have been lower at single-unit establishments than at multiunit establishments of the same size, it is quite possible that the impact of regulations differs between these two kinds of establishments and therefore between smaller and larger firms.

TABLE 6.16
F-Tests of Regulatory Variables

	Regression		
Variables	*Average Establishment Size*	*Number of Small Establishments*	*Number of Large Establishments*
All regulatory variables	2.9575*	3.3177*	2.4244*
Inspection variables	2.1212	5.2310*	5.3525*
Pollution operating cost variables	0.4667	1.6852	0.4555
All regulatory variables except pollution operating cost variables	3.7415*	5.3148*	3.7525*

*Variables are statistically significantly different from zero at 5 percent level of statistical significance.

7

SUMMARY AND CONCLUSIONS

Small businesses serve many useful purposes. They provide specialized products and services often ignored by larger businesses. They pioneer and create new markets for innovative products. By competing with each other and with larger businesses they hold prices down. Because they grow more rapidly and are more labor intensive than bigger firms they create new jobs. Most importantly, they are the seeds from which new industries will arise and from which the industrial giants of tomorrow will grow.

Are small businesses vanishing from the economic scene? Clearly not. The number of businesses that file tax returns more than doubled from 1947, when there were 8.1 million firms, to 1980, when there were 16.8 million firms. The vast majority of these firms are small.

Although small businesses are not in danger of imminent extinction, their relative economic importance has decreased significantly over time. The share of value added contributed by businesses with fewer than five hundred employees declined from 51 percent in 1958 to 47 percent in 1977. This 8 percent relative decline in the small business share masks two fundamental changes in the relative importance of small business in the economy over the last quarter-century.

First, small business–dominated industries such as services have increased their share of the economic pie while large business–dominated industries such as manufacturing have decreased their share of the economic pie. If small business had maintained its share of value added within each industry between 1958 and 1977, the small business share of value added for the economy would have increased from 51 percent to 54 percent.

Second, the small business share of value added has declined in every industry including those dominated by small businesses. Between 1958 and 1977 the relative decline in the small business share of value added was 42 percent in mining, 29 percent in manufacturing, 20 percent in retail trade, 10 percent in wholesale trade, 8 percent in services and construction, 5 percent in transportation, communications, and utilities, and 2 percent in finance, insurance, and real estate. If each of these industries had maintained its relative importance in the overall economy between 1958 and 1977, the small business share would have experienced a relative decline of 14 percent, from 51 percent in 1958 to 44 percent in 1977. The shift in the economy from manufacturing to services has clearly leavened the decrease in the small business share of value added.

It is difficult to say whether small business will continue to decrease in importance or at what rate. Continued decreases in heavy industries such as steel and continued increases in service industries such as health care will stem the decline. Continued increases in labor-saving technological changes and thus in capital intensity may accelerate the decline.

With the recent wave of merger mania, the rising burden of government regulations and taxes on all firms, and the declining importance of small businesses in every major economic sector, it is not surprising that policy makers are expressing increasing concern over the state of small business in the economy. Four major pieces of legislation that favor small business were passed in 1980 alone. This legislation has led to the preparation of a major presidential report on the state of small business each year, the wholesale review of regulations that may have a serious adverse impact on small business, and the requirement that regulatory agencies examine the impact of new rules on small businesses.

Is this concern misplaced? Generally, no. Small businesses play two important roles in the economy. First, they produce many specialized products that consumers desire and that large businesses cannot produce efficiently. Second, they enable entrepreneurs to learn about their business abilities at minimum risk: especially able entrepreneurs will expand their businesses and found the economy's future industrial giants; especially poor entrepreneurs will dissolve their businesses and move on to other pursuits. Government policies that hinder small businesses from playing these roles decrease social welfare.

Government policies affect the formation, dissolution, and growth of small businesses in many complicated ways. An excess profits tax illustrates one set of forces at play. Most small businesses are marginally profitable at best. They would be exempt from the tax. Bigger firms would bear the tax burden. At first blush this tax policy appears to favor small businesses. But unprofitable small businesses hope to become profitable big businesses and thereby obtain compensation for the risks they have borne and the losses they have incurred while small and young. By reducing after-tax profits for big businesses, an excess profits tax blunts the incentives of the young entrepreneur to establish and expand a small business. Although stagnant small businesses gain, dynamic small businesses ultimately lose from seemingly progressive tax schemes like an excess profits tax.

Regulations that impose fixed and variable costs illustrate another set of forces at play. Fixed regulatory costs bear more heavily on smaller than on larger businesses. These costs force extremely small businesses to close down, thereby reducing industry output at current price and releasing managers into the work force. The price for industry output rises (because output has fallen), and the wage for industry workers falls (because the supply of workers increases). Remaining firms expand production. For the largest firms, the increased profits due to higher prices and lower wages may more than offset the decreased profits due to the regulatory cost. Therefore, bigger firms are more likely than smaller firms to favor regulatory schemes that impose a high proportion of fixed costs. Among equally costly schemes, bigger firms will favor those that require large-scale technologies and heavy administrative costs, for these schemes will bear more heavily on their smaller competitors.

Policy makers have recognized that fixed regulatory costs place smaller firms at a competitive disadvantage and may force smaller firms out of business. In response, they have tiered many regulations so that smaller firms face lighter regulatory burdens than do larger firms. Smaller firms often face lighter substantive requirements, have lighter recordkeeping requirements, are inspected less frequently, and pay lighter fines than larger firms. Sometimes smaller firms are exempted from substantive requirements, recordkeeping requirements, or inspection programs.

Although in theory some form of tiering is desirable when regulations impose fixed costs, in practice it is a delicate question whether tiered regulations are better than untiered regulations. Existing tiered regulations generally impose lighter regulatory requirements on firms below some size level and impose heavier regulatory requirements on firms above some size level. Such tiering may save some efficient small businesses that contribute to social welfare but that would fail if they had to comply fully with regulations. But it has two drawbacks. First, it preserves inefficient small businesses, whose operation decreases social welfare. Second, it encourages larger businesses to become smaller in order to avail themselves of the lighter regulatory requirements for smaller firms.

The ideal tiering scheme must balance the social loss from inducing inefficient big business contractions and from preserving inefficient small businesses against the social gain from preserving efficient small businesses. It is beyond the scope of this book to determine how close existing tiering schemes come to this ideal.

Several modifications to existing tiering schemes might strike a better balance. Regulators should consider incorporating a mechanism for eliminating inefficient firms. Society gains nothing by saving marginally profitable egregious polluters. Regulators should also consider increasing regulatory requirements gradually for firms that are past the exemption level. Such gradual tightening would lessen inefficient business contractions. Regulators could minimize the two adverse consequences of tiering mentioned above by using a U-shaped enforcement plan. Inefficient small firms would face stiff enforcement. Efficient small firms would face light enforcement. Larger firms would face stiff enforcement.

There are several rules of thumb for determining whether an industry is a good candidate for tiering. Small business exemptions are more desirable

- the greater the degree of scale economies in regulatory compliance;
- the smaller the social cost of the activity being discouraged by regulation relative to the social value of the product whose production is subjected to regulation;
- the more inelastic the demand for the product whose production is subjected to regulation;
- the greater the number of small businesses that would dissolve as a result of the regulation.

There are reasonable grounds for suspecting that regulations have a disparate impact on small business. Some regulations have extensive reporting and recordkeeping requirements that bear heavily on small firms. Indeed, the average cost of complying with paperwork-intensive pension and banking regulations is roughly ten times as high for small firms as for large firms. Firms must learn about the requirements they face. It is plausible that there the average cost of learning decreases with firm size. Many regulations require firms to adopt certain procedures or to install particular equipment. Several observers claim that these requirements are not sensitive to firm size and therefore place smaller firms at a disadvantage.

Although there are almost surely specific cases where regulations have a disparate impact on small businesses—pension and banking regulations are two well-documented instances—several factors suggest that as a general matter regulations do not place smaller businesses at a competitive disadvantage. First, even before the passage of the Regulatory Flexibility Act, many regulations imposed lighter regulatory burdens on smaller than on larger businesses. Second, regulators have strong incentives to skew enforcement efforts toward larger businesses. Compliance rates are probably lower among smaller than larger businesses. Third, the surest way to attract political heat is to regulate a lot of small firms out of existence. Regulators who want to minimize congressional opposition to their programs and minimize the number of trips they must make to Capitol Hill will avoid imposing or enforcing regulations that bankrupt businesses.

Although existing studies of the differential impact of regulations across business size are far from definitive, it is possible to draw three tentative conclusions from them. First, there is reliable evidence that paperwork-intensive regulations cause substantial scale economies in regulatory compliance. Second, some regulations have a disparate impact on smaller businesses not because they impose fixed costs but rather because smaller businesses are more likely than are larger businesses to engage in the activity the regulations seek to discourage. Third, the available evidence indicates that there are no scale economies in complying with environmental regulations. If anything, small businesses have substantially lower average regulatory costs than large businesses.

The fact that regulations have not generally placed smaller businesses at a competitive disadvantage does not mean that tiering is unjustified or that the Regulatory Flexibility Act was ill conceived. It suggests instead that explicit and tacit tiering by regulators has reduced the disparate impact on smaller businesses. When properly designed, tiering enables government agencies to achieve regulatory goals more efficiently.

NOTES

Chapter 1

1. Stephen Breyer, *Regulation and Its Reform* (Cambridge: Harvard University Press, 1982), p. 1.

2. Robert DeFina, "Public and Private Expenditures for Federal Regulation of Business," Working Paper no. 22 (St. Louis: Center for the Study of American Business, Washington University, 1977).

3. Arthur Andersen, *Cost of Government Regulations: Study for the Business Roundtable* (Chicago: Arthur Andersen, March 1979).

4. Council on Environmental Quality, *Report of the Council on Environmental Quality: 1977* (Washington, D.C.: Government Printing Office, 1978).

5. U.S. Department of the Treasury, Internal Revenue Service, *Statistics of Corporate Income: 1977* (Washington, D.C.: Government Printing Office, 1981).

6. U.S. Regulatory Council, *Tiering Regulations: A Practical Guide* (Washington, D.C.: U.S. Regulatory Council, March 1981).

7. More on small businesses in the antitrust law in Chapter 2.

8. Formally, smaller businesses are those on the left-hand tail of the size distribution of businesses. We could define this precisely in terms of the businesses that are some number of standard deviations smaller than the mean or that are in the bottom quintile, let us say, of businesses. But for reasons that will become clearer in Chapter 3, such fine distinctions are not necessary.

9. For an excellent survey of alternative theories of the regulatory process, see Paul Joskow and Roger Noll, "Theory and Practice in Public Regulation: A Current Overview," in *Studies in Public Relation,* ed. G. Fromm (Cambridge: MIT Press, 1981), chap. 1.

10. See Robert W. Hahn and Roger G. Noll, "Barriers to Implementing Tradeable Air Pollution Permits: Problems of Regulatory Interactions," *Yale Journal of Regulation* 1, no. 1 (1983): 63–92.

11. Although we do not address the positive theory of regulation in this book, much in this book is positive economics in the sense that we examine the consequences of regulation without necessarily judging whether these consequences are good or bad.

Chapter 2

1. Executive Office of the President, *The State of Small Business: A Report of the President* (Washington, D.C.: Government Printing Office, 1983), p. 28. This figure is based on Internal Revenue Service estimates reported in the annual *Statistics of Income,* published by the Department of the Treasury, Internal Revenue Service.

2. *Ibid.*

3. Almost half of the sole proprietorships reported receipts of less than $5,000 in 1980; almost half of the partnerships reported receipts of less than $25,000 in 1980; and more than a fifth of the corporations reported receipts of less than $25,000 in 1980. See *ibid.,* tables A2.1, A2.2, and A2.3, pp. 199–200.

4. The Internal Revenue Service reports summary data on businesses that file tax returns but prohibits researchers and other government agencies from seeing individual data.

5. The Census Bureau survey queries all firms that are covered by the Federal Insurance Contributions Act, i.e., all firms that pay social security taxes. It therefore excludes self-employed persons, and thus most sole proprietorships, and various agricultural and railroad firms. Data from the 1982 survey were not available at the time of this writing.

6. The Small Business Administration has developed a data base on small businesses that relies largely on the DMI. The figures reported below are based on SBA analyses of these data. See *ibid.* for details.

7. Computation by Bruce D. Phillips of the Small Business Administration.

8. Of the businesses surveyed for the 1977 *Enterprise Statistics,* 58 percent had gross sales of less than $50,000. *Enterprise Statistics* contains data on many more tiny businesses than does the SBDB because it includes many sole proprietorships. Almost 3 million businesses included in the 1977 *Enterprise Statistics* had no employees; most of these were sole proprietorships.

9. Data for 1977 reported in Executive Office of the President, *The State of Small Business: A Report of the President* (Washington, D.C.: Government Printing Office, 1982), p. 189.

10. Based on data reported in *ibid.,* table A1.4, p. 190.

11. *Ibid.,* p. 39.

12. On average, these businesses have forty-two subordinate establishments. *Ibid.,* p. 39.

13. The reader can test this proposition by examining the turnover of stalls and boutiques at some of the new inner-city malls such as Quincy Market in Boston.

14. For example, see the *1981 Dun and Bradstreet Business Record* (New York: Dun and Bradstreet, 1983).

15. Of course, accounting profits may be poor indicators of economic profits, and profits per dollar of sale may be a particularly poor indicator of economic profits. See Thomas R. Stauffer, "The Measurement of Corporate Rates of Return: A Generalized Formulation," *Bell Journal of Economics* 2 (Autumn 1971): 434–469 for a discussion of the biases in accounting rates of return. Also see Franklin M. Fisher and John J. McGowan, "On the Misuse of Accounting Rates of Returns to Infer Monopoly Profits," *American Economic Review* 73 (March 1983): 82–97, for the argument that accounting rates of return provide no information about economic rates of return.

16. Based upon data from the Dun and Bradstreet Financial Statement files in 1978. See Executive Office of the President, *The State of Small Business* 1982, pp. 215–216, for further details. Note that the financial data upon which this statement is based are available for less than 15 percent of the firms surveyed by Dun and Bradstreet and therefore may not accurately represent the population of firms.

17. It is of interest, however, that profits are not generally higher in smaller firms for retail trade, the industry in which smaller firms are most dominant.

18. Alexander Stuart, "The Airlines Are Flying in a Fog," *Fortune* (October 20, 1980): 51–56.

19. U.S. Department of the Treasury, Internal Revenue Service, *1980 Proprietorship Returns* (Washington, D.C.: Government Printing Office, 1982), p. 205.

20. See William A. Brock and David S. Evans, *An Economic Analysis of Local Building*

Codes, prepared for the Federal Trade Commission (Chicago: CERA, May 1982); and Eli Noam, "Does Independence Matter? An Analysis of Regulatory Behavior," *Quarterly Review of Economics and Business* 22, no. 4 (Winter 1982): 53–60.

21. Ruth Ryon, "Discount Realty Companies on the Rise in Southland," *Los Angeles Times,* October 22, 1978, for a discussion.

22. See Owen R. Phillips, "Residential Real Estate Market in Texas: Prices, Quality, and Regulation," Working Paper no. 81–2 (College Station: Department of Economics, Texas A&M University, April 1981), and the references cited therein for a good survey of competition in real estate markets.

23. These data are based on the 4 million firms included in the 1980 DMI. Because they exclude roughly 12.8 million businesses, most of which are extremely small, they underrepresent the share of sales made by small businesses.

24. Value added includes rents, which are excluded from gross product.

25. Lawrence J. White, "The Determinants of the Relative Importance of Small Businesses," *Review of Economics and Statistics* (February 1982): 42–49. Small businesses are those with fewer than five hundred employees.

26. He used several alternative transformations of the small business share, including a logit specification. These alternative specifications yielded similar results. The industries were defined at the 3-digit SIC code level.

27. White's findings are best viewed as describing the typical characteristics of small business–dominated industries rather than as identifying underlying cause-and-effect relationships. By definition, vertically integrated, capital-intensive, national industries will have large firms. The more fundamental question is why large firms are more efficient in some industries than in others and what determines the change in the small business share over time. The stochastic theory discussed in Chapter 3, for example, suggests that the small business share will decrease over time as lucky firms expand and increase their dominance over industries. Technological changes may arrest these tendencies. The steel industry is a good example. An interesting recent development in this traditionally large business–dominated industry is the formation of small specialty steel companies. Small steel mills now account for 15 percent of domestic steel output. They are more cost competitive with foreign producers than are large steel mills for two reasons. First, they use reprocessed scrap steel. Second, they are generally nonunionized. See Data Resources, Inc., *The DRI Report on Manufacturing Industries* (Washington, D.C.: Small Business Administration, January 1984).

28. Internal Revenue Service, *Statistics of Income,* 1958 and 1980.

29. Internal Revenue Service, *Statistics of Income,* various years.

30. Based on data reported in Executive Office of the President, *The State of Small Business,* 1983, p. 213. This particular measure of value added, called gross product originating, does not include rents.

31. From data reported in *ibid.*

32. Lawrence White, *Measuring the Importance of Small Business in the American Economy,* Monograph Series in Finance and Economics (New York: Salomon Brothers Center for the Study of Financial Institutions, Graduate School of Business Administration, New York University, 1981).

33. This section arbitrarily defines small businesses as those with fewer than five hundred employees or with business receipts of $5 million or less. Defining small businesses as those with fewer than one hundred employees or with business receipts of $500,000 or less leads to the same qualitative results.

34. Let w_i equal the share of industry i in the total, and let s_i denote the small business share for industry i. Then the small business share for the economy is simply $S = \Sigma w_i s_i$. Totally differentiate S to obtain $dS = \Sigma w_i ds_i + \Sigma s_i dw_i + \Sigma ds_i dw_i$. In general, the third term

in this expression is small and can be ignored. Thus the change in the small business share can be decomposed into the change due to intraindustry changes in the small business share (the first term on the right-hand side of the equation) and the change due to the changing industrial composition of the economy (the second term on the right-hand side of the equation).

35. Some of the decrease in the small business share is the artificial result of inflation. Between 1958 and 1979, the GNP deflator, an index of average prices in the economy, increased by 150 percent. Consequently, a size level of $5,000,000 in 1958 dollars implies a size level of roughly $12,250,000 in 1979 dollars. Data were not available on the fraction of business receipts for firms with receipts of $12,250,000 or less. Between 1958 and 1975, the GNP deflator increased by 93 percent. Consequently, a size level of $5,000,000 in 1958 dollars implies a size level of $9,650,000 in 1975 dollars. In order to obtain a rough idea of the impact of inflation on the small business share of receipts, we can compare the share of business receipts obtained by firms with receipts of $5 million or less in 1958 with the share of business receipts obtained by firms with receipts of $10 million or less in 1975. The share of business receipts obtained by firms with receipts of $10 million or less was 36 percent in 1975. The share of business receipts obtained by firms with receipts of $5 million or less was 31 percent. Thus, even after accounting for inflation, the small business share of business receipts has declined quite substantially. See White, *Measuring,* pp. 20–22, for further discussion of inflation adjustments.

36. Farmers comprise the most important group of small businesses. Congress has bestowed numerous favors on the agriculture industry over the years. These favors include cheap agricultural loans, subsidies, partial exemptions from the antitrust laws, and price supports.

37. For a good overview of small business legislation, see Paul R. Verkuil, "A Critical Guide to the Regulatory Flexibility Act," *Duke Law Journal* (April 1982): 216–219.

38. P.L., 94–305.

39. *Ibid.,* p. 217.

40. *Ibid.*

41. The concern expressed by Congress and the White House, which supported these bills, was stimulated at least in part by the increasing strength of the small business lobby and by the pressures of an upcoming election.

42. Verkuil, *op. cit.,* "A Critical Guide," p. 218.

43. See *ibid.* for an extensive discussion of the objectives and implementation of the Regulatory Flexibility Act (P.L. 96–554).

44. *United States* v. *Trans-Missouri Freight Ass'n.,* 166 U.S. 323 (1897). Quoted by Robert H. Bork, *The Antitrust Paradox* (New York: Basic Books, 1978), p. 25.

45. A. D. Neale, *The Antitrust Laws of the United States,* 2d ed. (New York: Cambridge University Press, 1970), p. 478.

46. *Ibid.*

47. Bork, *Antitrust Paradox,* p. 54.

48. Carl Kaysen and Donald Turner, *Antitrust Policy* (Cambridge: Harvard University Press, 1958) p. 92.

49. Neale, *Antitrust Laws,* p. 467.

50. Donald Turner, "Conglomerate Mergers and Section 7 of the Clayton Act," *Harvard Law Review* 78 (1965): 1313–1347.

51. Neale, *Antitrust Laws,* p. 471.

52. Adam Smith, *The Wealth of Nations* (New York: Modern Library, 1937), p. 423.

53. F. M. Scherer, *Industrial Market Structure and Economic Performance,* 2d ed. (Boston: Houghton Mifflin, 1980), p. 546.

54. See the discussion in Chapter 2 about real estate and building codes.

55. Thomas J. Peters and Robert H. Waterman, *In Search of Excellence* (New York: Harper & Row, 1982).

56. *Ibid.*, p. 271. Also see Bradley L. Schiller, "Corporate Kidnap," *Public Interest* (Fall 1983).

57. Peters and Waterman, *In Search of Excellence,* p. 293.

58. David S. Evans and Sanford J. Grossman, "Integration," pp. 95–126, in David S. Evans, ed., *Breaking up Bell: Essays on Industrial Organization and Regulation,* (New York: North Holland, 1983).

59. See Morton Kamien and Nancy Schwartz, *Market Structure and Innovation* (New York: Cambridge University Press, 1982), for an excellent survey of recent empirical and theoretical work on innovation and market structure. A recent study found that small firms produce twice as many innovations per employee as large firms. See Gellman Research, *The Relationship Between Industrial Concentration, Firm Size, and Technological Innovation* (Washington, D.C.: Office of Advocacy, Small Business Administration, May 11, 1982) Also see John Bound et al., "Who Does R & D and Who Patents," pp. 21–54, in *Patents, R & D, and Productivity,* ed. Zvi Griliches (Chicago: The University of Chicago Press, 1984), for evidence based on a sample of roughly 2500 large firms.

60. See David S. Evans and James J. Heckman, "A Test for Subadditivity of the Cost Function with an Application to the Bell System," *American Economic Review* (September 1984): 615–623, for evidence on the telephone industry, and Laurits R. Christensen and William Greene, "Scale Economies in U.S. Electric Power Generation," *Journal of Political Economy* (August 1976): 655–676, for evidence on the electric utility industry.

61. This belief was the basis for the FCC's decision to encourage competition in the telephone industry. For a discussion, see Gerald Brock, *Telecommunications Industry* (Cambridge: Harvard University Press, 1981).

62. For a discussion of this tendency for the telecommunications industry, see Evans, *Breaking up Bell,* chaps. 3, 4.

63. See, generally, Alfred E. Kahn, "The Passing of the Public Utility Concept," pp. 3–37, in *Telecommunications Regulation Today and Tomorrow,* ed. Eli Noam. (New York: Law and Business, 1983).

64. On the other hand, deregulation has increased merger activity and increased concentration in the banking industry. See Bruce D. Phillips, "The Effect of Industry Deregulation on the Small Business Sector," presented at National Association of Business Economists, Altanta, Georgia, September 1984.

65. See, for example, Richard Nelson and Sidney Winter, *An Evolutionary Theory of Economic Change* (Cambridge: Harvard University Press, 1982).

66. Israel M. Kirzner, *Competition and Entrepreneurship* (Chicago: University of Chicago Press, 1973), p. 21.

67. Joseph R. Schumpeter, *Capitalism, Socialism and Democracy,* 3d ed. (New York: Harper & Row, 1950), p. 132.

68. Calvin A. Kent, Donald L. Saxton, and Karl H. Vesper, eds., *Encyclopedia of Entrepreneurship* (Englewood Cliffs, N.J.: Prentice-Hall, 1982).

69. The relative share created by smaller businesses rises in recessions, when large firms contract (1974–1976, 1980–1982), and falls when large firms expand (1978–1980). See Executive Office of the President, *The State of Small Business,* 1983, chap. 3; Catherine

Armington and Marjorie Odle, "Small Business—How Many Jobs?" *Brookings Economic Review* (Winter 1982): 1–14; and David L. Birch, *The Job Generation Process* (Cambridge: Center for the Study of Neighborhood and Regional Change, MIT, 1979).

70. See David Mills, "Fluctuations and Firm Size," *Journal of Industrial Economics* (in press); and Thomas A. Gray and Bruce D. Phillips, "The Role of Small Firms in Understanding the Magnitude of Fluctuations in the Economy" (Paper presented at the Atlantic Economic Society Meetings, Philadelphia, October 1983).

71. Scherer, *Industrial Market Structure,* p. 92.

72. M. Hall and L. Weiss, "Firm Size and Profitability," *Review of Economics and Statistics* 49, no. 3 (August 1967): 319–331.

73. S. S. Alexander, "The Effect of Size of Manufacturing Corporations on the Distribution of the Rate of Return," *Review of Economics and Statistics* 31, no. 3 (August 1949): 229–235; H. O. Stekler, "The Variability of Profitability with Size of Firm: 1947–1958," *Journal of the American Statistical Association* 59, no. 308 (December 1964): 1183–1193; George Stigler, *Capital and Rates of Return in Manufacturing Industries* (Princeton: Princeton University Press, 1963).

74. M. Marcus, "Profitability and Size of Firm," *Review of Economics and Statistics* 51, no. 1 (February 1969): 104–107.

75. Alexander, "The Effect of Size."

76. P. E. Hart and S. J. Prais, "The Analysis of Business Concentration: A Statistical Approach," *Journal of the Royal Statistical Society* 119, pt. 2 (1956): 150–191.

77. Herbert A. Simon and Charles P. Bonini, "The Size Distribution of Business Firms," *American Economic Review* 48 (September 1958).

78. Stephen Hymer and Peter Pashigian, "Firm Size and Rate of Growth," *Journal of Political Economy* 70 (April 1976): 556–569.

79. Edwin Mansfield, "Entry, Gibrat's Law, Innovation, and the Growth of Firms," *American Economic Review* 52 (December 1962), 1031–1051; David S. Evans," "Tests of Alternative Theories of Industry Evolution," unpublished manuscript, November 1985.

80. Hart and Prais, "Analysis"; Edwin Mansfield, "Entry," *American Economic Review* 52 (December 1962): 1031–1051; Gunnar DuRietz, "New Firm Entry in Swedish Manufacturing Industries During the Post-War Period" (doctoral diss., University of Stockholm, 1975).

81. David Birch, *Job Generation Process* (Cambridge: Program on Neighborhood and Regional Change, MIT, 1979).Also see Evans, "Industry Evolution" and Chapter 6 of this book for estimates which show that the probability of dissolution is a decreasing function of firm size and age.

82. Simon and Bonini, Hart and Prais, *op. cit.*

83. Richard E. Quandt, "On the Size Distribution of Firms," *American Economic Review* 56, no. 3 (March 1966): 416–432.

84. He tested several alternative forms of the Pareto distribution, the lognormal distribution, and several other exponential distributions.

85. A composite distribution based on an exponential distribution did slightly better—twenty-three out of a possible thirty good fits—and another exponential distribution performed as well as the lognormal distribution. The intuitive appeal of the lognormal distribution and the fact that it has a number of useful properties therefore suggests that it provides a good first approximation to the size distribution of businesses for many industries. For a useful summary of the recent literature, see Roger Clarke, "On the Lognormality of Firm and Plant Size Distributions: Some U.K. Evidence," *Applied Economics* (December 1979): 415–435. Further research needs to be done using larger samples, including a wider spectrum of firm sizes and examining more industries, including nonmanufacturing industries.

Chapter 3

1. This theory is primarily due to Alfred Marshall, *Principles of Economics* (London: Macmillan, 1925), and Jacob Viner, "Cost Curves and Supply Curves," *Zeitschrift fur Nationalekonomie* 3 (1932): 23–46.

2. Richard Kihlstrom and Jean-Jacques Laffont, "A General Equilibrium Entrepreneurial Theory of Firm Formation Based on Risk Aversion," *Journal of Political Economy* 59 (August 1979): 719–748.

3. Robert E. Lucas, "On the Size Distribution of Business Firms," *Bell Journal of Economics* 9 (August 1978): 508–523.

4. Incorporating a theory of expectations into the model is important not only for theoretical consistency but also to obtain valid empirical predictions of the effects of policy changes. Entrepreneurs base entry and exit decisions on expectations of, among other things, certain governmental policies being in effect. Empirical estimates of the rate of entry and exit that are based on a distributed lag or cost of adjustment framework but that are not based on explicit consideration of the underlying formation of expectations are susceptible to Lucas's well-known critique of econometric policy evaluation. This critique says that an unanticipated change in policy will alter the observed behavior of rational economic agents. In particular, this change will alter the distributed lag coefficients, which agents use implicitly in formulating future actions. These distributed lag coefficients, which the econometrician recovers when he estimates a distributed lag equation on time series data for one policy regime, will not be applicable under a different policy regime. The implicit rational expectations mechanism used by the economic agent is confounded in the estimates of the distributed lag coefficients much as the structural coefficients are confounded in reduced form estimation. The way around this problem is to model the parameters underlying this formulation explicitly. This is done in William A. Brock, "On Models of Expectations that Arise from Maximizing Behavior of Economic Agents Over Time," *Journal of Economic Theory* (December 1972): 348–376. Brock's paper does not contain a theory of the size distribution of business firms. Therefore, we use the related Jovanovic model referred to in note 53 below.

5. For a critical review of the role of enterpreneurs in economic theory, see William A. Baumol, "Entrepreneurship in Economic Theory," *American Economic Review* 58, no. 2 (May 1968): 63–69. The entrepreneur has been neglected by modern theory largely because this theory focuses on the general equilibrium for the economy. The importance of the entrepreneur lies in upsetting economic equilibria and setting the forces of change into motion. The entrepreneur plays a central role in the Austrian economic theory that focuses on the competitive process that continually transforms the economy over time. See our discussion in Chapter 2 on the Austrian theory.

6. Most economists view as entrepreneurs anyone who has control over the direction and operation of a business and bears risk as the residual claimant on business profits. This definition, which is due to Frank Knight (*Risk, Uncertainty and Profit* [New York: Houghton Mifflin, 1921]), obviously includes most small businessmen. This definition has been criticized for being overly broad and not capturing the essential features of the entrepreneur. The Austrians discussed in Chapter 2 view the entrepreneur as a spotter of opportunities. The entrepreneur can shift risks onto the capitalist (although he may choose not to). Consequently, risk bearing is not essential to entrepreneurship. We believe this argument has substantial merit. But the Schumpeterian definition is too narrow for our purposes. It would exclude many small businessmen who operate fairly standard businesses and cannot claim to have developed a new product or service, the hallmark of the entrepreneur. Moreover, we suspect there are insurmountable observational problems in determining whether a particular small businessman is a "spotter" or just a "risk bearer." Most empirical studies of entrepreneurs are plagued by arbitrary criteria for selecting the sample of entrepreneurs.

7. In William Miller, ed., *Men in Business* (New York: Harper & Row, 1962), see William Miller, "The Business Elite in Business Bureaucracies," and "The Recruitment of the Business Elite," and Frances Gregory and Irene Neu, "The American Industrial Elite in the 1870's." Also see Jocelyn Maynard Ghent and Frederic Cople Jaher, "The Chicago Business Elite: 1830–1930," *Business History Review* 50, no. 3 (Autumn 1976): 288–328.

8. Erik Dahmen, *Entrepreneurial Activity and the Development of Swedish Industry,* trans. Axel Leijonhufvud (Homewood, Ill.: Richard D. Irwin, 1970).

9. David McClelland and David Winter, *Motivating Economic Achievement* (New York: Free Press, 1969); D. F. Collins, D. G. Moore, and D. B. Unvalla, *The Enterprising Man* (East Lansing: Michigan State University Press, 1964); and Albert Shapero, "The Displaced Uncomfortable Entrepreneur," *Psychology Today* (November 1975): 83–88. The scientific validity of these studies, which are seldom based on random samples and often use ambiguous or overly inclusive definitions of an entrepreneur, is open to question. The regularities reported below, however, appear fairly robust across studies and therefore provide useful working hypotheses concerning who becomes an entrepreneur. See David S. Evans, *Entrepreneurial Choice and Success,* prepared for the Small Business Administration (Washington, D.C.: Small Business Administration, 1985) for tests of these hypotheses based on 1980 census data. We report some preliminary tests of these hypotheses in Chapter 6.

10. In a study of twenty-two R&D companies that were no more than ten years old, Henry Schrage found that the successful entrepreneur has "accurate perceptions of the market's response to his firm's products or services as well as a keen understanding of the determinants of his employee's morale." The most successful entrepreneurs (as measured by the profitability of their companies) were high in achievement motivation, low in power motivation, and high in total awareness of their business environment. See Henry Schrage, "The R&D Entrepreneur: Profile of Success," *Harvard Business Review* 43 (December 1965): 56–69.

11. Merril E. Douglas, "Relating Education to Entrepreneurial Success," *Business Horizons* 19 (December 1976): 40–44. He studied 153 entrepreneurs in the Atlanta metropolitan area who had been in business for at least three years and who had no more than thirty employees. He found that 40 percent of the college-educated entrepreneurs major in business or economics. Interestingly, he also found that there was no statistically significant correlation between education and success (as measured by firm size or sales growth; he had no data on profitability) among the entrepreneurs he studied. The most successful group of entrepreneurs (according to his criteria) were those with some college but without a degree.

12. William Copulsky and Herbert McNulty, *Entrepreneurship and the Corporation* (New York: AMACOM, 1974).

13. F. M. Scherer, *Industrial Market Structure and Economic Performance* (Boston: Houghton Mifflin, 1980), pp. 145–150.

14. These parameters reflect the experience of 369 companies on the 1953 Fortune 500 Industrials between 1954 and 1960.

15. See Chapter 2 for a discussion of these studies.

16. See Yuji Ijiri and Herbert A. Simon, *Skew Distributions and the Sizes of Business Firms* (Amsterdam: North Holland, 1977).

17. Yuji Ijiri and Herbert A. Simon, "Interpretations of Departures from the Pareto Curve Firm-Size Distributions," *Journal of Political Economy* 82 (March–April 1974).

18. Edwin Mansfield, "Entry, Gibrat's Law, Innovation, and the Growth of Firms," *American Economic Review* (December 1962): 1023–1051. Current research by one of the authors, however, finds that even after correcting for sample selection bias due to the exit of some firms, smaller firms have higher growth rates than larger firms. Moreover, growth rates are not independent of size even for larger firms. See David S. Evans, "Tests of Alternative Theories of Industry Evolution," unpublished manuscript, November 1985, and our discus-

sion of this work in Chapter 6. Evans also shows that Gibrat's Law fails for large manufacturing firms observed between 1976 and 1982.

19. Lucas, "Size Distribution."

20. Lucas assumes that managerial ability is exogenously given. Individuals cannot invest in acquiring managerial ability. We discuss this assumption later in this section.

21. Lucas assumes that individuals have access to a common constant-returns-to-scale production technology with which the "typical" manager can produce h(1,k) units of output. Individuals have differing managerial technologies that are characterized by diminishing returns to scale (or decreasing "span of control"). The production-cum-managerial technology is described by $q = ag[f(1,k)]$, where a is the ability level of the manager and g exhibits diminishing returns to scale. In our notation, $h(1,k) = g[f(1,k)]$.

22. This statement assumes, of course, that market demand is large at a price equal to the minimum average cost of the best manager.

23. $G(a)$ is by definition the fraction of individuals with $0 < a < a$.

24. See Lucas, "Size Distribution," pp. 514–517, for a detailed discussion.

25. In terms of note 21, Gibrat's Law implies that g( ) has the Cobb-Douglas form $A[h(l,k)\}^{-\beta}$, where $0 < \beta < 1$. If f(l,k) is a constant-return-to-scale Cobb-Douglas function, then the fact that g( ) is Cobb-Douglas with decreasing returns to scale implies that h(1,k) is a decreasing-returns-to-scale production function.

26. For evidence that the elasticity of substitution is less than unity see Robert E. Lucas, "Labor-Capital Substitution in U.S. Manufacturing," in *The Taxation of Income from Capital,* ed. A. C. Harberger and M. J. Bailey (Washington, D.C.: Brookings Institution, 1969), pp. 223–274. When the elasticity of substitution is greater than unity, average firm size is a decreasing function of the wealth of the economy.

27. He used three alternative definitions of firms: Dun and Bradstreet concerns for 1900–1970; Bureau of the Census firms for 1929–1963; and Bureau of the Census manufacturing firms for 1929–1963. Depending upon the series he used, the estimated elasticity ranged from 0.8 to 1.0 percent. See *ibid.*, tables 1 and 2, for further details.

28. Of course, the Lucas model is much too abstract and depends upon too many questionable assumptions for us to place much faith in this explanation. For example, the evidence in support of Gibrat's Law and in support of the elasticity of substitution between capital and labor being less than unity is less solid than we would like.

29. Since we have not said what x is at this point, we can make these assumptions concerning the partial derivatives of c with respect to x without any loss of generality.

30. Stanley Fischer and Rudiger Dornbusch, *Economics* (New York: McGraw-Hill, 1983), p. 255. Data were incomplete for firms with less than $10 million in assets, although the rate of return for reporting in this size category firms was 7.7 percent. See Chapter 2 for further discussion of the evidence on this relationship between profitability and firm size; like most empirical evidence in industrial organization, this evidence is more dubious than most economists, including ourselves, would like.

31. See Chapter 2 for further discussion of evidence on this well-documented relationship.

32. See Table 2.14.

33. This may be stretching our case a bit. The second regularity mentioned above says that exits and entrants are more likely to be small—a probabilistic relationship that our deterministic model cannot faithfully reproduce—not that they are all small.

34. On this point, see Edward Prescott and R. Vischer, "Organization Capital," *Journal of Political Economy* 88, no. 3 (June 1980): pp. 446–461.

35. Let x′ index managerial ability in some other industry. Then across individuals in the population $Cov(x,x') = 0$.

36. Let us note the importance of this implication for the applications of this model in the

remaining chapters. The basic conclusion of Chapter 4 is that it is optimal to exempt businesses with larger values of x under certain circumstances. This result holds (although not necessarily always to the same degree) as long as average costs are positively correlated with x. In order to derive any policy implications from this result there must be some correlation between x and observable quantities. Given the correlation between rates of return, business failures, and size, and given the increasing exemption of small businesses from regulations, the case where there is a negative correlation between x and output is of considerable interest for both economists and policy makers. It is straightforward to carry out the analysis when x depends on a number of variables. For example, the Jovanovic model discussed below suggests that x is correlated with the output, age, and profit history of a business.

37. It is important in this regard to distinguish between managers of production technologies and managers of portfolios of financial assets. We suspect there is substantial movement of largely financial managers between conglomerates that cover different sets of industries. There is little evidence, however, that conglomerate mergers yield synergies between the merged firms and thereby fundamentally alter the basic production technologies of these firms. Many conglomerates decentralize by shifting administrative responsibilities and financial risk onto the managers of production technologies. See R. Vancil, *Decentralization: Managerial Ambiquity by Design* (Homewood, Ill.: Dow Jones-Irwin, 1978). Thus, it seems more sensible to identify firms with production technologies themselves rather than with the institutions having financial claims over the returns generated by these production technologies or with the institutions that have ultimate legal control over the assets used by these production technologies.

38. Note that the output supply function and the maximum profit function now have w as an argument. We are implicitly assuming here that capital is supplied to the industry perfectly elastically at rental rate r.

39. Workers bear risk over their life cycle as well. An individual beginning his career is uncertain about how quickly he will advance and thus about the income stream he will receive in the future. But casual observation suggests that this risk is less severe than that for an entrepreneur. Moreover, the worker is certain of the wage he will receive for an hour of labor, whereas the entrepreneur is less certain of the profit he will retain from an hour of entrepreneurship.

40. This model was developed by Kihlstrom and Laffont, "General Equilibrium."

41. U_I and $U_{II} \leq 0$ exist and are continuous. Marginal utility is positive and decreasing so that $U_{II} \leq 0$.

42. Formally, the absolute risk aversion measure $r(I, \rho) = -U_{II}/U_I$ is nondecreasing in ρ.

43. See the discussion earlier in this chapter about the characteristics of entrepreneurs.

44. In order to prevent the possibility of bankruptcy, Kihlstrom and Laffont assume that individuals begin with A units of income and are constrained to hire fewer than A/w workers.

45. One special case where the random variable would affect output and the marginal product of labor in the same way is where output is multiplicative in the random variable, $f(1,v) = vh(1)$.

46. See Kihlstrom and Laffont, "General Equilibrium," theorem 4, p. 730, for the precise conditions under which this result holds.

47. The decrease in the demand for workers holds only when the previous proposition holds.

48. The equilibrium is inefficient in the sense that a benevolent social dictator could select an allocation of individuals and a distribution of income under which at least one individual would be better off and no individual would be worse off than under the equilibrium allocation.

49. This inefficiency would not arise if all individuals were indifferent to risk.

50. Kihlstrom and Laffont consider several special cases. When all individuals have the same degree of risk aversion it is possible to show that there are too many enterpreneurs in equilibrium. A special case where this occurs is when the production technology exhibits constant returns to scale. In this case it is optimal to have only one firm. But the desire of individuals to avoid risk will lead to the creation of more than one firm. When all individuals are indifferent to risk it is possible to show that there will be the correct number of entrepreneurs in equilibrium. See Kihlstrom and Laffont, "General Equilibrium," pp. 740–743.

51. In the model discussed above, the fixed cost is the w that the entrepreneur must forgo when he entrepreneurs instead of works.

52. In reality stock markets are not entirely efficient because entrepreneurs differ in their abilities and because investors do not have perfect information concerning these abilities. Moreover, because there are substantial fixed costs in floating stock it is difficult for entrepreneurs running small firms to diversify their risk through a stock sale.

53. Boyan Jovanovic, "Selection and Evolution of Industry," *Econometrica* 50, no. 3 (May 1982): 649–670.

54. Jovanovic assumes that individuals use Bayes' Law to update their forecasts of their abilities. It is straightforward, however, to extend his model to cases where individuals use some other learning process.

55. We abstract here from situations in which one entrepreneur gets a head start perhaps because he invented the product upon which the industry is based. For the sake of simplicity we concentrate on an industry that perhaps comes into being because of new demand for a product produced with existing technology (a taste change) or because of a technology not available to all producers has been developed for producing a new product like the personal computer.

56. With a Bayesian learning process, people form a new estimate, roughly speaking, by averaging their estimate from last period and an estimate based on an observation for this period. The estimate based on an actual observation for this period is formed by inverting the cost function and solving for ability.

57. See Jovanovic, "Selection and Evolution," for the Bayesian formula for this new estimate.

58. This assumption is unrealistic and could, at the price of considerable technical complexity, be relaxed so that the supply of potential entrepreneurs is more inelastic or so that individuals do not start with a common estimate of their abilities.

59. The concavity of $c(q,x)$ in x is sufficient but not necessary.

60. A necessary but not sufficient condition for this is that $c(q,x)$ is convex in x.

61. We have not, however, worked out this equilibration process rigorously.

62. This is a consequence of some simple statistical principles; see Jovanovic, "Selection and Evolution," for proof. Evans, "Industry Evolution," finds that several implications of Jovanovic's model are consistent with the data for smaller, entrepreneurial-based firms: firm growth rates decrease with firm age; the probability of firm failure decreases firm size and age; and the variability of firm growth rates decreases with firm age. Firm growth increases with firm age for larger firms. See Chapter 6 for further discussion.

63. As measured by the Herfindhal Index or the Gini Coefficient.

64. Executive Office of the President, *The State of Small Business* (Washington, D.C.: Government Printing Office, March 1982), p. 133.

65. For example, Manville Corporation has sought shelter under the bankruptcy laws from workers who claimed to have suffered from asbestos exposure.

66. We recognize that policy makers sometimes pay little heed to the economic approach to regulation. See Steven J. Kelman, "Economic Incentives and Environmental Policy: Politics, Ideology, and Philosophy," pp. 291–332, in *Incentives for Environmental Protection,* ed. Thomas Schelling (Cambridge: MIT Press, 1983).

67. We discuss this situation in great detail in Chapter 4.

68. There are few costs that are purely fixed or purely variable. Nevertheless, this taxonomy provides a useful way to examine the differential impact of regulations across business sizes.

69. Whether this situation actually occurs depends upon the price demand, cost, and regulatory situation of the industry and upon the distribution of managerial efficiency for the industry. In the first variant of Lucas's model the supply of workers and managers is perfectly elastic. Because the imposition of regulations will not alter the wage rate (by assumption), larger businesses are less likely to gain from the imposition of regulations with heavy fixed costs.

70. Normal profit here is analogous to the competitive rate of return on capital in textbook models.

71. No new considerations enter with the Jovanovic's model. We therefore leave it to the reader to work out the impact of a profits tax on industry evolution in the Jovanovic model.

72. That is, at given p and w, managers with $x < x < z$ withdraw, where z is the marginal manager before the tax ($\pi = w$) and x' is the marginal manager after the tax ($(1 - t)\,\pi' = w$).

73. Inexperienced and hence marginal managers must expect to just break even in equilibrium because if they expected to make money they would all enter and bid price down and if they expected to lose money marginal managers would exit and bid price up. At an equilibrium price and managerial cutoff level, the marginal inexperienced manager must expect to just break even.

74. We distinguish here among barriers to entry such as scale economies that do not necessarily decrease efficiency and barriers to entry in which bigger firms can produce more efficiently than smaller firms can and barriers to entry such as government entry restrictions (taxi markets in most cities, for example) that by artificially restricting competition decrease efficiency. See C. C. Von Weisacker, "Barriers to Entry," *Bell Journal of Economics* 11 (Autumn 1980): 399–420.

75. We conjecture that many other industries dominated by small firms such as automobile repair and pharmacies are much less competitive than they might appear on first inspection. These industries consist of many small local markets that are largely insulated from one another.

Chapter 4

1. For an extensive discussion of tiering, see U.S. Regulatory Council, *Tiering Regulations: A Practical Guide* (Washington, D.C.: U.S. Regulatory Council, March 1981).

2. See Paul R. Verkuil, "A Critical Guide to the Regulatory Flexibility Act," *Duke Law Journal* (April 1982): 225.

3. See U. S. Regulatory Council, *Tiering,* for forty-three examples of tiering. Also see Leah Hertz, *In Search of a Small Business Definition* (Washington, D.C.: University Press of America, 1982), for further examples in this and other countries.

4. 5 U.S.C. 601–612 (Supp. IV 1980).

5. The RFA applies to small public institutions (such as small colleges) and small municipalities as well as to small businesses.

6. For proposed rules, agencies (1) must either certify that the rule will not have a

significant impact on small businesses or prepare a regulatory flexibility analysis that examines the benefits and costs of applying the rule to small businesses and (2) must hold hearings on the effect of the rule on small businesses. Agencies must review the impact of existing rules on small businesses within ten years of the passage of the act (President Reagan has directed agencies to complete these reviews within five years). Progress reports on these reviews have been published since 1981 in the April and October issues of the *Federal Register* as part of the *Unified Agenda of Federal Regulations.*

7. See Chapter 5 for further discussion of the impact of fixed compliance costs on smaller businesses.

8. Federal Home Loan Bank Board, "Industry Reporting Requirements: Benefits or Burden?" *Federal Home Loan Bank Board Journal* (March 1977): 7–12. See Chapter 5 below for details.

9. Arthur Andersen & Co., *Cost of Government Regulation: Study for the Business Roundtable* (Chicago: Arthur Andersen & Co., March 1979). See Chapter 5 below for details.

10. Also see Todd Morrison, *Economies of Scale in Regulatory Compliance: Evidence of the Differential Impacts of Regulation by Firm Size*. Prepared by Jack Faucett Associates for the Small Business Administration (Washington, D.C.: Office of Advocacy, Small Business Administration, December 1984). The prevalence of tiering may explain the lack of reliable evidence that federal regulations have had a widespread disparate impact on smaller firms. See Chapter 5 for a critical review of studies of scale economies in regulatory compliance. In addition to explicit tiering, regulatory agencies may also tacitly tier regulations by skewing monitoring and enforcement efforts toward large businesses.

11. The model we use for most of this chapter is the first version of Lucas's model, where the supply of labor is perfectly elastic. See our discussion of the Lucas Model in Chapter 3.

12. Society would like these entrepreneurs to produce at the point where social marginal cost equals price. But in order to maximize private profit these entrepreneurs produce at the point where private marginal cost equals price. The latter output level is higher than the former.

13. And of course, most regulatory schemes entail similar requirements.

14. The sequel considers the more general case where administrative costs are a weakly increasing function of the tax rate and the tax burden.

15. Disregard the asterisks in front of some entries for the time being. As we explain below, these asterisks identify businesses that society would like to see closed down.

16. It is also difficult to measure the other parameters of the model, such as the cost structure of the firm, the social cost of the externality, and the relationship between administrative costs and taxes, but these measurement problems afflict the design of all regulatory schemes and are not unique to the particular scheme we propose.

17. Let us put this assumption in more practical terms. Production costs vary across firms. It would be prohibitively expensive for regulators to estimate the cost structure for every firm. But perhaps regulators could estimate the cost structure for a sample of firms in the industry and from these estimates infer the distribution of costs across the population of firms. The estimated distribution of costs provides sufficient information for implementing the tax schedule discussed below.

18. Information is imperfect here, of course, because we do not know each entrepreneur's ability level.

19. This exemption level is found by calculating the ability exemption level from the second line of (4.15) and calculating the output that an entrepreneur with an ability just equal to the cutoff level would produce from (4.2).

20. $\$20 \times 33 - \$2 \times 0.1 \times 33^2 - \$40 - \$10 = \$392$.

21. Regulators would like to exempt entrepreneurs with $x \leq .15$.

22. This problem is not a mere abstraction. As discussed in a later section, a Department of Energy subsidy program for small refineries encouraged the construction of inefficiently small refineries that could take advantage of the subsidy.

23. By flat-rate tax we mean that the firm pays the same tax rate on all units of output. The section on optimal regulation with imperfect information considers the case where the tax rate varies with output.

24. D. Spulber, "Spatial Nonlinear Pricing," *American Economic Review* 71, no. 5 (December 1981): 923–933.

25. Readers who are more interested in applications than in technical details may wish to proceed directly to the application and summary sections at the end of this chapter.

26. See Chapter 2 for a discussion of the assumptions behind this model.

27. A. Mitchell Polinsky and Steven Shavell, "Pigouvian Taxation with Administrative Costs," *Journal of Public Economics* 19, no. 3 (December 1982): 385–390 show that the optimal flat tax is less (greater) than the flat tax of s when the fixed administrative cost is borne solely by the firm (government). Unlike our analysis, they do not entertain nonlinear taxes and therefore do not obtain a tax schedule that is optimal within this broader class. As we show below, the optimal nonlinear tax schedule generally involves an exemption for smaller businesses, a rate that may increase with business size, and a license fee (or other mechanism) to discourage inefficient entry.

28. More generally, F and R are designed to capture any regulatory costs that are independent of business size or the level of emissions. For example, the cost of installing certain emission control equipment required by regulators may be roughly independent of firm size and the cost of government inspections and prosecutions may be independent of the level of emissions involved.

29. Note that Problem 1 is analogous to Spulber's problem of a spatial monopolist who price discriminates according to location. See Spulber, "Spatial Nonlinear Pricing."

30. If regulators cannot use lump-sum taxes or subsidies in designing the tax schedule t(a), they must take into account the incentive for inefficient entry.

31. It is straightforward but tedious to establish from primitive concepts that these conditions must hold. We assume these conditions directly rather than throwing a mess of derivatives at the reader.

32. For proofs of this and subsequent propositions, see William A. Brock and David S. Evans, "The Economics of Regulatory Tiering," *Rand Journal of Economics* 16, no. 3 (Fall 1985): 398–409.

33. The assumptions concerning the profit function imply that the marginal physical product of the externality input is larger and decreases less rapidly with increases in the externality input for more able managers.

34. Monotonicity of J(t(a),a) is needed for this result because if J falls for $a > a^*$, the license fee of L on all firms will drive socially efficient firms out of business when $J(t(a^*),a^*) > J(t(a),a)$. Also note that if entrepreneurial ability is perfectly observable then regulators could prohibit entry by inefficient firms ($a < a^*$). Whether the license fee is preferable to entry prohibition depends upon the administrative cost of the two alternatives. It is straightforward and natural to introduce administrative costs that are borne at both the government and the firm level for lump-sum charges. But in order to keep our problem notationally manageable, we shall continue to assume that the administrative costs for the license fee are zero.

35. There may, of course, be many situations when it is desirable to exempt some small businesses from the tax but not the license fee. The optimal tax rate $t^*(a)$ may be zero for some a.

36. W. P. Heller and K. Shell, "On Optimal Taxation with Costly Administration," *American Economic Review* 61, no.2 (May 1974): 338–345.

37. Or perhaps the regulator can observe magnitudes such as the output of the firm or the use of externality-causing inputs that are closely correlated with the output of externalities.

38. See James Mirrlees, "An Exploration in the Theory of Optimal Income Taxation," *Review of Economic Studies* 38, no. 3 (1971): 175–208; James Mirrlees, "Optimal Tax Theory: A Synthesis," *Journal of Public Economics* (1976): 327–358; and E. Maskin and J. Riley, "Income v. Leisure Taxes," Discussion Paper no. 174 (Los Angeles: Department of Economics, University of California at Los Angeles, August 1980).

39. See Spulber, "Spatial Nonlinear Pricing."

40. Y′ denotes the first derivative of Y throughout.

41. A discussion of the solution technique may be found in our technical paper, William A. Brock and David S. Evans, "Optimal Regulatory Design with Heterogeneous Firms and Administrative Costs," SSRI Working Paper (Madison, Wisc.: Social Systems Research Institute, December 1983).

42. See, for example, E. Joeres and M. David, "Buying a Better Environment: Cost-Effective Regulation Through Permit Trading," and M. David and E. Joeres, "Flexibility with Quality: Implementation of Transferable Permits for Wisconsin Rivers," unpublished mss. (Madison: Department of Economics, University of Wisconsin at Madison, July 1983).

43. Whether the regulatory requirements should be strictly progressive depends upon the precise relationship between administrative costs and regulatory requirements and upon the regulatory instrument (e.g., ability-specific flat taxes, multipart tariffs, performance requirements, marketable permits) used by regulators.

44. Tiered regulations as well as untiered regulations may tacitly vary regulatory requirements across firm sizes by varying the probability of enforcement. See, for example, Carol Adaire Jones, "Agency Enforcement and Company Compliance Behavior: An Empirical Study of the OSHA Asbestos Standard" (Cambridge: Harvard School of Public Health [1983]).

45. Table 4.2 is based on forty-three examples of tiering compiled by the U.S. Regulatory Council, *Tiering,* from federal programs in existence prior to 1981; fourteen of the forty-three examples either did not apply to small businesses or were under consideration rather than actually implemented.

46. Our schemes achieve the largest social surplus possible under the assumptions we made. Other schemes necessarily achieve lower social surplus.

47. Our deduction-laden progressive income tax system imposes enormous administrative costs on taxpayers as well as on the Internal Revenue Service. A flat-tax system with no deductions could almost surely raise the same tax revenues at a lower social cost.

48. U.S. Regulatory Council, *Tiering,* pp. 20–21.

49. See Evans, *Regulation, Fixed Costs, and the Size Distribution of Businesses* (Ph.D. dissertation, University of Chicago, 1983), for a formal statement of the maximization problem for the first scheme.

50. This proposition assumes that there are no pure fixed regulatory costs imposed on the firm and that administrative costs are zero for the government.

51. This proposition may be seen by noting that the externalities drag wages and profits down. In the extreme case of fixed proportions in production this effect may be strong enough that the community would rather have no regulation at all. We assume that no other community is injured.

52. An example is *ex ante* free entry followed by *ex post* tacit collusion on price. Some professions may fit this model where professional ethics prevent price-cutting competition

but cannot prevent price-cutting in other dimensions such as entry. See William A. Brock and José A. Scheinkman, *Review of Economic Studies* 27, no. 3 (July 1985): 371–382.

Chapter 5

1. Murray Weidenbaum, *The Future of Business Regulation* (New York: AMACOM, 1979), p. 151.

2. Robert E. Berney, "The Cost of Government Regulation for Small Businesses: An Update" (Unpublished paper, September 1980).

3. Executive Office of the President, *The State of Small Business: A Report of the President* (Washington, D.C.: Government Printing Office, March 1982).

4. *Ibid*. p. 151, notes, "The fact that smaller businesses spread these [regulatory] burdens across a smaller sales base eventually led to the conclusion that these disproportionate economic burdens on small business were key contributors to the decline in productivity, competition, innovation, and the relative market shares of small business."

5. P.L. 96-354, September 19, 1980, 5 U.S.C. 601. See Paul Verkuil, "A Critical Guide to the Regulatory Flexibility Act," *Duke Law Journal* (April 1982): 2

6. Executive Office of the President, *The State of Small Business*, p. 155.

7. B. Peter Pashigian, "A Theory of Prevention and Legal Defence with an Application to the Legal Costs of Companies," *Journal of Law and Economics* (October 1982): 247–270.

8. See our discussion in Chapter 3.

9. The trucking industry has experienced both increased entry by smaller firms and some consolidation of larger firms. Regulation of the banking industry has led primarily to mergers that have consolidated local banks into larger regional banks. See Bruce D. Phillips, "The Effect of Industry Deregulation on the Small Business Sector." Presented at the annual meeting of the National Association of Business Economists, Atlanta, Georgia, September 1984.

10. Arthur D. Little, *The Impact of Premanufacture Notification Requirements on the Chemical Industry,* prepared for the Environmental Protection Agency (Cambridge: Arthur D. Little, 1979). Charles River Associates, *The Impact of OSHA Lead Standards on the Lead Industry,* prepared for the Lead Industries Association (Boston: Charles River Associates, 1978). Also see Jack Faucett Associates, *Economies of Scale in Regulatory Compliance: Evidence of the Differential Impacts of Regulation by Firm Size,* prepared for Small Business Administration (Washington, D.C.: Small Business Administration, November 1984) for an excellent survey of a number of such *ex ante* studies.

11. Booz-Allen & Hamilton, *Impact of Environmental Regulations on Small Business* (Bethesda, Md.: Booz-Allen & Hamilton, May 24, 1982).

12. B. Peter Pashigian, "The Effect of Environmental Regulation on Optimal Plant Size and Factor Shares," *Journal of Law and Economics* (April 1984): pp. 1–22.

13. Roland J. Cole and Paul Sommers, *The Impact of Government Regulations on Small Business in Washington State* (Seattle: Battelle Human Affairs Research Center, 1978), and *Complying with Government Requirements: The Costs to Small and Larger Businesses* (Seattle: Battelle Human Affairs Research Center, 1981).

14. Booz-Allen & Hamilton, *Impact,* p. III–5.

15. *Ibid.*, p. III–6.

16. Booz-Allen ranked industries by capital costs of complying with environmental regulations. It is useful to compare these industries with those chosen by Pashigian, reported in Table 5.6, on the basis of operating costs of complying with environmental regulations. Only

six industries are the same on both lists of heavily regulated industries. Since the major impact of environmental regulations was to force firms to purchase pollution control equipment and since these capital investments are the most likely source of scale economies in compliance, the Booz-Allen ranking appears more sensible than the Pashigian ranking.

17. Wayne B. Gray, "The Impact of OSHA and EPA Regulation in Productivity." NBER Working Paper no. 1405 (Cambridge: National Bureau of Economic Research, July 3, 1984), Table 2.1.

18. Booz-Allen argues that environmental regulations increased the demand for capital and thereby created a "capital shortage" that hurt all firms. This argument is not convincing. See Booz-Allen, p. IV-5.

19. It is important to recognize that Pashigian analyzes establishment data, not company data. Larger companies typically own several establishments. The implication of Pashigian's analysis for the size distribution of companies is highly problematic. We cannot know from his analysis, for example, whether small establishments owned by small single-establishment companies have been affected in the same way as small establishments owned by large multi-establishment companies. The former but perhaps not the latter may have received tacit or explicit exemptions from the regulations. Evidence reported in the next chapter on the average pollution abatement cost incurred by single-unit and multiunit establishments indicates that the average pollution abatement cost for establishments operated by single-establishment companies is generally less than the average pollution abatement cost for establishments operated by multiestablishment companies.

20. This list was constructed by rank ordering the ratio of pollution abatement costs to value added for the industries in his sample for the years 1974–1978.

21. The inclusion of these other variables made the coefficient of the regulatory dummy variable less negative and less statistically significant in the regressions for small plants.

22. Pashigian did not control for changes in the size of the market in these regressions. Pashigian recognizes in the appendix to his paper that increases in the size of the market may decrease the market share of small firms as small firms expand to meet increased demand. According to data reported in Table 4 of Pashigian, *op. cit.*, heavily regulated industries were growing more rapidly than lightly regulated industries between 1972 and 1977 (84.5 percent versus 64.1 percent using industry value added). Therefore differential growth in demand rather than the imposition of regulations may explain Pashigian's finding.

23. Gray, "The Impact of OSHA and EPA."

24. See C. Radhakrishna Rao, *Linear Statistical Inference and Its Applications*, 2nd ed. (New York: John Wiley & Sons, 1973), pp. 463–464.

25. His *Journal of Law and Economics* article uses number of establishments but his longer working paper also uses value added.

26. An alternative approach for obtaining valid test statistics in the face of heteroskedastic disturbances in a regression framework is given by Halbert White, "A Heteroskedasticity-Consistent Covariance Matrix Estimator and a Direct Test for Heteroskedasticity," *Econometrica* (May 1980): 817–828.

27. Pashigian, "The Effect of Environmental Regulations," Table 10, p. 21.

28. Pashigian, *ibid.*, p. 26.

29. Pashigian also used labor's share in value added as a dependent variable in order to determine whether regulations increased the capital-intensity of establishments. He also includes this variable as a regressor in the number of establishments and average establishment size regressions. If the disturbance term in the labor share equation is correlated with the disturbance term in the number of establishments and average establishment size equations, as seems plausible, the estimates of the latter two equations, which include labor

share as a regressor, will suffer from simultaneous equations bias. Little credence should therefore be placed in the estimates reported in the fourth and sixth columns of Table 5.10.

30. Pashigian excludes the industry size variable from the average plant size regression. This exclusion is unfortunate since increases in industry demand are met by the expansion of existing plants. Since heavily regulated industries grew more rapidly than lightly regulated industries over the sample period Pashigian examines, his finding that increases in plant size were positively correlated with high levels of regulatory costs may be spurious.

31. Average pollution abatement costs are deflated by industry value added.

32. The level of pollution abatement cost in 1977 would be the same as the change in pollution abatement costs between 1972 and 1977 if costs were zero in 1972. But such is not the case. State and federal environmental controls as well as voluntary controls were in place well before 1972. Pollution abatement operating costs were $2,235.3 million in 1973 and $5,425 million in 1977 for all industries. See U.S. Bureau of the Census, *Pollution Abatement Costs and Expenditures* (Washington, D.C.: Government Printing Office, 1973 and 1977).

33. See the appendix to Pashigian's "The Effect of Environmental Regulations."

34. Pashigian, *ibid.*, p. 27.

35. Arthur Andersen, *Analysis of Regulatory Costs*, p. 13.

36. *Ibid.*, p. 9.

37. Cole and Sommers, *Costs of Compliance*.

38. See the discussion of this statistical problem in the section of this chapter concerning Pashigian's study.

39. See Cole and Sommers, *Complying with Government Requirements*.

40. Peter Linneman, "The Effects of Consumer Safety Standards: The 1973 Mattress Flammability Standard," *Journal of Law and Economics* (October 1980): 461–479.

41. George R. Neumann and Jon P. Nelson, "Safety Regulation and Firm Size: Effects of the Coal Mine Health and Safety Act of 1969," *Journal of Law and Economics* (October 1982): 183–199.

42. Frank Crowne, "Industry Reporting Requirements: Benefits or Burden?" *Federal Home Loan Bank Board Journal* (March 1977): 7–12; Arthur Andersen, *Cost of Government Regulation;* and Bruce D. Phillips and William Knight, "The Davis-Bacon Act Reconsidered: A "New" Small Business Tax," in *Proceedings* (1982 Small Business Research Conference, Bentley College, Waltham, Mass., March 1982), pp. 330–352.

43. The survey was distributed in the ABC's March 19, 1981, newsletter. The ABC is a trade association of construction firms.

44. See Phillips and Knight, "Davis-Bacon Act" pp. 5–6, for further details. Firms with five hundred or more employees are underrepresented in the survey data. Only 0.5 percent of the respondents had five hundred or more employeees, while 15.4 of the construction firms listed on Dun and Bradstreet had five hundred or more employees.

45. A General Accounting Office study found that in 1977 the Davis-Bacon Act imposed costs of $200 million on private construction firms. Of this amount, $190 million was for increased labor cost and $10 million was for administrative costs. Therefore, there appear to be scale economies in the most expensive portion of the program. See U.S. General Accounting Office, "The Davis-Bacon Act Should Be Repealed" (Washington, D.C.: Government Printing Office, 1979).

46. The original purpose of the act was to discourage the bidding down of wage rates on construction contracts. The way in which government administrators of the act have defined "prevailing wages" in recent years has tended to favor unionized commercial contractors, whose wages are generally higher than those of smaller, typically nonunionized, construction companies.

47. Arthur Andersen, *Cost of Government Regulation,* p. 107. Unfortunately, they do not provide a cost breakdown by firm size.

48. Pashigian controlled for industry size in examining average business size but not in examining the small business share.

49. Nor do they provide enough data for other researchers to do so.

50. As mentioned earlier, Pashigian used an erroneous testing procedure in rejecting this hypothesis.

51. Linneman and Knight and Phillips relied on survey data collected by other researchers and had no control over sample design or response rates.

52. In addition, responding firms may tend to exaggerate their regulatory costs in order to influence policy makers.

53. In principle it is possible to test and correct for selectivity bias using the procedure outlined by James J. Heckman, "The Common Structure of Statistical Models of Truncation, Sample Selection, and Limited Dependent Variables and a Simple Estimator for Such Models," *Annals of Economic and Social Measurement,* no. 5 (1976): 475–492. The procedure requires sufficient information on both respondents and nonrespondents to predict the probability that a typical firm in the industry will respond.

Chapter 6

1. Our objective in reporting preliminary results here is to illustrate how the models discussed in Chapter 3 together with the data sources we describe can be used to investigate a number of questions concerning entrepreneurs and small businesses. This chapter is written mainly for our fellow researchers. The nontechnical reader will find this chapter rough going and may wish to proceed directly to our concluding chapter.

2. For extensions and refinements, see David S. Evans, "Tests of Alternative Theories of Industry Evolution," unpublished manuscript, November 1985.

3. See David S. Evans, *Entrepreneurial Choice and Success* (Washington, D.C.: Office of Advocacy, Small Business Administration, October 1984) for further details.

4. For extensions and refinements, see David S. Evans, "The Cost of Complying with Environmental Regulations across Plant and Firm Sizes in the Manufacturing Industries," unpublished manuscript, September 1985.

5. Boyan Jovanovic, "Selection and Evolution of Industry," *Econometrica* (May 1982): 649–670.

6. See Jovanovic, *ibid.,* for proof.

7. See Jovanovic, *ibid,* for proofs of these two propositions.

8. Let $\dot{q}$, $\dot{p}$, and $\dot{a}$ denote logarithmic changes between two time periods in firm output, industry price, and a vector of factor prices and shift variables in the cost function $c(q;\dot{a})$ respectively. Then the structural model is

$$\dot{q}_{it} = \delta[\dot{p}_t] - \delta[\beta\dot{a}_t] + \lambda T + u_{it}$$

where T denotes the cohort to which the firm belongs and the variance of the u_{it} varies by cohort. This model can be estimated with the kind of panel data discussed below.

9. Ignore selectivity bias issues for the time being.

10. We attempted to test alternative functional forms for this expansion by regressing the dependent variable in the equation (6.2) against Box-Cox transforms of the levels, squares, and cross products of age and size but failed to achieve convergence in the likelihood function. We tested the double-log specification in equation (6.2) against a semi-log specifica-

tion (where the exogenous variables are measured in levels). The mean square error for the double-log specification was slightly lower than the mean square error for the semi-log specification. Apparently the likelihood function is relatively flat with respect to the Box-Cox transform parameter. Results for the semi-log equation were similar to the results for the double-log equation.

11. See Executive Office of the President, *The State of Small Business: 1983* (Washington, D.C.: Government Printing Office, 1984), pp. 405–438 for further details.

12. Most firms have employment data on a quarterly basis for FICA reporting whereas sales data are often available on a yearly basis. Consequently, the employment data reported to Dun and Bradstreet interviewers are more likely to be up to date and accurate than are the sales data.

13. Results based on sales are similar to those based on employment.

14. For 1980, the data set contains 4 million firms from all industries whereas the Internal Revenue Service lists 13.3 firms filing tax returns. The breakdowns by sales size are: $1 million or more–0.5 million firms for SBA and 0.5 million firms for IRS; $100,000–$999,999–2.1 vs. 2.3; $25,000–$99,999–1.1 vs. 2.7; and $0–$25,000–0.25 vs. 7.8. Most firms with sales of under $100,000 do not have employees other than the owner; many are not full-time concerns. See *Small Business,* p. 417 for further details.

15. Results are similar, however, when all firms are included.

16. The age of the data is reported in three-month intervals.

17. The lognormal approximation overpredicts that fraction of firms in the tail of the distribution.

18. The average length of time between observations was 5.8 years with a standard deviation of 0.5 years.

19. The growth rate equals the expression in (6.3).

20. An exit may mean that the firm failed, dissolved, or merged with another firm.

21. Empirical work by Stephen Hymer and B. Peter Pashigian, "Firm Size and Rate of Growth," *Journal of Political Economy* (April 1962): 556–569 and Edwin Mansfield, "Entry, Gibrat's Law, Innovation, and the Growth of Firms," *American Economic Review* (December 1962): 1031–1051 finds that smaller firms have a higher variance of growth rates. Theoretical work by Jovanovic suggests that younger firms have a higher variance of growth rates. See Chapters 2 and 3 for further discussion.

22. The procedure suggested by White involves regressing the squared residuals from the estimated equation 6.2 against the cross products of the exogenous variables in 6.2 and then testing whether the coefficients of these variables are jointly zero. The x^2-statistic was 252.34 leading to rejection of the null hypothesis of homoskedasticity at the .0001 level of statistical significance. See Halbert White, "A Heteroskedasticity Consistent Covariance Matrix Estimator and a Direct Test for Heteroskedasticity," *Econometrica* (May 1980): 817–830.

23. The Jovanovic model with the two assumptions discussed earlier implies just such a relationship.

24. For the size-weighting scheme, the R^2 of the regression was .00074 with six independent variables giving us a test statistic of 10.68 compared to a critical level of 16.81 at the .01 level. It is, however, barely possible to reject the null hypothesis at the .05 percent level of statistical significance which has a critical level of 10.64. The important point to note here is that the deviations of the residuals from homoskedasticity are of a trivial magnitude when the weighting scheme is used. Such trivial deviations, even if statistically significant, will not seriously bias the estimated standard errors. Furthermore, given the size of the sample used in this study, the level of statistical significance for rejecting a hypothesis should be larger than 0.05.

25. Hymer and Pashigian and Mansfield use a regression framework similar to the one used in this paper to test Gibrat's Law. Although both sets of authors recognize that the variance of firm growth rates varies systematically with firm size, their regression estimates assume homoskedastic disturbances. Their reported test statistics are therefore biased. (Hymer and Pashigian recognize this bias but do not correct for it.) See Hymer and Pashigian, "Firm Size and Rate of Growth," and Mansfield, "Entry, Gibrat's Law, Innovation, and the Growth of Firms."

26. James Heckman, "Sample Selection Bias as a Specification Error," *Econometrica* (February 1979): 153–161.

27. Because of software limitations, the probit estimation and selectivity correction were performed for a sample of approximately 11,000 firms drawn randomly from the sample discussed above. Note that equation (6.2) is weighted by the square root of employment size in both stages of the estimation. See Evans, "Tests of Alternative Theories" for more detailed estimates and discussion.

28. The generalized least squares estimate of the coefficient of the Mill's ratio (denoted by lambda in Table 6.5) is 6.85 with a standard error of 4.22. The estimated correlation of the disturbance term in the growth equation with the disturbance term in the probit of survival equation is 0.1760. The fact that the estimated correlation coefficient is positive implies, as one would expect, that firms that have unusually high growth rates (after controlling for their size and age) have an unusually high probability of survival (after controlling for their size and age). The fact that this correlation is small and statistically insignificant suggests that there is little correlation between unobservable variables that lead to high growth and unobservable variables that cause a high likelihood of survival.

29. It is also possible to reject the hypotheses that firm growth is independent of firm size for firms in the same age cohort and for mature firms. See Evans, "Tests of Alternative Theories" for details.

30. These estimates were obtained by regressing an estimate of the variance of the log firm growth rate against the same variables used in the growth equation. The estimate of the variance was obtained from employment data for 1976, 1978, 1980, and 1982 which yields three observations from which to calculate the variance of growth for each firm. No correction was made for selection bias in securing the regression estimates. Estimates are available from the second author upon request.

31. See Evans, "Tests of Alternative Theories" for discusssion of possible objection to these results. He shows that the results hold when growth is measured by sales rather than employment and when the time period 1969–1974 rather than 1976–1982 is considered.

32. Based on 1981 data for employed workers from U.S. Bureau of the Census, *Statistical Abstract of the United States: 1982–83* (Washington, D.C.: Government Printing Office, 1982), p. 385.

33. There were somewhat more than 16 million businesses in 1981, including 12 million sole proprietorships. Many of these businesses are either not active or are operated on a part-time basis by people who are primarily wage earners. See *ibid.*, p. 529).

34. See our discussion of entrepreneurs in Chapter 3.

35. The major studies in these other disciplines are reviewed below.

36. See our discussion of the Lucas and Kihlstrom and Laffont models in Chapter 3.

37. Robert Lucas, "On the Size Distribution of Business Firms," *Bell Journal of Economics*, (August 1978): 508–523.

38. Richard Kihlstrom and Jean-Jacques Laffont, "A General Equilibrium Entrepreneurial Theory of Firm Formation Based on Risk Aversion," *Journal of Politial Economy* (August 1979): 719–748 and S. Kanbur, "Of Risk Taking and the Personal Distribution of Income," *Journal of Political Economy* (October 1979): 769–797.

39. Nevertheless, the reader should note that these theories were developed primarily to study general equilibrium issues and have limited empirical content.

40. See the discussion of the Austrian theory in Chapters 2 and 3.

41. Victor Fuchs, "Self-Employment and Labor Force Participation of Older Males," *Journal of Human Resources* (September 1982): 339–357 and Thomas Gray and David Hirschberg, "Shifts in the Employment Status of Proprietors, 1960–1975," paper presented at the Eastern Economics Association Meetings, March 1983 (Washington, D.C.: Office of Advocacy, Small Business Administration, undated), examine self-employed individuals. Fuchs examines the determinants of switches to self-employment among older workers only and does not examine the determinants of self-employment earnings. Gray and Hirschberg provide interesting information on the frequency of switches between self-employment and wage work but do not investigate the impact of demographic and human capital characteristics on these switches.

42. These implications follow directly from the psychological and sociological studies reviewed earlier.

43. These implications follow from Lucas's theory of entrepreneurship and from the psychological studies that find that successful enterpreneurs have different psychological profiles than other individuals.

44. These implications are from Kihlstrom and Laffont's and Kanbur's theories that entrepreneurs have a stronger taste for risk than nonentrepreneurs and from the psychological and sociological studies reviewed earlier.

45. The vectors x and z may have elements in common. Education, for example, may affect the "taste" for entrepreneurship as well as the entrepreneurial and wage earnings.

46. The random disturbances in (6.7) and (6.8) are not necessarily the same random disturbances observed by the econometrician.

47. The notion that entrepreneuring is riskier than working implies that for given expected earnings, $\ln w(x) = \ln e(x)$, $\sigma_{ee} > \sigma_{ww}$.

48. Further research will test this assumption.

49. Note that we are assuming that the expected value of log earnings is the same from the standpoint of the individual as it is from the standpoint of the analyst although the variance of log earnings may be different for the individual than for the analyst. This assumption could be relaxed (by including an unobserved component of log earnings in (6.23) and (6.24)) without materially affecting the analysis.

50. The structural parameters of the general model given by (6.12)–(6.16) and (6.25) are generally not identified. But the general model and the reduced form equations it implies nevertheless provide a useful framework for testing alternative specifications that are identified.

51. For example, when constant across individuals, the c's are identified only up to a constant of proportionality. The four c's give us four nonlinear equations in the four structural parameters plus the proportionality constant. Further research is testing special cases of the utility function where the structural parameters are identified.

52. See Stephen R. Coslett, "Efficient Estimation of Discrete Choice Models," in Charles Manski and Daniel McFadden, *Structural Analysis of Discrete Data with Econometric Applications* (Boston: MIT Press, 1980), pp. 51–113.

53. Full-time workers are defined to be those who worked more than 40 weeks out of the year and who worked at least an average of 36 hours per week.

54. See Fuchs, "Self Employment," *op. cit.*, for evidence on self-employment among retired individuals.

55. See Fuchs, *ibid.*

56. For a discussion of the linear probability model see Jan Kmenta, *Elements of Econometrics* (New York: Macmillan, 1971). As is well known, the simple linear probability model has heteroskedastic errors so that test statistics from standard regression programs are not valid. We correct the heteroskedasticity using the generalized least squares method discussed in Kmenta.

57. The sample was constructed by taking all the wage earners from the sample and a random sample of all self-employed workers where the sampling proportion for self-employed workers reflects the true representation of self-employed workers in the population. See Evans, "Entrepreneurial Choice," for the regression and test results.

58. C. Manski and S. Lerman, "The Estimation of Choice Probabilities from Choice-Based Samples," *Econometrica* (November 1977): 1977–1988.

59. See the discussion of Shapero's theory in Chapter 3.

60. This assumption may be criticized as too stringent. But it is the basis for virtually all econometric estimation and is not unique to this study.

61. The method was devised by James Heckman and has been used extensively in the labor economics literature to estimate earnings equations for women from samples of women who have self-selected themselves into the labor force. See Heckman, "Sample Selection Bias."

62. Lambda is calculated from the estimates of the reduced-form probability model reported in Table 6.10.

63. And, equivalently, that a 10 percent change in age leads to a 15 percent change in entrepreneurial earnings.

64. They are not statistically significantly different from zero, but given that there are few self-employed blacks and Asians in our sample this lack of statistical significance may simply reflect the lack of data necessary for precise estimates.

65. The calculations reported below are for a 42-year-old man. The earnings differences would be smaller for younger men. They incorporate the coefficients on the educational attainment dummies, the coefficient on education times age, and the coefficient on education times veteran status.

66. In interpreting this result, recall that our sample excludes professionals such as doctors and lawyers.

67. Note than 80 percent of the men in our sample live in urban areas.

68. We considered men who were younger than 34 years in 1979 and therefore 18 or younger in 1964.

69. Arthur Andersen & Co., *Analysis of Regulatory Costs by Establishment Size* (Chicago: Arthur Andersen & Co., November 1979) and Frank Crowne, "Industry Reporting Requirements: Benefits or Burden?", *Federal Home Loan Bank Board Journal,* March 1979. Also see the discussion of Regulation Z in Jack Faucett and Associates, *Economies of Scale in Regulatory Compliance* prepared for the Small Business Administration (Chevy Chase, Md.: Jack Faucett and Associates, November 1984).

70. Arthur Andersen & Co., *Costs of Government Regulation: Study for the Business Roundtable* (Chicago: Arthur Andersen & Co., March 1979).

71. Booz-Allen & Hamilton, *The Impact of Environmental Regulations on Small Businesses* (Bethesda, Md.: Booz-Allen & Hamilton, May 1982).

72. B. Peter Pashigian, "Effect of Environmental Regulations on Optimal Plant Size and Factor Shares," *Journal of Law and Economics* (April 1984): 1–28.

73. The sample is stratified by establishment size and industry and then weighted to obtain population estimates.

74. The tabulations also include statistics which enable us to calculate the regression of

log pollution abatement costs against log employment size. For further details and data for 1974–1981 see David S. Evans, *The Differential Impact of EPA and OSHA Regulations across Firm and Establishment Sizes* (Washington, D.C.: Small Business Administration, 1985) and Evans, "Costs of Complying."

75. Evans, "Costs of Complying" reports regression estimates for 403 4-digit SIC code industries. These estimates show diseconomies of scale in most industries.

76. It is possible, however, that although existing small businesses did not incur a cost disadvantage, potential small businesses would. Regulators might grandfather existing small firms in order to lessen politically undesirable firm closures but not give any preferential treatment to small businesses that enter after the regulations are imposed.

77. See the previous note for further discussion of this important possibility.

78. For further description of the sources and construction of these data see Wayne Gray, "The Impact of OSHA and EPA Regulation on Productivity," NBER Working Paper no. 1405 (Cambridge: National Bureau of Economic Research, July 1984).

79. It is important to recognize that we are now assuming that a manager is attached to an establishment rather than a firm.

80. Jovanovic's model discussed above and in Chapter 3 would yield similar reduced form equations.

81. For simplicity we treat I as a single variable for the time being.

82. These industries had consistent industry definitions between 1963 and 1977.

BIBLIOGRAPHY

Alexander, S. S. "The Effect of Size of Manufacturing Corporations on the Distribution of the Rate of Return." *Review of Economics and Statistics* 31, no. 3 (August 1949): 229–235.

Andersen, Arthur & Co. *Analysis of Regulatory Costs by Establishment Size*. Prepared for the Small Business Administration. Chicago: Arthur Andersen & Co., November 1979.

———. *Cost of Government Regulation: Study for the Business Roundtable*. Chicago: Arthur Andersen & Co., March 1979.

Armington, Catherine, and Odle, Marjorie. "Small Business—How Many Jobs?" *Brookings Economic Review* (Winter 1982): 1–14.

Baumol, William A. "Entrepreneurship in Economic Theory." *American Economic Review* 58, no. 2 (May 1968): 63–69.

Benveniste, U., and Scheinkman, Jose A. "Duality Theory for Dynamic Optimization Models in Economics: The Continuous Time Case." *Journal of Economic Theory* 27, no. 1 (June 1982): 1–19.

Berney, Robert E. "The Cost of Government Regulation for Small Businesses: An Update." Unpublished paper. September 1980.

Birch, David L. *The Job Generation Process.* Cambridge:Center for the Study of Neighborhood and Regional Change, MIT, 1979.

Booz-Allen & Hamilton, Inc. *Impact of Environmental Regulations on Small Business.* Bethesda, Md.: Booz-Allen & Hamilton, May 24, 1982.

Bork, Robert. *The Antitrust Paradox*. New York: Basic Books, 1978.

Breyer, Stephen. *Regulation and Its Reform*. Cambridge: Harvard University Press, 1982.

Brock, Gerald. *Telecommunications Industry.* Cambridge: Harvard University Press, 1981.

Brock, William A. "On Models of Expectations That Arise from Maximizing Behavior of Economic Agents over Time." *Journal of Economic Theory* (December 1972): 348–376.

Brock, William A., and Dechert, William D. "Dynamic Ramsey Pricing." *International Economic Review* (October 1985): 569–591.

———. "On the Theoretical Foundations of Optimal Nonlinear Taxation." Unpublished manuscript. Departments of Economics, University of Wisconsin at Madison and State University of New York at Buffalo, September 1983.

———."Ramsey Pricing with Costly Administration Under Self-Selection Constraints." Unpublished manuscript Departments of Economics, University of Wisconsin at Madison and State University of New York at Buffalo. October 1983.

Brock, William A., and Evans, David S. *The Impact of Federal Taxes and Regulations on Business Formations, Dissolutions, and Growth.* Preliminary Report to the Small Business Administration. Chicago: CERA, March 1981.

———.*Economic Analysis of Building Codes.* Washington, D.C.: Federal Trade Commission, May 1982.

———. *Federal Regulation of Small Business.* Washington, D.C.: U.S. Small Business Administration, May 1982.

Bryson A., and Ho, Y. *Applied Optimal Control.* New York: Wiley, 1975.

Charles River Associates. *The Impact of OSHA Lead Standards on the Lead Industry.* Prepared for the Lead Industries Association. Boston: Charles River Associates, 1978.

Christensen, Laurits R., and Greene, William. "Scale Economies in U.S. Electric Power Generation." *Journal of Political Economy* (August 1976): 655–576.

Clarke, Roger. "On the Lognormality of Firm and Plant Size Distributions: Some U.K. Evidence." *Applied Economics* (December 1979): 415–435.

Cole, Roland, Jr., and Sommers, Paul. *Complying with Government Requirements: The Costs to Small and Larger Businesses.* Seattle: Battelle Human Affairs Research Center, 1981.

———. *The Impact of Government Regulations on Small Business in Washington State.* Seattle: Battelle Human Affairs Research Center, 1978.

Collins, D. F.; Moore, D. G.; and Unvalla, D. B. *The Enterprising Man.* East Lansing: Michigan State University Press, 1964.

Copulsky, William, and McNulty, Herbert. *Entrepreneurship and the Corporation.* New York: AMACOM, 1974.

Council on Environmental Quality. *Report of the Council on Environmental Quality: 1977.* Washington, D.C.: Government Printing Office, 1978.

Crowne, Frank. "Industry Reporting Requirements: Benefits or Burden?" *Federal Home Loan Bank Board Journal* (March 1977): 7–12.

Dahmen, Erik. *Entrepreneurial Activity and the Development of Swedish Industry.* Translated by Axel Leijonhufvud. Homewood, Ill.: Richard D. Irwin, 1970.

Data Resources, Inc. *The DRI Report on Manufacturing Industries.* Washington, D.C.: Small Business Administration, January 1984.

David, M., and Joeres, E., *Flexibility with Quality: Implementation of Transferable Permits for Wisconsin Rivers.* Department of Economics, University of Wisconsin at Madison, July 1983.

Douglas, Merril E. "Relating Education to Entrepreneurial Success." *Business Horizons* 19 (December 1976): 40–44.

Dun and Bradstreet. *1981 Dun and Bradstreet Business Record.* New York: Dun and Bradstreet, 1983.

DuRietz, Gunnar. "New Firm Entry in Swedish Manufacturing Industries During the Post-War Period." Doctoral dissertation, University of Stockholm, 1975.

Ekelund, I., and Scheinkman, Jose A. "Transversality Conditions for Some Infinite Horizon Discrete Time Optimization Problems." Department of Economics, University of Chicago, July 1983.

Evans, David S. "Regulations, Fixed Costs, and the Size Distribution of Businesses." Ph.D. thesis. University of Chicago, August 1983.

———. *Entrepreneurial Choice and Success.* Washington, D.C.: Small Business Administration, May 1985.

———. *The Differential Impact of EPA and OSHA Regulations across Firm and Establishment Sizes.* Washington, D.C.: Small Business Administration, September 1985.

———. "The Cost of Complying with Environmental Regulations across Plant and Firm Sizes in the Manufacturing Industries," unpublished manuscript, September 1985.

———. "Tests of Alternative Theories of Industry Evolution," unpublished manuscript, November 1985.

Evans, David S., and Grossman, Sanford J. "Integration," In *Breaking up Bell: Essays on*

Industrial Organization and Regulation, edited by David S. Evans. New York: North Holland, 1983, pp. 95–126.

Evans, David S., and Heckman, James J. "A Test for Subadditivity of the Cost Function with an Application to the Bell System." *American Economic Review* (September 1984): 615–623.

Fischer, Stanley, and Dornbusch, Rudiger. *Economics.* New York: McGraw-Hill, 1983.

Fisher, Franklin M., and McGowan, John J. "On the Misuse of Accounting Rates of Returns to Infer Monopoly Profits." *American Economic Review* 73 (March 1983): 82–97.

Gallant, A. Ronald. "Seemingly Unrelated Nonlinear Regression." *Journal of Econometrics* (April 1975): 35–50.

Gellman Research. *The Relationship Between Industrial Concentration, Firm Size, and Technological Innovation*. Washington, D.C.: U.S. Small Business Administration, May 11, 1982.

Ghent, Joceyln, and Jaher, Frederick Cople. "The Chicago Business Elite: 1830–1930." *Business History Review* 50, no. 3 (Autumn 1976): 288–382.

Gray, Thomas A., and Phillips, Bruce D. "The Role of Small Firms in Understanding the Magnitude of Fluctuations in the Economy." Paper presented at the Atlantic Economic Society Meetings, Philadelphia, October, 1983.

Gregory, Frances, and Neu, Irene. "The American Industrial Elite in the 1870's." In *Men in Business,* edited by William Miller. New York: Harper & Row, 1962.

Hahn, Roger W., and Noll, Roger G. "Barriers to Implementing Tradeable Air Pollution Permits: Problems of Regulatory Interactions." *Yale Journal of Regulation* 1, no. 1 (1983): 63–92.

Hall, M., and Weiss, L. "Firm Size and Profitability." *Review of Economics and Statistics* 49, no. 3 (August 1967): 319–331.

Hart, P. E., and Prais, S. J. "The Analysis of Business Concentration: A Statistical Approach." *Journal of the Royal Statistical Society* 119, pt. 2 (1956): 150–191.

Hymer, Stephen, and Pashigian, Peter. "Firm Size and Rate of Growth." *Journal of Political Economy* 70 (April 1976): 556–569.

Ijiri, Yuji, and Simon, Herbert A. "Interpretations of Departures from the Pareto Curve Firm-Size Distributions." *Journal of Political Economy* 82 (March–April 1974).

———. *Skew Distributions and the Sizes of Business Firms.* Amsterdam: North Holland, 1977.

Joeres, E., and David, M. *Buying a Better Environment: Cost-Effective Regulation Through Permit Trading.* Madison: University of Wisconsin Press, 1983.

Joskow, Paul, and Noll, Roger G. "Theory and Practice in Public Regulation: A Current Overview." In *Studies in Public Regulation,* Edited by G. Fromm. Cambridge: MIT Press, 1981, chap. 1.

Jovanovic, Boyan. "Selection and Evolution of Industry." *Econometrica* 50, no. 3 (May 1982): 649–670.

Kahn, Alfred E. "The Passing of the Public Utility Concept." In *Telecommunications Regulation Today and Tomorrow.* Edited by Eli Noam. New York: Law and Business, 1983, pp. 3–37.

Kamien, Morton, and Schwartz, Nancy. *Market Structure and Innovation.* New York: Cambridge University Press, 1982.

Kanbur, S. "Of Risk Taking and the Personal Distribution of Income." *Journal of Political Economy* 87, no. 4 (August 1979): 769–797.

Kaysen, Carl, and Turner, Donald. *Antitrust Policy.* Cambridge: Harvard University Press, 1958.

Kelman, Steven J. "Economic Incentives and Environmental Policy: Politics, Ideology, and Philosophy." In *Incentives for Environmental Protection*. Edited by Thomas Schelling. Cambridge: MIT Press, 1983, pp. 291–332.

Kent, Calvin A.; Saxton, Donald L.; and Vesper, Karl H., eds. *Encyclopedia of Entrepreneurship*. Englewood Cliffs, N.J.: Prentice-Hall, 1982.

Kihlstrom, Richard, and Laffont, Jean-Jacques. "A General Equilibrium Entrepreneurial Theory of Firm Formation Based on Risk Aversion." *Journal of Political Economy* 59 (August 1979): 719–748.

Kirzner, Israel M. *Competition and Entrepreneurship*. Chicago: University of Chicago Press, 1973.

Knight, Frank. *Risk, Uncertainty and Profit*. New York: Houghton Mifflin, 1921.

Linneman, Peter. "The Effects of Consumer Safety Standards: The 1973 Mattress Flammability Standard." *Journal of Law and Economics* (October 1980): 461–479.

Little, Arthur D. *The Impact of Premanufacture Notification Requirements on the Chemical Industry*. Prepared for the Environmental Protection Agency. Cambridge: Arthur D. Little, 1979.

Lollivier, Stefan, and Rochet, Jean-Charles. "Bunching and Second-Order Conditions: A Note on Optimal Tax Theory." *Journal of Economic Theory* 31, no.2 (December 1983): 392–400.

Lucas, Robert E. "Labor-Capital Substitution in U.S. Manufacturing," In *The Taxation of Income from Capital*. Edited by A. C. Harberger and M. J. Bailey. Washington, D.C.: Brookings Institution, 1969, pp. 223–274.

———. "On the Size Distribution of Business Firms." *Bell Journal of Economics* 9 (August 1978): 508–523.

Mansfield, Edwin. "Entry, Gibrat's Law, Innovation, and the Growth of Firms." *American Economic Review* 52 (December 1962): 1031–1051.

Marcus, M. "Profitability and Size of Firm." *Review of Economics and Statistics* 51, no. 1 (February 1969): 104–107.

Marshall, Alfred. *Principles of Economics*. London: Macmillan, 1925.

Maskin, E., and Riley, J. "Income vs. Leisure Taxes." Discussion Paper no. 174. Department of Economics, UCLA, August 1980.

McClelland, David, and Winter, David. *Motivating Economic Achievement*. New York: Free Press, 1969.

Miller, William. "The Business Elite in Business Bureaucracies." In *Men in Business*. Edited by William Miller. New York: Harper & Row, 1962.

———. "The Recruitment of the Business Elite." In *Men in Business*. Edited by William Miller. New York: Harper & Row, 1962.

Mills, David. "Fluctuations and Firm Size." *Journal of Industrial Economics* (in press).

Mirman, L., and Sibley, D. "Optimal Nonlinear Prices for Multiproduct Monopolies." *Bell Journal of Economics* 11, no. 2 (Autumn 1980): 639–670.

Mirrlees, James. "An Exploration in the Theory of Optimal Income Taxation." *Review of Economic Studies* 38 (1971): 175–208.

———. "Optimal Tax Theory: A Synthesis." *Journal of Public Economics* 6 (1976): 327–358.

———. "The Theory of Optimal Taxation." In *Handbook of Mathematical Economics*. Edited by Kenneth Arrow and Michael Intriligator. Amsterdam: North Holland, forthcoming.

Montgomery, W. D. "Markets in Licenses and Efficient Pollution Control Programs." *Journal of Economic Theory* 5, no. 3 (1972): 395–448.

Neale, A. D. *The Antitrust Laws of the United States.* 2d ed. New York: Cambridge University Press, 1970.

Nelson, Richard, and Winter, Sidney. *An Evolutionary Theory of Economic Change*. Cambridge: Harvard University Press, 1982.

Neumann, George R., and Nelson, Jon P. "Safety Regulation and Firm Size: Effects of the Coal Mine Health and Safety Act of 1969." *Journal of Law and Economics* (October 1982): 183–199.

Noam, Eli. "Does Independence Matter? An Analysis of Regulatory Behavior." *Quarterly Review of Economics and Business* 22, no. 4 (Winter 1982): 53–60.

O'Neill, W. "Transferable Discharge Permits and Economic Efficiency." *Journal of Environmental Economics and Management* 10 (1983).

Pashigian, B. Peter. "The Effect of Environmental Regulation on Optimal Plant Size and Factor Shares." *Journal of Law and Economics* (April 1984): 1–22.

———. "A Theory of Prevention and Legal Defence with an Application to the Legal Costs of Companies." *Journal of Law and Economics* (October 1982): 247–270.

Peters, Thomas J., and Waterman, Robert H. *In Search of Excellence*. New York: Harper & Row, 1982.

Phillips, Bruce D., and Knight, William. "The Davis-Bacon Act Reconsidered: A 'New' Small Business Tax." In *Proceedings,* 1982 Small Business Research Conference, Bentley College, Waltham, Mass., March 1982, pp. 330–352.

Phillips, Owen R. "Residential Real Estate Market in Texas: Prices, Quality, and Regulation." Working Paper no. 81–2. College Station: Department of Economics, Texas A&M University, April 1981.

Polinsky, A. Michael, and Shavell, Steven. "Pigouvian Taxation with Administrative Costs." *Journal of Public Economics* 19, no. 3 (December 1982): 385–390.

Popkin, Joel, and Company. *Estimates of Gross Product Originating in Small Business: 1977 Benchmark and Revisions of Intervening Years Since 1972*. Washington, D.C.: Small Business Administration, September 1982.

Prescott, Edward, and Vischer, R. "Organization Capital." *Journal of Political Economy* 88, no. 3 (June 1980): 446–461.

Quandt, Richard E. "On the Size Distribution of Firms." *American Economic Review* 56, no. 3 (March 1966): 416–432.

Rao, C. Radhakrishna. *Linear Statistical Inference and Its Applications.* 2d ed. New York: Wiley, 1973.

Ryon, Ruth. "Discount Realty Companies on the Rise in Southland." *Los Angeles Times,* October 22, 1978.

Scherer, F. M. *Industrial Market Structure and Economic Performance*. 2d ed. Boston: Houghton Mifflin, 1980.

Schiller, Bradley L. "Corporate Kidnap." *Public Interest* (Fall 1983).

Schrage, Henry. "The R&D Entrepreneur: Profile of Success." *Harvard Business Review* 43 (December 1965): 56–69.

Schumpeter, Joseph R. *Capitalism, Socialism and Democracy.* 3d ed. New York: Harper & Row, 1950.

Shapero, Albert. "The Displaced Uncomfortable Entrepreneur." *Psychology Today* (November 1975): 83–88.

Simon, Herbert A., and Bonini, Charles P. "The Size Distribution of Business Firms." *American Economic Review* 48 (September 1958): 607–617.

Smith, Adam. *The Wealth of Nations.* New York: Modern Library, 1937.

Spulber, D. "Spatial Nonlinear Pricing." *American Economic Review* 71, no. 5 (December 1981): 923–933.

Stauffer, Thomas R. "The Measurement of Corporate Rates of Return: A Generalized Formulation." *Bell Journal of Economics* 2 (Autumn 1971): 434–469.

Stekler, H. O. "The Variability of Profitability with Size of Firm: 1947–1958." *Journal of the American Statistical Association* 59, no. 308 (December 1964): 1183–1193.

Stigler, George. *Capital and Rates of Return in Manufacturing Industries.* Princeton: Princeton University Press, 1963.

Stuart, Alexander. "The Airlines Are Flying in a Fog." *Fortune* (October 20, 1980): 51–56.

Turner, Donald. "Conglomerate Mergers and Section 7 of the Clayton Act." *Harvard Law Review* 78 (1965): 1313–1347.

U.S. Department of Commerce. Bureau of the Census. *County Business Patterns.* Washington, D.C.: Government Printing Office, various issues.

———. *Enterprise Statistics.* Washington, D.C.: Government Printing Office, various issues.

U.S. Department of the Treasury. Internal Revenue Service. *Statistics of Income: Sole Proprietorships, Partnerships, and Corporations.* Washington, D.C.: Government Printing Office, various issues.

Vancil, R. *Decentralization: Managerial Ambiguity by Design.* Homewood, Ill.: Dow Jones-Irwin, 1978.

Verkuil, Paul R. "A Critical Guide to the Regulatory Flexibility Act." *Duke Law Journal* 1982, no. 2 (April 1982): 216–279.

Viner, Jacob. "Cost Curves and Supply Curves." *Zeitschrift fur Nationaleckonomie* 3 (1932): 23–46.

Weidenbaum, Murray. *The Future of Business Regulation.* New York: AMACOM, 1979.

Weisacker, C. C. Von. "Barriers to Entry." *Bell Journal of Economics* 11 (Autumn 1980): 399–420.

White, Lawrence J. "The Determinants of the Relative Importance of Small Businesses." *Review of Economics and Statistics* (February 1982): 42–49.

———. *Measuring the Importance of Small Business in the American Economy.* Monograph Series in Finance and Economics. New York: Salomon Brothers Center for the Study of Financial Institutions, Graduate School of Business Administration, New York University, 1981.

INDEX

ABOUT THE AUTHORS

WILLIAM A. BROCK is Frank P. Ramsey Professor of Economics at the University of Wisconsin at Madison. He is a general economic theorist who has authored and coauthored more than fifty articles and several books. He was elected Fellow of the Econometric Society in 1974, Sherman Fairchild Distinguished Scholar at the California Institute of Technology in 1979, and a Romnes Faculty Fellow at the University of Wisconsin at Madison in 1981. Mr. Brock received his B.A. from the University of Missouri and his Ph.D. from the University of California at Berkeley.

DAVID S. EVANS is Associate Professor of Economics and Adjunct Associate Professor of Law at Fordham University. As President of CERA, an economic research firm based in Greenwich, Connecticut, he has been a consultant to a number of federal agencies and business clients. Mr. Evans received his B.A. and Ph.D. degrees from the University of Chicago. His last book was *Breaking Up Bell: Essays in Industrial Organization and Regulation,* which he edited and coauthored.

BRUCE D. PHILLIPS is Director of Data Base Development and Senior Economist at the Office of Advocacy, U.S. Small Business Administration. Mr. Phillips, who holds a B.A. from the City College of New York and a Ph.D. from the University of Maryland, has written numerous articles on small businesses.